MW01194914

Introduction to Computer Programming and Numerical Methods

First Edition

Xudong Jia
Professor of Civil Engineering
California State Polytechnic University, Pomona

Shu Liu
Senior Software Engineer
DIRECTV

KENDALL/HUNT
PUBLISHING COMPANY

4050 Westmark Drive P.O. Box 1840 Dubuque, IA 52004 1-800-228-0810
©Kendall/Hunt Publishing Company. All Right Reserved

Copyright © 2007 by Xudong Jia and Shu Liu

ISBN 978-0-7575-3892-6

Kendall/Hunt Publishing Company has the exclusive rights to reproduce this work,
to prepare derivative works from this work, to publicly distribute this work,
to publicly perform this work and to publicly display this work.

All rights reserved. No part of this publication may be reproduced,
stored in a retrieval system, or transmitted, in any form or by any
means, electronic, mechanical, photocopying, recording, or otherwise,
without the prior written permission of the copyright owner.

Printed in the United States of America
10 9 8 7 6

Contents

Preface

Introduction to Computer Programming and Numerical Methods is primarily intended for use as a textbook in university-level courses that deal with computer programming and numerical methods. This book is aimed at integrating computer programming techniques and numerical methods in solving engineering problems. While giving focuses on basic computer programming and primary numerical methods, this book includes materials that are useful for students to write computer programs and develop numerical methods-related projects.

This is the first edition from the draft manuscripts that have been extensively tested in the classrooms at Cal Poly Pomona. The chapters in this book have been structured to reflect students' learning process. Key features of this book include:

- Visual Basic.Net is used to help students learn computer programming. The selection of VB.NET is based on the fact that VB.NET is the easiest object-oriented programming language for beginning-level students. The first seven chapters provide fundamentals of VB.Net programming.

- Computer simulation and animation techniques are introduced in Chapter 8-10. Students can learn how to generate and use random numbers that follow various probability distributions including uniform, Poisson, and normal distributions in Chapter 8. Monte Carlo simulation and traffic animation techniques are discussed in Chapters 9 and 10.

- Object-oriented programming is introduced in Chapters 11 and 12. We focus on principals of object-oriented programming and methods of creating, managing, and using objects for VB.Net applications.

- Numerical methods are commonly used to solve science or engineering problems. Chapters 13–19 introduce principles of numerical methods used to find roots of equations, calculate values for systems of linear equations, and understand paired data points through curve fitting, etc.

- MATLAB and EXCEL are used in this book to help students implement the numerical methods discussed in this book.

- A companion CD of this book contains the source code files and executable files for all the sample applications discussed in the book. Students can open these applications in VB.Net, MATLAB, and EXCEL and run them.

We are indebted to a number of faculty members at the Department of Civil Engineering who made valuable suggestions and contributions to this book. Dr. Ronald L Carlyle provided a rich set of information for Chapters 14, 15 and 16. Without the positive support from the faculty members, I would never have completed this book.

Many others also made significant contributions to the book. Students at Cal Poly University who used various draft manuscripts of this book from 1998 to 2006 have provided constructive comments and suggestions. These comments and suggestions have made the book useful and eliminate lots of errors in the book.

A special note of thanks goes to Shelly Walia and Ryan L. Schrodt for their wonderful help, advice, and support in producing this book, together with the team at Kendall Hunt Publishing.

The book cannot be error free. We would be especially grateful for suggestions, criticisms, and corrections that might improve this book.

Xudong Jia
Shu Liu

Diamond Bar, CA
October, 2006

Chapter 1
Visual Basic.Net Environment

Welcome to Introduction to Computer Programming and Numerical Methods. The objective of this chapter is to introduce Microsoft Visual Basic.Net (or VB.Net), the most useful computer programming language. You will learn step-by-step the Integrated Development Environment (IDE) inside VB.Net for creating, running and debugging VB.Net programs.

1.1   Getting Started

Assume you have a user account and a password for use of computers in a university or college lab. Now it is the time for you to enter the user account name and the password into a lab computer. [If you have a home computer where VB.Net and Windows XP is installed on it, you can also learn the VB.Net Integrated Development Environment using your home computer.] The procedures described in this chapter apply both your lab and home computers.

After you log on to a computer (lab or home), you are in the Windows XP operating system. You are encouraged to change the password to a new one for security reasons. Otherwise, someone may break into your account and delete your files accidentally or with some purposes.

The steps to change your password and start VB.Net are as follows:

❑   Press *Alt+Del+Ctrl* keys at the same time and follow the instructions provided in the window dialog to change your password.

❑   Click the *Start* button at the bottom of the *Desktop* using the left mouse button.

❑   Select *Programs-> Microsoft Visual Studio .Net 2003 -> Microsoft Visual Studio .Net 2003.*   You will be in the .Net development environment (see Figure 1-1). It is noted that the Visual Studio .Net 2003 version is used in this book. All the programs listed in this book are tested under this version and saved in the CD at the back of this book.

❑   Inside the .Net development environment, you will see three tabs listed in the middle of the environment. These three tabs are *Projects, Online Resources,* and *My Profile.* Click the *Projects* tab and *New Project* button.

❑   Highlight *Visual Basic Projects* in the *Project Type* window and *Windows Application* in the *Templates* window.

❑   Specify a name called **Lab1** and a location of the VB application to be developed. The location you specify is the place where your VB.Net project data and code is located.

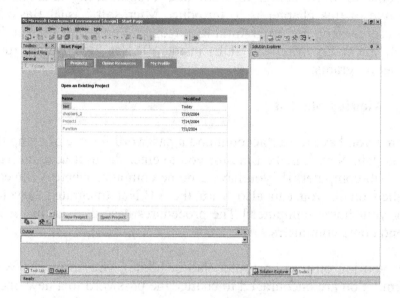

Figure 1-1 VB.NET Development Environnent

❑   Click **OK.** Now you are in the Visual Basic.Net Integrated Development Environment (IDE).

1.2   VB.Net Integrated Development Environment

The integrated development environment (IDE) is important in helping you create, run and debug VB.Net programs or applications. You can consider VB.Net IDE as Microsoft Word and VB.Net programs as Word documents. A Word document is created in Microsoft Word, while a VB.Net program is created in the VB.Net IDE.

The VB.Net IDE consists of a set of Graphical User Interfaces (GUIs) and components (see Figure 1-2). You need to understand this IDE because all VB.Net programs or applications are developed within this environment.

Let us look at this environment in detail. On the top of the window, you can see the following components:

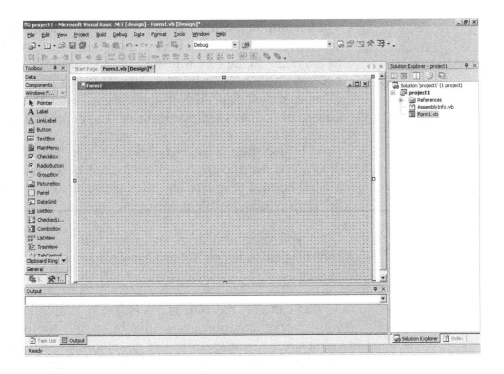

Figure 1-2   VB.Net Integrated Development Environment

Title Bar   It shows the title of the VB.Net project you are currently working on. The default project title is the project name you have specified when you create a new project. If you would like to change the project name or title to other name, you can change it through **Project -> Project Properties**.

Menu Bar   It consists of menus that help you manipulate VB.Net programs in the project. The menus are listed from left to right as **File, Edit, View, Project, Build, Debug, Tools, Window,** and **Help.**

Tool Bar   Two built-in tool bars are provided when you open the VB.Net IDE. You can add more toolbars. The steps to do that are

             Select Views->Toolbars
             Check on the names of the toolbars.

In addition to the above components, you should be aware of the five windows in the IDE when you are developing a VB.Net project or application. These five windows are as follows:

Toolbox window   The window is very important in the VB.Net IDE. It contains control templates or components that are available for you to use.

These components are similar to the engine and transmission in a car. They are well built. Just as people do not need to know how to build an engine or a transmission to assemble a car, you do not need to know how to build a component or a control template in order to develop a VB.Net application. Your job is just to know how to use control templates for a VB.Net program.

How to use these control templates? The solution is 'drag and drop'. You need to first click on a control template, for example, a label control template and then move the control template into the form window while pressing and holding the mouse.

Once you drag and drop an instance of an control template, a control that inherits the behavior of the control template is created.

As you can see, the IDE is a VB.Net assembling line that allows you to take components available in the toolbox to make an application. Similar to a car assembling line that allows car builders to select various engines and transmissions to make different cars, the IDE can allow you to access millions of control components that are available through Microsoft VB.Net built-in libraries, third-party software, and user-defined libraries.

Form Window

The window is a blank window (or form) on which you can place controls. The form and its controls constitute the graphical user interface (GUI) of a VB.Net program. They are the visual part of the program with which the user can interact.

Solution Explorer

The window contains a Windows Explorer-like tree view of all the customizable forms and general code (modules) that make up a VB.Net application.

The Solution Explorer provides you with an organized view of your project and program files associated with the project. A toolbar associated with this window lists a set of commands that allow you to see the graphical user interface (GUI) of your project and to see the code that supports the controls on the GUI.

Select the Solution Explorer on the **View** menu when you cannot find the Solution Explorer in your IDE.

Properties
Window

The properties window displays the properties for a form or a control. Properties describe attributes such as size, color, and font of a control. Each form or control has its own set of properties.

When you click on a control or the form, the properties will be listed in the *properties* window. There are two columns in the properties window. The first column lists the property names and the second column shows the current value of the property. The value can be changed at the design phase of the form or through the program code.

There are lots of properties associated with controls. You do not need to know all of them but understand how to use primary properties such as name, text, etc.

1.3   A Simple VB.Net Application

Creating a simple application is a process that implements a logic used in solving a problem. It involves the steps to create forms (or Graphic User Interfaces) and to write code to support the forms. Each form contains a set of controls "dragged and dropped" from control templates. Each control has a set of properties and a group of events or actions such as click, double-click, mouse-up, and key-press. Each event is supported by a sequence of VB.Net code to tell the computer what to do when an event of a control is trigged or activated.

Example 1.1   A Simple VB.Net Application

Suppose you have a command button control in the form window. The name of the control is called *aCommandButton*. You can go to the code window through *View ->Code*, select the *aCommandButton* control from the *control* list, and select the *click* event from the *event* list. After the operations, you can see the procedure template as follows:

```
Private Sub ACommandButton_Click(ByVal sender As System.Object,      _
          ByVal e As System.EventArgs) Handles                       _
          ACommandButton.Click
End Sub
```

Note that there are two arguments inside the parentheses. We will discuss these two arguments later. Now you just understand two arguments are important in this event procedure.

When you compare the above procedure to that created by your IDE, you see the above procedure has two "_" letters inserted between the two parentheses. Each "_" letter indicates that the line after the letter is the continuation of its previous line. For example, the first "_" letter indicates that `"ByVal e As System.EventArgs) Handles"` is considered as part of the first line. With the use of the two "_" letters, the first three lines are considered as one line in VB.Net IDE.

Type the following code between **Private Sub** and **End Sub.**

```
        Msgbox "Welcome to VB.Net"
```

The entire code looks like:

```
Private Sub ACommandButton_Click(ByVal sender As System.Object,    _
         ByVal e As System.EventArgs) Handles                      _
         ACommandButton.Click


         Msgbox "Welcome to VB.Net"

End Sub
```

Provided that the code has been written for the click event of the aCommandButton control, let us run the project and see what happens. You can find this simple application as Example 1_1 in Chapter 1 of CD.

❑ *Select Debug -> Start*

A window that represents the form you just have designed is prompted. Click the command button control and see what the program will do for you. Surprisingly, you will see another window. The window shows the message "Welcome to VB.Net." This message is created by the VB.Net statement `Msgbox "Welcome to VB.Net."` More discussions of VB.Net statements will be provided in later chapters.

From the above simple application, we can conclude that the VB.Net IDE takes the following steps to run a VB.Net program:

Step 1:   Visual Basic.Net monitors the forms and the controls in each form for all the possible events such as mouse movements, clicks, keystrokes and so on.

Step 2:   When VB.Net detects an event, it searches for a built-in response to the event. If there are not any built-in responses to the event, the VB.Net examines the program to see if an event procedure has been written for that event.

If an event procedure is written for that event, VB.Net executes the procedure. VB.Net statements within the procedure will be executed statement by statement from top to bottom. Once all the statements are executed, the program will go back to Step 1.

If an event procedure is not written for that event, VB.Net skips this event and waits for the next event and goes back to Step 1.

1.4   VB.Net Application Development Process

A VB.Net application development process involves five major steps, that is, 1) understand the logic needed to solve the problem by a VB.Net program, 2) design form(s) to implement the logic, 3) write program code to support the controls in the form(s), 4) debug the program, and 5) deliver the program to users.

Example 1.2   Quadratic Equation VB. Net Application

Let us use an example to describe the development process. Suppose we need to develop a VB.Net program to solve the following quadratic equation and find two real roots if they exist:

$$f(x) = ax^2 + bx + c = 0$$
Where $a \neq 0$ and $b \neq 0$

Two logical flows can be developed for the program. These two flows are:

Logical Flow #1:   A user is prompted a window on which three input boxes for parameters a, b, and c are listed. The user then enters a numerical value in each of these input boxes and clicks a button called **Calculate.** The program will find two real roots if they exist. The user terminates the execution of the program by clicking on a button called **Cancel.** We name this logical flow the simple flow.

Logical Flow #2:   A user is asked to enter a full quadratic function (like 1x^2+2x+1) into an input box. Once the user presses the **Enter** key, the three parameters (a, b, and c) will be parsed (or extracted) out from the function expression and displayed in the input boxes. The user then clicks a button called **Calculate**. The program will find two real roots if they exist. The user terminates the execution of the program by clicking on a button called **Cancel.** We name this logical flow the complex flow.

These two logic flows will make the development of a VB.Net application different. Here we only concentrate on the VB.Net implementation of the simple logic and leave the complex logic in later chapters. Example1_2 within Chapter 1 of the CD is the VB.Net application for the simple logic.

The development process to implement the simple logic flow involves the following steps:

1) Form design
2) Program coding
3) Debugging and testing
4) Program packaging and delivery

Let us go through these four basic steps:

Step 1:   Form Design

The form design is a process that implements the logic for the program. For the simple logic flow, we need to develop the form as shown in Figure 1-3. Within this form, you can find a form control, five label controls, five text box controls, and two command controls.

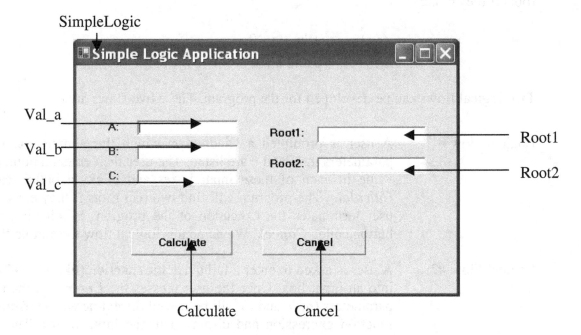

Figure 1-3   Form Designed for the Simple Logic Flow

These controls are defined with the following names:

```
Form Control:            SimpleLogic

Textbox for a:           val_a
Textbox for b:           val_b
Textbox for c:           val_c
Textbox for root1:       root1
Textbox for root2:       root2
Calculate button:        calculate
Cancel button:           cancel

Label for a:             Label1
Label for b:             Label2
```

```
Label for c:              Label3
Label for root1:          Label4
Label for root2:          label5
```

These names must follow the VB.Net rules and conventions listed below:

1)   Each control must have a unique name that can be no more than 40 characters long.

2)   Each control name must start with a letter. The remaining characters can be any letters, numerical characters, or underscores. You cannot have spaces, special symbols, or punctuation characters in a control name.

3)   It is a good practice to name a control to reflect the logic of the application. For example, we define Val_a, Val_b, and Val_c to represent the three parameters of a quadratic equation.

The procedures to create these controls are as follows:

1)   Within the VB.IDE, click the empty form and change its name to be **SimpleLogic** (see Figure 1-4). Also replace **Form1** in the **Text** property by **Simple Logic Application**.

2)   Highlight the **Textbox** template within the **Toolbox** window. Press and hold the cursor and drag the cursor into the **Form** window. Release the cursor. You will see a textbox control is created (see Figure 1-5).

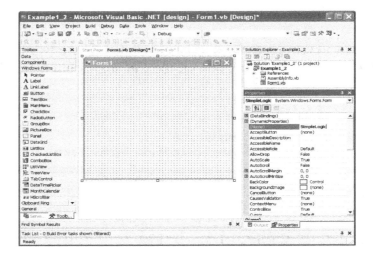

Figure 1-4 Form Window for Example1_2

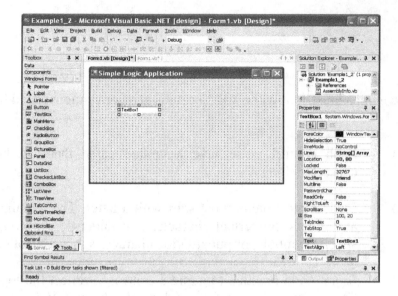

Figure 1-5 Create a Textbox Control

3) Note that the name of the textbox control created in 2) is **Textbox1**. Change it to **Val_a**. Also Clear the **Text** property.

4) Follow the same way to create other control names. Note that you do not need to change the label control names since they are not used in the program code.

Step 2:   Program Coding

There are two event procedures to be developed. These two procedures will respond to two **click** actions (or events), one on the **Calculate** button and the other on the **Cancel** button.

```
Public Class quadradic_equation
        Inherits System.Windows.Forms.Form

    ┌─────────────────────────────────────────────┐
    │ Windows Form Designer Generated Code        │
    └─────────────────────────────────────────────┘

Private Sub cancel_Click(ByVal sender As System.Object,   _
        ByVal e As System.EventArgs)                       _
        Handles cancel.Click
    End
End Sub
```

```
Private Sub calculate_Click(ByVal sender As  System.Object,  _
                    ByVal e As System.EventArgs)                 _
                    Handles calculate.Click
     Dim a As Single
     Dim b As Single
     Dim c As Single
     Dim rt1 As Double
     Dim rt2 As Double
     Dim chk As Double

     a = Val(val_a.Text)
     b = Val(val_b.Text)
     c = Val(val_c.Text)

     chk = b ^ 2 - 4 * a * c

     If chk < 0 Then
         MsgBox("no real roots exist")
         Exit Sub
     Else
         rt1 = (-b + Math.Sqrt(chk)) / (2 * a)
         rt2 = (-b - Math.Sqrt(chk)) / (2 * a)
     End If
     root1.Text = Str(Rt1)
     root2.Text = Str(rt2)
   End Sub
End Class
```

As you can see the two procedures all begin with **Private Sub** and end at the **End Sub**.
Between **Private Sub** and **End Sub**, there are various VB.Net statements. We will learn
these statements one-by-one in later chapters. You do not need to know these
statements right now.

❑ Enter the above two procedures into the code window and name the project
   SimpleLogic.

Step 3:   Debugging and Testing

Debugging and testing a VB.Net application is a tedious task that often involves a
systematic way of checking various potential errors in the application. You can read the
article entitled "Testing of a Windows-Based Transportation Application: The LRSEdit
Experience." for more information on how to do the testing on Windows-based
applications. The article was published on the ITE Journal on the Web, February 1999
and can be found as **testing.pdf** in the CD.

The application developed in step 2 is a simple application. It does not involve a lot of
testing efforts. However you need to know tools provided in VB.Net for the debugging
and testing of programs. The tools can be accessed through the Debug menu in the
VB.Net IDE.

It is noted that this simple application does have some errors. What happens if a non-numeric value is entered into the Val_a, Val_b or Val_c textbox? When you enter "abc" into the Val_a textbox, the program will be terminated abnormally. In later chapters, we will add more VB.Net statements into this simple application to deal with various "what if" cases.

Step 4:   Project Packaging and Product Delivery

Once the project is tested error free, it is the time to package the project and deliver it as a software product to users. The software product contains not only the executable program but also various documentations that guide users for installation and execution of the product.

The professional product, once packaged, will have a setup program that allows users to install the product into any computers, even the ones without VB.Net. After installation, the product can be executed in a window environment.

1.5   Questions

Q1.   Explore Internet to see how many versions Visual Basic.Net has. Hint: Go to Microsoft web site or use Google search engine. You may see that VB.Net has Learning Version, Professional Version, and Enterprise Version.

Q2.   What is the difference between Visual Basic and Visual Basic .Net?

Q3.   Develop a VB.Net application that gets input from the user about the radius of a circle, calculates the diameter, circumference, and area of the circle, and displays the results in three textboxes. The three textboxes should be disabled for user input. A logic flow and the form that implements the flow are required for this problem.

Q4.   List the five windows inside the VB.Net IDE and describe the functions of each window.

Q5.   List all the properties for a textbox control, a label control, and a command button control.

Q6.   What are the steps for the development of a VB.Net Application? Explain each step briefly?

Q7.   Why do we need the "_" letter in VB.Net code? Hint: See the explanation in this chapter.

Q8.   List three VB.Net rules that should be considered when a control name is defined.

Q9.   What is the difference between a control template and a control?

Q10.   What is VB.Net IDE?

Q11.   Assume you have a command button control named **Clear** created in the **Form** window. When you double click on the button, you will see the empty event procedure created in the **Code** window. Can you write down the first line and last line of the empty procedure without looking at the procedure in the **Code** window?

Q12   List steps required to create a VB.Net project called **FirstProject** and save the project files into **C:\temp** folder.

Q13.   Assume you have already created a VB.Net project called **SecondProject** and saved it in the **C:\temp** folder. How many files are there within the **SecondProject** folder? What is the file type of each file in the **SecondProject** folder?

Q14.   When you find a file in the Windows Explorer whose type is Visual Basic .Net Project, what happens when you click on it? Hint: Assume you create a project called **SecondProject** in Q13, you find the **SecondProject** file in the **C:\temp\SecondProject** folder whose type is Visual Basic .Net Project.

Q15.   How many controls are there in Figure 1.3? List these controls and explain their control type.

Q16.   How to change your password in Windows XP?

Q17.   What is a GUI?

Chapter 2
Exploration of a Visual Basic.Net Application

We will discuss in this chapter the structure of a typical Visual Basic.Net application and provide you with a simple project that describes the relationships of forms. In addition, we will explore a number of control templates or components that are listed in the VB.Net IDE.

2.1   Structure of a VB.Net Application

The Visual Basic.Net IDE organizes a VB.Net application as a solution to a problem. A large VB.Net application may have one or more VB.Net projects in which each project is responsible for a single, well-defined task. Figure 2-1 shows the relationships among a VB.Net application, its solution, and its VB.Net projects. As you can see from Figure 2.1, the Application A has two VB.Net projects and Application B has one VB.Net project.

In this book we assume each VB.Net application requires a solution that only contains one VB.Net project. With this assumption, VB.Net application and VB.Net project are used interchangeably in this book.

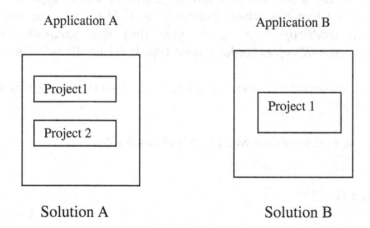

Figure 2-1   VB.Net Application, Solution, and VB.Net Projects

A VB.Net project consists of one or more forms. Each form, as discussed in Chapter 1, is a graphical user interface (GUI). It has a form file to store controls.

Example 2.1   House Orientation Application

Assume you create a VB.Net application or project called *House Orientation* that contains three forms *House*, *Room1* and *Room2.* When you open this project in the VB.Net IDE, you can see the *Solution* is named as *House Orientation* in the *Solution Explorer* window. The *Solution Explorer* window contains a tree that lists all the form files inside the project *House Orientation*. It provides access to the form files and manipulates these files visually (see Figure 2.2).   This application is saved as Example2_1 in Chapter 2 of CD.

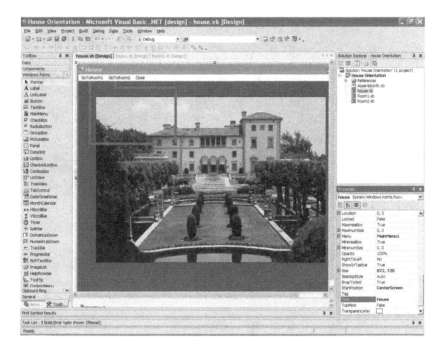

Figure 2-2   Three Form Files Listed in the Solution Explorer Window

As shown in Figure 2-2, all of the controls on the *House* form are saved into a form file called *House.vb*. Similarly, the *Room1* and *Room2* forms have their corresponding form file called *Room1.vb* and *Room2.vb*, respectively. VB is the short name for "Visual Basic".

The executable file of the *House Orientation* project can be found as *HouseOientation.exe* in Chapter 2 of the CD. When you run this executable file, the *House* window as shown in Figure 2-3 will appear. If you click the *GoToRoom1* menu, the *Room1* window as shown in Figure 2-4 shows up. If you click the *BacktoHouse* menu of the *Room1* window, the *House* window will appear again.

If you click the **GoToRoom2** menu of the **House** window, you will see the **Room2** window as shown in Figure 2-5. When you click the **Close** menu of the **Room2** window, the program terminates normally.

Figure 2-3   House Window

Figure 2-4   Room1 Window

Figure 2-5   Room2 Window

Figure 2-6 shows the detailed structure of the **House Orientation** project. Clearly, the project consists of three forms and code modules that support the forms. Each form is internally grouped as a form class. We will discuss the concept of a class in later chapters. Here we just assume a class is equivalent to a form that has a group of controls.

Each project has a starting form. If you have several forms in your project, you need to define which form is your starting form. From the starting form, the application can navigate to any other forms.

Provided that you are already in the VB.Net IDE environment, the procedure to set up the starting form for the VB.Net project **House Orientation** is as follows:

- In the VB.Net IDE, Select **Project -> House Orientation Properties**. You will see the following window (see Figure 2-7):

- The **Startup Object** box is the place where you can specify a form as the start-up form. In the above window, type **House** in the **Start Object** box to specify the **House** form is the start-up form.

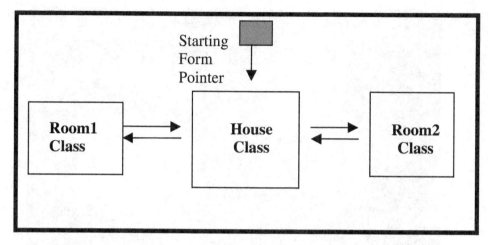

Figure 2-6   Structure of the *House Orientation* Project

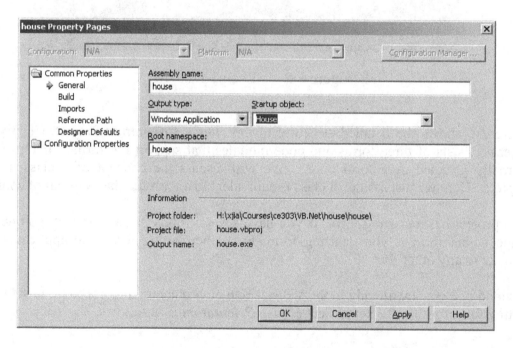

Figure 2-7 Project Properties Window for Specifying the Start-up Form

2.2   Developing the House Orientation Application

In the previous section we describe the *House Orientation* executable application. Now you need to develop this application from scratch.

The development of this application involves four primary steps: 1) form design, 2) program coding, 3) debugging and testing and 4) program packaging and delivery.

Before you develop this application, you need to get three image files from the CD. The three files are called *house.jpeg*, *room1.jpeg*, and *room2.jpeg*. You have to copy these files into your working folder or the folder where the *House Orientation* project is located.

With the image files available, let us go through the below steps for this application.

2.2.1   Form Design

Step 1: *House* Form Design

First, follow the same steps as used to create a VB.Net project called *Example1_2* in Chapter 1. You name the new project as *House Orientation* and save all the files associated with the project in your working folder (or a folder you like to store your *House Orientation* project files.)

When you are in the VB.Net IDE, note that the empty form has a default name *Form1*. Change the value of the *Name* property to *House*. Now your form is named *House.*

Figure 2-8 shows the layout of the *House* form. As you can see, the form has a total of ten controls: one *Form* control, one *PictureBox* control, five *Label* controls that represent lines, and three *Menu Item* controls derived from the *MainMenu* control template. As the label controls just show where the rooms are, we do not need to worry about their properties. The rest of controls should be created with the properties listed in Table 2-1.

a)   Create Menu Items

In order to create the *GoToRoom1*, *GoToRoom2*, and *Close1* menu items, you need to do the following:

    1)   Highlight the *MainMenu* in the *Toolbox* window.
    2)   Hold and Drag the *MainMenu* template into the *House* form
    3)   Change the text of the first menu item to be *Go To Room1* and the name
           of the control to be *GoToRoom1*. Note that the name of the control is one
           word and no space is inserted between "Go", "To" and "Room1".

           Do the same way to get *GoToRoom2* and *Close1* controls. It is noted that
           Close is a reserved word in VB.Net. We cannot use it to name a control.
           Instead we use *Close1* to name a menu item for the project.

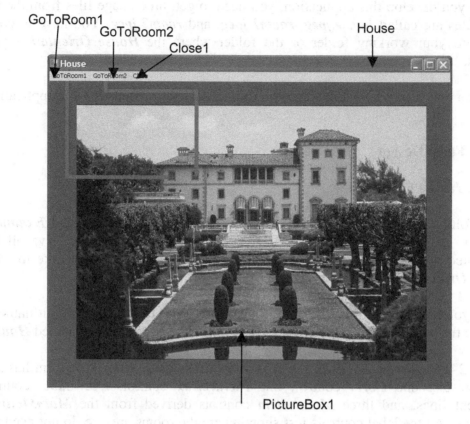

Form 2-8 House Form

Table 2-1   Control Name Table for the House Form

Control Name:	GoToRoom1	Control Name:	House
Control Type:	Menu Item from MainMenu	Control Type:	Form
Text:	Go to Room1	Text:	House
Control Name:	GoToRoom2	Control Name:	PictureBox1
Control Type:	Menu Item from MainMenu	Control Type:	PictureBox
Text:	Go to Room2	Image:	House.jpeg
Control Name:	Close1		
Control Type:	Menu Item from MainMenu		
Text:	Close		

b)   Create a *PictureBox* Control

    1)   Highlight the *PictureBox* control template in the *Toolbox* window.

    2)   Hold and Drag a *PictureBox* control in the *House* form.

    3)   In the *Image* property of the *PictureBox* control, click on the icon ⬚⬚⬚ , browse to the folder where *house.jpeg* is located, and load the image into the *PictureBox* control.

    4)   Set the **SizeMode** to be *StretchImage.*

When you finish the design of the *House* form, it will look like Figure 2-8.

Step 2: *Room1* Form Design

Do the following to create the *Room1* form:

    Go to *Project -> Add Windows Form*
    Select the *Windows Form* option
    Set the name of the new form as *Room1.vb* in the Name textbox.
    Select *Open*

Right now, the form is empty. Add one *PictureBox* control and two *Menu Item* controls on the form. The definition of these controls and their properties are listed in Table 2-2. Figure 2-9 shows the layout of the form.

Note that the image to be loaded into the *PictureBox1* control is *room1.jpeg*. Also note that the *PictureBox* controls on *House* and *Room1* forms has the same name. Although they are same, they work on different form.

Table 2-2   Control Name Table for the *Room1* Form

Control Name:	BacktoHouse	Control Name:	Close1
Control Type:	Menu Item	Control Type:	Menu Item
Text:	Back to House	Text:	Close
Control Name:	PictureBox1	Control Name:	Room1
Control Type:	PictureBox	Control Type:	Form
Image:	room1.jpeg	Text:	Room1

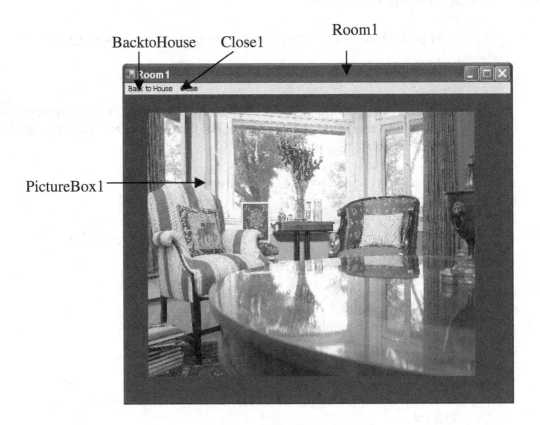

Figure 2-9 Room1 Form

Step 3: Room2 Form Design

Do the following to create the **Room2** form:

> Go to **Project -> Add Windows Form**
> Select the **Windows Form** option
> Set the form as **Room2.vb** in the Name textbox.
> Select **Open**

Right now, the form is empty. Add one **PictureBox** control and two **Menu Item** controls on the form. The definition of these controls and their properties are listed in Table 2-3. Figure 2-10 shows the layout of the form.

Table 2-3   Control Name Table for the Room2 Form

Control Name:	BacktoHouse	Control Name:	Close1
Control Type:	Menu Item	Control Type:	Menu Item
Text:	Back to House	Text:	Close
Control Name:	PictureBox1	Control Name:	Room2
Control Type:	PictureBox	Control Type:	Form
Image:	room2.jpeg	Text:	Room2

BackToHouse   Close1   Room2

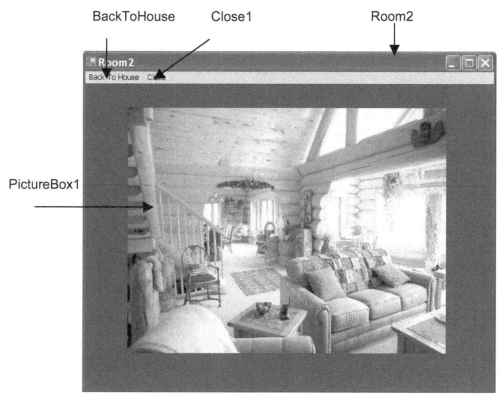

Figure 2-10   Room2 Form

2.2.2   Program Coding

a)   Code for House form

Below is the code used in the *House* form. Please copy it into the *Code* window for the House form:

Public Class House

```
    Inherits System.Windows.Forms.Form

    ┌────────────────────────────────────────┐
    │ Windows Form Designer Generated Code   │
    └────────────────────────────────────────┘
Private Sub GoToRoom1_Click(ByVal sender As Object, _
            ByVal e As System.EventArgs) Handles _
            GoToRoom1.Click
    Dim myRoom1 As New Room1
    Me.Hide()
    myRoom1.Show()
End Sub

Private Sub GoToRoom2_Click(ByVal sender As Object, _
            ByVal e As System.EventArgs) Handles _
        GoToRoom2.Click
    Dim myRoom2 As New Room2
    Me.Hide()
```

```
      myRoom2.Show()
   End Sub


   Private Sub Close1_Click(ByVal sender As Object, _
         ByVal e As System.EventArgs) Handles Close1.Click
      End
   End Sub
End Class
```

The *House* form has a class called *House*. Within this class you have three event procedures. These procedures are coded to respond to user clicking actions on *Close1 Menu Item*, *GotoRoom1 Menu Item*, and *GoToRoom2 Menu Item*, respectively.

In the above three event procedures, you see a statement called *Me.Hide*. The term *Me* refers to the form or class it resides. As the term *Me* is in the *House* form, so the *Me* refers to the *House* form. The *Hide* method enforces the *House* form to be hidden. Users cannot see this form on the computer screen.

Note that there is a *Dim* statement in the following event procedure:

```
Private Sub GotoRoom1_Click(ByVal sender As System.Object, _
                             ByVal e As System.EventArgs) _
                             Handles GotoRoom1.Click
         Dim myRoom1 As New Room1
         Me.Hide()
         myRoom1.Show()

End Sub
```

This *Dim* statement uses the *Room1* class as its data type. In VB.Net, whenever you want to declare a variable to be of a class data type, you have to use *New* in the *Dim* statement. The term *New* tells the VB.Net IDE that the event procedure should have a variable to refer to the form or the form class. More discussions on Dim statements and their data types will be discussed in later chapters.

Once you declare a variable to refer to a form, you can use the follow statements to show or hide the form:

```
MyRoom1.Show        ' MyRoom1 refers to the Room1 form
                    ' The Show method invokes the display of the
                    ' Room1 form
MyRoom1.Hide        ' MyRoom1 refers to the Room1 form
                    ' The Hide method hides the Room1 form
```

b)   Code for Room1 Form

Below is the code used in the ***Room1*** form. Please copy it into the ***Code*** window for the Room1 form:

```
Public Class Room1

    Inherits System.Windows.Forms.Form

    ┌─────────────────────────────────────────────┐
    │ Windows Form Designer Generated Code        │
    └─────────────────────────────────────────────┘

    Private Sub BackToHouse_Click(ByVal sender As Object, _
            ByVal e As System.EventArgs) Handles    _
        BackToHouse.Click
      Dim myhouse As New house
      Me.Hide()
      myhouse.Show()
    End Sub


    Private Sub Close1_Click(ByVal sender As Object, _
            ByVal e As System.EventArgs)  _
                Handles Close.Click

      End
    End Sub
End Class
```

The ***BackToHouse_Click*** event procedure, when executed, first displays the ***House*** form and then hides the ***Room1*** form. Since the procedure is tied to the ***Room1*** form, you should be aware that the procedure cannot be copied into the code window of the ***House*** form.

c)   Code for Room2 Form

Below is the code used in the **Room2** form. Please copy it into the ***Code*** window for Room2 form:

```
Public Class Room2
        Inherits System.Windows.Forms.Form

    ┌─────────────────────────────────────────────┐
    │ Windows Form Designer Generated Code        │
    └─────────────────────────────────────────────┘

    Private Sub BackToHouse_Click(ByVal sender As Object, _
            ByVal e As System.EventArgs) Handles    _
        BackToHouse.Click
      Dim myhouse As New house
      Me.Hide()
      myhouse.Show()
    End Sub

    Private Sub Close1_Click(ByVal sender As Object, _
            ByVal e As System.EventArgs)           _
```

```
                     Handles Close.Click
         End
      End Sub
End Class
```

2.2.3   Debugging and Testing

Once you finish the coding part of the *House Orientation* project, the next step is to run and test if the project executes and gets the results as you expect. Before we debug the *House Orientation* application, let us learn some concepts and terms used for debugging.

Expectation

Flow   Once an event procedure is activated, the VB.Net statements within the procedure are executed statement by statement from top to bottom.

Breakpoints   Breakpoints are the markers that can be set at any executable line of code. When a program executes to the breakpoint, it pauses and allows you to examine the state of program and ensure that everything is working as expected.

❏   Click the executable line in the code window. A solid dot will appear at the beginning of the line. The dot indicates that the breakpoint has been set for the line.

❏   When the executable line is marked with a dot, click the line. The dot will disappear.

❏   Debug -> Start to check how the breakpoint works.

Step Over   The *Step Over* button executes the next executable line of code.

You are encouraged to apply the debugging tools to test the *House Orientation* application.

2.2.4   Product Delivery

After successfully debugging the application and ensuring that the application is error free, you can package the application as a Windows product. There are many product packaging and releasing software and references available commercially. You can learn how to package a VB.Net program by reading relevant references or textbooks.

The *House Orientation* project is a simple VB.Net application. We do not need to have a complicated product that has a *setup* program to install this application. A simple executable file created from this application is enough to allow users to run this application on a computer that has VB.Net.

A quick way to create an executable file for your **House Orientation** project is as follows:

>Go to **Build -> Build House Orientation**
>Go to **Solution Explorer** window and highlight **House Orientation**
>Check the project path listed in the **Project Folder**
>Open a **Windows Explorer** and browse to the **Project Folder**
>Go to **Bin folder** within the **Project Folder**

You will see an executable file called **House Orientation** in the folder. Its file type is **Application**. Copy this executable file to a computer with VB.Net and run this executable file. You will see the same results as those generated by the executable file you get in the CD.

2.3 Questions

Q1. Suppose you are developing a VB.Net application that has four forms called FormA, FormB, FormC, and FormD. According to your understanding of the application logic, you would like to set up the FormC form to be the starting form. How do you do that?

Q2. Can a VB.Net application contain different projects? If you have a VB.Net application has two projects, **Project1** and **Project2**, describe steps on how to get the two projects into the VB.Net IDE for the application.

Q3. If you have a VB.Net application that has two projects, can you see them in the **Solutions Explorer** window?

Q4. What form is the starting form within the **House Orientation** application?

Q5. Given the below Room2 class

```
Public Class Room2
Inherits System.Windows.Forms.Form

Windows Form Designer Generated Code

Private Sub BackToHouse_Click(ByVal sender As Object,  _
           ByVal e As System.EventArgs)              _     Handles
           BackToHouse.Click
      Dim myhouse As New house
      Me.Hide()
      myhouse.Show()
  End Sub

End Class
```

What do the following VB.Net statements do?

```
Me.Hide()
myhouse.Show()
```

Q6. Assume you have two forms within a VB.Net application. These two forms are called **Form1** and **Form2**. A command button (its name is called **GoToRoom2**) appears when the **Form1** form is activated. Write an event procedure that responds to this command button. When this button is clicked, the **Form1** form will be hidden and the **Form2** form will show up.

Q7. Design a VB.Net form that has the following menus:

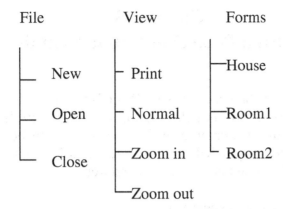

Q8.   Write the first and last line of an event procedure that responds to the click event of a command button called **Chapter2.**

Q9.   Assume you have an image file called ***Background.jpg*** in the ***c:\temp*** folder. List the steps to set this image as the background image of a form called ***Test.***

Q10.   Assume you have a VB.Net application, list steps to create an executable file for the application.

Chapter 3
Visual Basic.Net Fundamentals

As you see in the previous chapters, a Visual Basic.Net application is made of a group of forms and modules. Each form is a class and has its own controls. Each control has a number of events that are encountered during the interaction between users and the program. An event is often responded by a procedure that tells what to do for the event. This chapter discusses the contents of event procedures.

3.1   Structure of An Event Procedure

Typically an event procedure has the following structure:

```
Private Sub ControlName_EventName (parameters)

     VB.Net Statement
     VB.Net Statement
     VB.Net Statement
     .
     .
     .
     VB.Net Statement
End Sub
```

It begins with *Private Sub* and ends with *End Sub*. It has a set of VB.Net statements that respond to an event (defined by the EventName) of an control (defined by the ControlName). When this event procedure is trigged to run, the statements will be executed one by one from top to bottom. The first statement will be called for execution. After the first statement, the second statement will be called and executed. The procedure keeps the same pattern for execution until it reaches to *End Sub*.

Take the below event procedure as an example:

```
Private Sub Calculate_Click (ByVal sender As System.Object, _
                    ByVal e As System.EventArgs)            _
                    Handles Calculate.Click

   REM This is a comment statement
   REM Below are variables a, b, c, rt1, rt2 and
   REM chk declared within this procedure

   Dim a as integer
   Dim b as integer
   Dim c as integer
   Dim rt1 as Double
   Dim rt2 as Double
   Dim chk as Long
   Dim Response as integer
```

```
' The below three statements are used to check
' if the values of the textboxes are numeric values.
' If they are not, send messages out and terminate
' the execution of the procedure.

If Not IsNumeric(Val_a.text) or Val_a.Text = "" then
     Messagebox.Show ("Please enter a numeric value")
     Exit Sub
End If

If Not IsNumeric(Val_a.text) or Val_a.Text = "" then
     Messagebox.Show ("Please enter a numeric value")
     Exit Sub
End If

If Not IsNumeric(Val_c.text) or Val_c.Text = "" then
     Messagebox.Show ("Please enter a numeric value")
     Exit Sub
End If


' The below three statements get user inputs
' of a, b, and c from the textboxes on the
' form after the numeric value check.

A = val(val_a.text)
B = val(val_b.text)
C = val(val_c.text)

' The below two statements are used to check
' if real roots exist. If there are real
' roots, calculate the roots and assign them
' to two variables called rt1 and rt2.

Chk = b^2 - 4*a*c

If chk <  0 then

        Response = Msgbox ("No real roots exist", _
                       VBYesNo, "Example")
        If response = vbYes then
             Exit Sub
        End if

Else
        Rt1 = (-b+Math.sqrt(chk))/(2*a)
        Rt2 = (-b-Math.sqrt(chk))/(2*a)
End If

' Output the calculated roots onto the two
' textboxes on the form so that users
' can see the roots.

Root1.text = str(rt1)
Root2.text = str(rt2)
End Sub
```

This event procedure responds to the *Click* event of the control called *Calculate*.

3.2   VB.Net Statements

In this section we will discuss the comment statement, the Dim statements, the assignment statements, and the if-Then-Else-End If statement used to find roots for a quadratic equation. Discussion of other VB.Net statements will be provided in later chapters.

3.2.1   Comment Statements

Comment statements are the statements that start with a single quotation mark (') or REM. They help explain the logic of the code. Since they are not executable statements, they will be skipped during the execution of the event procedure.

3.2.2   Dim Statements

The Dim statement declares a "room" in the computer memory with a name. Its syntax is as follows:

```
Dim   <variable> As <Data Type>
```

In this syntax, <variable> is a placeholder for the name of a room. A room contains a group of memory cells allocated to store various values. The words Dim and As are the keywords reserved for VB.Net applications.

How big is the "room" represented by a variable? Dim statements use data type to define the size of the room. When a variable is declared to be of *Integer* data type, the room for the variable is sized with two bytes.

Table 3-1 lists a group of data types commonly used in VB.Net. The *Long Integer* data type takes 4 bytes to size variables that store whole numbers without any factional portion. The *Single* and *Double* data types take 4 and 8 bytes respectively to represent float numbers. The *Currency* or *Date* data type specifies the values of a variable in the format of currency or date. The *String* data type specifies a variable to have a string of characters. The *Boolean* data type takes 2 bytes to store values either *TRUE* or *FALSE*. The *Object* data type is a compounded data type. We will discuss this data type when we use it in later chapters.

Table 3-1 List of Data Types

Data type	Description	Range
Byte	1-byte binary data	0 to 255.
Integer	2-byte integer	- 32,768 to 32,767.
Long	4-byte integer	- 2,147,483,648 to 2,147,483,647.
Single	4-byte floating-point number	- 3.402823E38 to - 1.401298E - 45 (negative values). 1.401298E - 45 to 3.402823E38 (positive values).
Double	8-byte floating-point number	- 1.79769313486231E308 to - 4.94065645841247E - 324 (negative values). 4.94065645841247E - 324 to 1.79769313486231E308 (positive values).
Currency	8-byte number with a fixed decimal point	- 922,337,203,685,477.5808 to 922,337,203,685,477.5807.
String	String of characters	Zero to approximately two billion characters.
Boolean	2 bytes	TRUE or FALSE
Date	8-byte date/time value	January 1, 100 to December 31, 9999.
Object	4 bytes	Any object reference.

Examples of *Dim* statements are listed below:

```
Dim        StudentName As String
Dim        Tuition As Currency
Dim        StudentAddress As String, StudentID As Long
Dim        a, b, c as Integer
```

The first statement declares the variable ***StudentName***. Its data type is ***String***. The second statement declares the variable ***Tuition***. It has the ***Currency*** data type. The third statement combines multiple declarations in one line and separates them by commas. The last statement defines three variables. The first two variables *a* and *b* are specified as the ***Object*** data type. The last variable *c* is specified as the ***Integer*** data type.

A variable is often named to reflect its use. When you declare a variable to store a value for the parameter A of a quadratic equation, it is suggested to name it as ***ParameterA, a,*** or ***CoefficientA***. The variable name cannot begin with a numeric letter. You cannot name a variable as ***123ABC***. Additionally, two identical variable names cannot be used in a form. Otherwise, you may run into errors when you execute the form. Also variable names cannot be the same as control names.

3.2.3 Assignment Statements

An assignment statement gives a variable a value by setting it equal either to an existing quantity or to a value computed by a mathematical expression. Its syntax is as follows:

```
Control Property
Or                    = value, variable, expression, or property
Variable
```

Note that the control property or variable being assigned a value always appears on the left side of the "=" sign. One and only one control property or variable can be placed on the right side of the "=" sign and is assigned by a value.

Example assignment statements are listed below:

```
A  =  4
B  =  A
C = val(val_c.text) + A + B
Root1.text = rt1
```

The first assignment statement assigns 4 to variable *A*. The format of this assignment statement is:

```
Variable = value
```

The second assignment statement assigns the current value of variable *A* to variable *B*. Before this statement is executed, variable A must have a value. Otherwise running errors will occur. The format of the statement is:

```
Variable = variable
```

The third assignment statement assigns the value computed from the expression "Val (val_c.Text) + A + B" to variable *C*. Its format is:

```
Variable = expression
```

Note that the expression is made of the text property of the textbox control *val_c*, variables *A* and *B*.

The fourth statement assigns the current value of variable *rt1* to the text property of the textbox control *root1*.

Note that on the right side there are values, variables, expressions, properties or combination of them. On the left side there are one and only one variable or a control property. You cannot find a valid assignment statement as shown below:

```
X+Y = A + B
```

The above statement has two variables combined on the left side of the "=" sign and violates the definition of the assignment statement.

3.2.3.1 Dot Notion

A dot notion is used to link a property to a control. The general format of the dot notion is **Object.Property**. A control is considered an object in VB.Net. The above format for a control is then shown as **Control.Property**. For example, **Root1.text** indicates the text property of the control **Root1**.

3.2.3.2 Expression

An expression defined in VB.Net is a combination of two or more variables, control properties and/or constants with operators. It is the VB.Net implementation of a mathematical expression in algebra. To understand the definition of an expression in VB.Net, we need to discuss three key terms: constants, operators, and functions.

Constants

Constants are values that do not change within a VB.Net application. Numbers and strings are constants. For example, 100 and 3.1415926 are the number constants, while **"Real roots do not exist"** and **"Please enter parameter a"** are the string constants.

VB.Net allows the use of symbolic constants (or named constants) for actual numbers or strings. Assigning a name to a constant follows the below syntax:

```
CONST <Constant-Name> AS <Data-Type> =     _
      <Value> or <Expression>
```

For example,

```
CONST PI as Single = 3.1215926
CONST Year as INTEGER = 365
```

In the above examples, the CONST and AS are the keywords reserved in VB.Net. The <Constant-Name>, <Data-Type>, <Value>, and <Expression> are the placeholders. You can use any name for a constant as long as the name follows the VB.Net naming convention. Data types used here are the same as those in Dim statements. The value can be a string constant, a number or an expression.

Operators

Operators are symbols used for carrying out mathematical operations. There are four types of operators in a VB.Net expression: arithmetic, concatenation, comparison, and logical.

1)   Arithmetic Operators

Arithmetic operations are listed in Table 3-2. They are used for arithmetic calculations. Note that all of these operators are the same as those in algebra. You should be able to handle them easily.

Table 3-2   Arithmetic Operators

Operator	Example	Description
( )	(a+b+c)	Group operating elements.
^	Radius ^2	Get exponential value of Radius
*	4* A	Multiply 4 by the value stored in variable A
/	Tuition/4	Divide tuition by 4
\	Number\7	Perform an integer division of number by 7
Mod	Days mod 7	Get reminder from dividing days by 2
+	a+b+c	Sum a, b and c together
–	a–b	Subtract b from a

Here we just review the integer division and mod operations. The integer division rounds divisor and dividend to integers before the division operation is executed. Further the quotient is truncated to an integer. For example,

```
A = 4.1415926
B = 13.345
C = B\A
D = B mod A
```

The B\A operation will first round the value in A to be 4 and value in B to be 13, then perform the division of 13 by 4, get the result to be 3.25, and truncate the result to be 3. Finally the variable C is assigned with 3.

The mod operation finds the integer reminder that results from the integer division of two operands. Given the above example, the B mod A operation will yield a value of 3 with reminder of 1. Therefore the variable D is assigned with 1.

Operations in an expression follow the below order (or the same order as in algebra):

1) Parenthesis
2) Exponentiation
3) Multiplication or division
4) Integer division
5) Modulus
6) Addition or subtraction

In case there are elements in the same execution level, the order will be from left to right.

2)   Concatenating Operators

Concatenating operators are string operators because they are applied only to string constants and string variables. There are two string operators available in VB.Net: "+" and "&". They both append the second string value to the first one. For example,

```
Dim A as String
Dim B as String
Dim C as string
A = "Please enter "
B = "a value for the program"

C = A & B
D = A + B
E = C + ", OK?"
```

The string variable A is assigned with a string constant "Please enter ", while the variable B is assigned with a constant "a value for the program." The C and D variables will get the same result as "Please enter a value for the program." even with two different string operations. The last statement shows the concatenation operation of a string variable and a constant string ", Ok?"

3)   Comparison Operators and Logical Expression

There are six comparison operators used in VB.Net for comparison of any two variables, constants, expressions or control properties. Table 3-3 lists these six operators.

Comparison operators in VB.Net are the same as those in mathematics. However there are several issues programmers should be aware of. First, the symbols for the "greater than or equal to" and "less than or equal to" operators are ">=" and "<=" respectively, different from ≥ and ≤ in mathematics. In addition, the "not equal to operator" is symbolized as <> instead of ≠. Second, when variables, constants, expressions, or control properties are compared using the above operators, they should be with the same data type. You cannot compare a string value with a numerical value. Third, the result of comparison is a Boolean value, that is, either TRUE or FALSE.

Using comparison operations, we can form simple logical conditions as shown in Table 3-3.

Table 3-3 List of Comparison Operators

Operator	Example	Description
=	StudentID = 1567001	Equal to
>	Score > 90	Grater than
>=	Score >= 90	Grater than or equal to
<	Score < 60	Less than
<=	Score <= 60	Less than or equal to
<>	Score <> 100	Not equal to

4)   Logical Operators

Simple logical conditions can be combined to form a compound logical condition using logical operators *And, Or, Not*, and *Xor* (see Table 3-4). Using the *And* operator we can represent the mathematical expression 15 < y < 100 by two simple logical conditions 15 < y and y < 100.

Table 3-4 List of Logical Operations

Operator	Example	Description
And	Score > 90 and Grade = A	Both logical operands must be true for the entire condition to be true.
Or	X > 20 or Y < 0	One or both logical operands must be true for entire condition to be true.
Not	Not (Score > 90)	Reverse the logical condition. Whatever is true will be false, whatever is false will be true.
Xor	X > Y Xor A > B	One and only one condition is true.

Functions

A VB.Net function is an operation that takes one or more arguments and returns a single value. Its syntax is as follows:

```
Function_Name (arg1, arg2, …., argn)
```

Where `arg1, arg2, … argn` are the list of arguments.

VB.Net has implemented or embedded lots of functions including math functions, string extraction and manipulation functions, date and time functions, and so on. In the below section, we just discuss functions that are often used in later chapters.

Sqrt() Function

Sqrt () function returns the square root of a number in *Double* format. Its syntax is Sqrt (*number*). The *number* argument is a Double type value that is greater than or equal to zero.

Examples of Sqrt function are as follows:

```
Dim aSqureRoot as Double
aSqureRoot  = Math.Sqrt(4)          ' Returns 2.
Chk         = Math.sqrt(B^2-4*A*C)  'returns based on a, b, and c
```

Val() Function

Val () function converts alphabetical numbers in a string to a numeric value. Its syntax is Val(*string*). The *string* argument is any valid string expression. Examples of Val() function are as follows:

```
Dim aValue as Integer
aValue = Val("24571")            ' Returns 24571.
aValue = Val(" 2 45 7 1")        ' Returns 24571.
aValue = Val("25 and 571")       ' Returns 25.
aValue = Val(" +  2 45 7 1")     ' Returns +24571.
aValue = Val("  -  25 and 571")  ' Returns -25.
```

Val() function stops reading the string when it cannot recognize a character as part of a number. Symbols and characters that are often considered parts of a numeric value in math, such as dollar signs and commas, are not recognized as part of a numerical value in VB.Net. Blanks, tabs, and linefeed characters are skipped from the argument.

The following Val () function returns the value of 3801:

```
Val("  3801 Temple Ave.")
```

In addition, Val() function recognizes only the first period (.) as a valid decimal separator.

Very often we use Val() function to convert a value of the text property from a string to a number, which is then assigned to a numeric variable. Take the below statements as an example,

```
A = val(val_a.text)
B = val(val_b.text)
C = val(val_c.text)
```

The first statement uses the Val() function to convert the user input (which is a string) into a numeric value and assigns the value to variable A. The second and third statements convert user inputs in the textbox controls into numerical values and assign them to variables B and C, respectively.

MsgBox() Function

Msgbox () function displays a message in a dialog box, waits for the user to click a button, and returns an Integer indicating which button is clicked by the user. Its syntax is

MsgBox(*prompt* [, *buttons*] [, *title*])

The description of arguments in the function is as follows:

Prompt   Required. It is a string expression that will appear as the message in the dialog box.

Buttons   Optional. It is a numerical expression that sums the values used to specify the number and type of buttons to display, the icon style to use, the identity of the default button, and the modality of the message box. The default value for *buttons* is 0 when this argument is omitted.

Title   Optional. It is a string expression that will appear in the title bar of the dialog box. The application name is placed in the title bar when this argument is omitted.

The key *buttons* settings are:

Constant	Value	Description
vbOKOnly	0	Display **OK** button only.
vbOKCancel	1	Display **OK** and **Cancel** buttons.
vbAbortRetryIgnore	2	Display **Abort, Retry,** and **Ignore** buttons.
vbYesNoCancel	3	Display **Yes, No,** and **Cancel** buttons.
vbYesNo	4	Display **Yes** and **No** buttons.
vbRetryCancel	5	Display **Retry** and **Cancel** buttons.
vbCritical	16	Display **Critical Message** icon.
vbApplicationModal	0	Application modal; the user must respond to the message box before continuing work in the current application.
vbSystemModal	4096	System modal; all applications are suspended until the user responds to the message box.

The Return Values can be one of the values in the list below:

Constant	Value	Description
vbOK	1	OK
vbCancel	2	Cancel
vbAbort	3	Abort
vbRetry	4	Retry
vbIgnore	5	Ignore
vbYes	6	Yes
vbNo	7	No

An example of the *MsgBox* () function is as follows:

```
Response = Msgbox ("No real roots exist", VBYesNo, _
     "Example")
If response = vbYes then
     Exit Sub
End if
```

The *MsgBox()* function asks the user to respond by clicking on the *Yes* or *No* button (see Figure 3-1). If the user clicks the *Yes* button, the value of 6 (or *VbYes*) will be returned and assigned to the variable *response*. The next statement will check if the return value is *VBYes*. If it is *VBYes*, then the program executes the *Exit Sub* statement and exits the procedure.

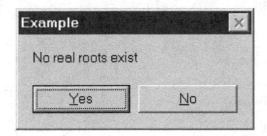

Figure 3-1 Example of a Msgbox() Function

Str() Function

Str () function returns a String value converted from a number. Its syntax is **Str**(*number*). The *number* argument is a *Long*-type argument containing any valid numeric expression. Below are examples that use the Str() function to return a string representation of a number.

```
Dim MyString as string
MyString = Str(4591)          ' Returns " 4591".
MyString = Str(-4591.65)      ' Returns "-4591.65".
MyString = Str(4591.001)      ' Returns " 4591.001".
```

When numbers are converted to strings, a leading space is always reserved for the sign of *number*. If *number* is positive, the returned string contains a leading space and the plus sign is implied. The Str() function is just the reverse operation of Val() function.

InStr() Function

It returns a Long-type value that specifies the position of the first occurrence of one string within another. Its syntax is InStr([*Start,*] *String1*, *String2*)

The InStr () function syntax has these arguments:

Start   Optional. It is a numerical expression that tells the starting position for search. If this argument is omitted, search starts at the first character position. An error occurs when this argument contains Null.

String1   Required. It is the string expression to be searched from.

String2   Required. It is the string expression to be searched for.

Below are examples that show the use of the InStr() function to get the position of the first occurrence of one string within another.

```
Dim SearchSource as String, SearchKey as String
Dim Position as Integer

SearchSource = "Civil Engineering Program is a Nice Program"
SearchKey = "Program"

' Search starts at position 5. Returns 19.
Position = Instr(5, SearchSource, SearchKey)

' Search starts at position 20. Returns 37.
Position = Instr(20, SearchSource, SearchKey)
```

The InStr() function is useful for extracting a subset of a string. Suppose you have a form with a textbox control. The user can input a quadratic expression such as $10005x^2 - 2222x + 1$ into the textbox control. You can use the following InStr() function to check where the string "x^2" starts.

```
Position = instr(val_a.text, "x^2")
```

Note that the `val_a` is the name of the textbox control. A string "x^2" is the search key. The position will be assigned with 6 for the above example.

Mid() Function

It returns a String value that contains a specified number of characters from a string. Its syntax is *Mid(String, Star t[, Length])*. It has three arguments listed below:

String   Required. It is a string expression from which characters are returned.

Start   Required. It specifies the character position in *String* at which a subset to be taken begins. This function returns a zero-length string ("") when *Start* is greater than the number of characters in *String*.

Length   Optional. It specifies the number of characters to be extracted out of *String*. If it is omitted, all characters from the *Start* position to the end of the string are returned. Also if the number of characters in *String* (including the character at *Start)* is less than the *Length* value, all the characters after the *Start* position (including the *Start* character) is returned.

The below example uses the Mid () function to return a specified number of characters from a string.

```
Dim Astring as String
Dim FirstString as String
Dim LastString as String
Dim MidString as String

Astring = "Jason is a good kid."

' The below Mid() returns "Jason".

FirstString = Mid(AString, 1, 5)

' The below Mid() returns "is".
LastString = Mid(AString, 7, 2)

'The below Mid returns "is a good kid."

MidString  = Mid(AString, 7)
```

The second example uses both the InStr() and Mid() functions to extract parameter *a* from a textbox that stores a quadratic equation expression.

```
Dim Position as Integer
Dim para_a as String

Position = Instr(func.text, "x^2")
Para_a = Mid(func.Text, position -1)
Val_a.Text = Para_a
```

In this example, the quadratic expression is stored in the text property of the textbox control *func*. The extracted value is then sent to the text property of the textbox *val_a*.

3.2.4   If-Then-Else and If-Then Statements

If-Then-Else statement is a compound VB.Net statement that controls the flow of the program's execution. Normally a program's logic is to flow through statements from left to right, and from top to bottom. When an If-Then-Else statement is used, it conditionally executes a group of statements depending on the value of a logical expression.

The syntax of If-Then-Else statements is as follows:

```
If <Logical Expression> Then

        VB.Net Statements 1
Else

        VB.Net Statements 2


End If
```

When the logical expression is *True*, then the VB.Net statements 1 will be executed. Otherwise, the VB.Net statements 2 will be executed. In detail, the execution flow can be described by a flow chat in Figure 3-2.

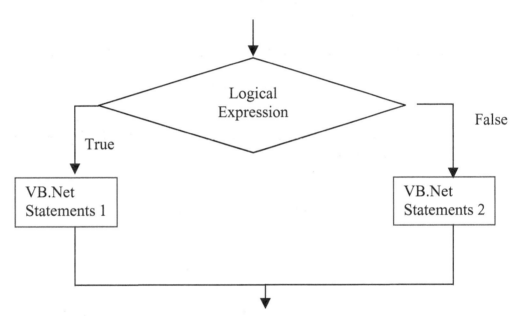

Figure 3-2 Execution Flow of an If-Then-Else Statement

When no VB.Net statements 2 are used in the *Else* part, the If-Then-Else statement will become an If-Then statement. Its syntax is as follows:

```
If Logical Expression Then

        VB.Net Statements 1

End If
```

An example of If-Then-Else statements is as follows:

```
Chk = b^2 - 4*a*c
If chk < 0 then
      MessageBox.Show ("No real roots exist")
      Exit Sub
Else
      Rt1 = (-b+Math.sqrt(chk))/(2*a)
      Rt2 = (-b-Math.sqrt(chk))/(2*a)
End If
```

This example shows that the logical expression is *chk < 0*, where variable *chk* is assigned a value before the execution of the logical expression. If the expression returns *True*, the following two statements will be executed.

```
MessageBox.Show ("No real roots exist")
Exit Sub
```

Otherwise, the below two assignment statements will be executed.

```
Rt1 = (-b+Math.sqrt(chk))/(2*a)
Rt2 = (-b-Math.sqrt(chk))/(2*a)
```

Note that *MessageBox.Show ()* is a VB.Net statement. It displays a message box window to inform users "No real roots exits".

The flow chart for the above example is shown in Figure 3-3.

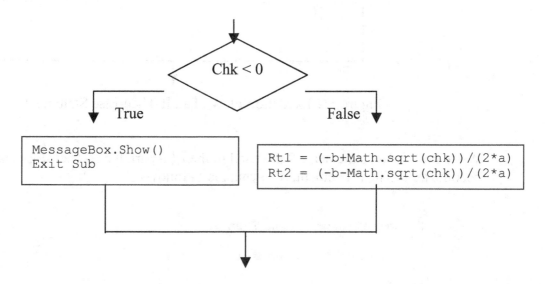

Figure 3-3 Flow Chart of the Example If-Then-Else Statement

An example of If-Then statements is as follows:

```
If A > 0 Then
        A = A + 1
        C = B + A
        C = C + B
End If
```

The flow chart for the above example is shown in Figure 3-4.

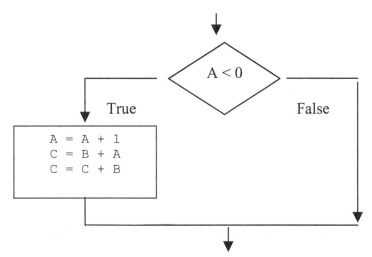

Figure 3-4 Flow Chart of the Example If-Then Statement

You can use the single-line form to have multiple statements executed when the logical expression is **_True_**. All statements must be on the same line and separated by colons, as in the following statement:

```
If A > 0 Then A = A + 1 : C = B + A : C = C + B
```

The above statement is equivalent to the following statement:

```
If A > 0 Then
        A = A + 1
        C = B + A
        C = C + B
End If
```

An If-Then-Else statement can be nested with another If-Then-Else or If-Then statement. This is allowed since the outer If-Then-Else statement considers the inner If-Then-Else or If-then statement as a VB.Net statement.

For example,

```
If chk <  0 then

      Response = Msgbox (      "No real roots exist", _
                              VBYesNo, "Example")
      If response = vbYes then
            Exit Sub
      End if

Else
      Rt1 = (-b+Math.sqrt(chk))/(2*a)
      Rt2 = (-b-Math.sqrt(chk))/(2*a)
End If
```

The below VB.Net statement is embedded inside the outer If-Then-Else statement:

```
If response = vbYes then
      Exit Sub
End if
```

3.3   Questions

Q1.   Determine the data type for each of the following variables:

```
Variable expected to store 1,2,3, 67, 56, 49
Variable expected to store 12345, 45678, 346784
Variable expected to store True and False
Variable expected to store $100.87, $299,000.00
Variable expected to store 12233.234, 2345.009, 3456.998
```

Q2.   VB.Net provides a set of built-in functions such as those discussed in this chapter. Use the VB.Net Help to explore the functions called *Inputbox()* and *format()*. Develop a program that illustrates the use of them.

Q3.   Determine the execution order of the following expression

```
7+3*3+a+b^2
Math.sin(x) + Math.cos(x)  * Math.exp(x)
Math.exp(x) + Math.sqrt(Math.abs(x))
-5 - 5\2+3
10 mod 2 ^2 +3
```

Note that *Exp(x)* and *Abs(x)* are the VB.Net functions that calculate the exponential and absolute values of x, respectively. Also note that *Sin(x), Cos(x), Exp(x), Sqrt(x),* and *Abs(x)* are the mathematical functions. Therefore, each of them is prefixed with **Math** in VB.Net applications.

Q4.   Identify and correct the following variables:

```
DIM true As Integer
DIM variable as Long
DIM 123Lotus as String
DIM a,b,c as Integers
```

Q5.   Write a VB.Net program that allows users to enter a series of numbers
           (separated by a coma) in a text box called *series*. When the users clicks the
           command button called *Average,* the program extracts the number one by one
           from the series and calculates the average, and outputs the average onto a
           textbox called *Result.* When the user clicks on the command button called
           Cancel, the program terminates normally.

Q6.   Given the following procedure, develop its execution flow chart

```
Private Sub Calculate_Click ( ByVal sender As            _
                 System.Object,                           _
                 ByVal e As System.EventArgs)             _
                 Handles Calculate.Click

   ' This is a comment statement
   ' Below are Variables a, b, c, rt1, rt2 and
   ' chk declared within this procedure

     Dim a as integer
     Dim b as integer
     Dim c as integer
     Dim rt1 as Doubl
     Dim rt2 as Double
     Dim chk as Long
     Dim response as integer

     ' The below three statements get user inputs
     ' of a, b, and c from the textboxes on the
     ' form.

   A = val(val_a.text)
   B = val(val_b.text)
   C = val(val_c.text)

     ' The below two statements are used to check
     ' if real roots exist. If there are real
     ' roots, calculate the roots and assign them
     ' to two variables called rt1 and rt2.

   Chk = b^2 - 4*a*c

   If chk <  0 then

         Msgbox ("No real roots exist"
         Exit Sub
```

```
        Else
                Rt1 = (-b+Math.sqrt(chk))/(2*a)
                Rt2 = (-b-Math.sqrt(chk))/(2*a)
        End If

        Root1.text = str(rt1)
        Root2.text = str(rt2)
End Sub
```

Q7.   Develop a program that can calculate the below function:

$$y = 1.5e^{-1.2t} + \sqrt{t} + e^{-2.0t} \ (t \geq 0 \ and \ t < 5)$$
$$y = 2.5\cos(t) + 1.2\sin(t) + \log_{10}(t) \ (t \geq 5)$$
$$y = 0 \ (t < 0)$$

You need to design a graphic user interface that allows users to enter the value for t, calculate the y value and display the y value on the interface. A user should be able to clear the t and y values anytime and terminate the program when the user clicks on the *Cancel* button. [Hint: Go to VB.Net online help to search functions for e^t and $\log_{10}(t)$.

Q8.   Given the below program, please answer the following questions:

a)   List variables used in the below event procedure
b)   List built-in functions in the event procedure
c)   List all the dot notations that combine a control name and a property name with a dot.
d)   Which control does the event procedure respond to?
e)   If you type `123` into text box "`a_box`", what are the values of `a_box.Text` and `a_val` respectively?
f)   If the value of variable "`Temp1`" is `457.900`, what is the value of `Root1.Text`?

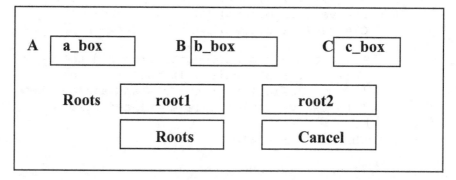

Control Names: Names in boxes are the control names.

```
Private Sub Roots_Click (ByVal sender As                _
                System.Object,                          _
                ByVal e As System.EventArgs)            _
                Handles Roots.Click

      Dim Check as Double
      Dim A_val, b_val, c_val as double
      Dim Temp1, Temp2 as double
      Dim Root1_val, root2_val as double

      A_val = val(a_box.Text)
      B_val = val(b_box.Text)
      C_val = val(C_box.Text)

      Check =  b_val * b_val - a_val *c_val * 4

      If check < 0 then
            Msgbox "No root exists"
      Else

            Temp1 =(-b_val+Math.sqrt(check))/(2*a_val)
            Temp2 =(-b_val-Math.sqrt(check))/(2*a_val)

            Root1.Text = str(temp1)
            Root2.Text = str(temp2)
      End if
End Sub
```

Q9.   List all the VB.Net statements discussed in this chapter.

Q10.   What is the difference between the following statements?

```
Msgbox "This is a test"
Messagebox.Show "This is a test"
```

Q11.   Given the below statements, what is the value of *position*?

```
Dim Position as Integer
Position = Instr ("Welcome to VB.Net", "come")
```

Q12.   Given the below statements, what is the value of *test*?

```
Dim Position as Integer, Test as string
Position = Instr ("x^2 - 2x + 1", "x")
Test = mid("x^2 - 2x + 1", 1, Position - 1)
```

Q13. The below chart shows the execution flow that determines the roots of a quadratic equation: ax^2+bx+c = 0. If parameter a does not exists, enter 0 in its textbox. Follow the same rule for parameters b and c.

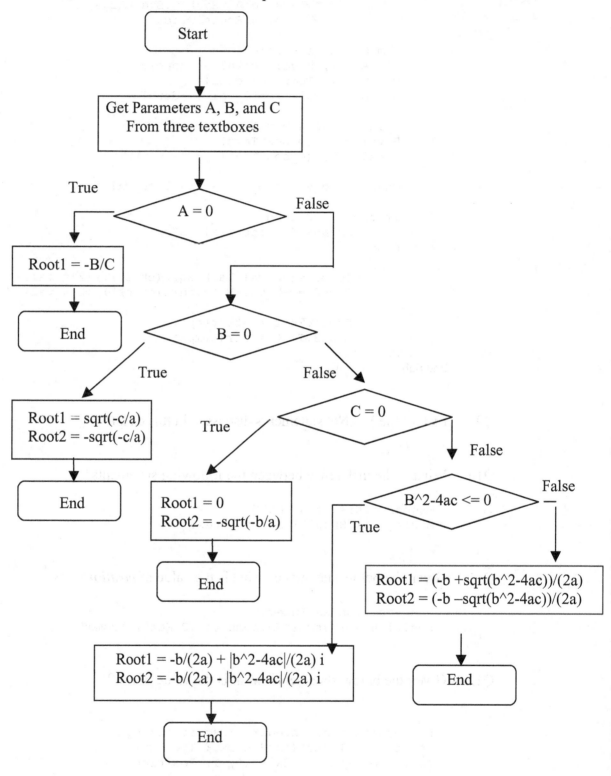

Chapter 4
Development of VB.Net Applications I

This chapter presents two problems with which you can develop VB.Net applications. The first problem is related to the calculation of area and perimeter of three given points. The second problem is related to the solution of a quadratic equation. The quadratic equation is entered in the form of $f(x) = ax^2 + bx + c = 0$. You need to develop a VB.Net application that can get the real or imaginary roots for any given quadratic equation.

4.1   Project I: Area and Perimeter of Three Given Points

You are asked to develop an <u>error free</u> VB.Net application that can calculate the area and perimeter of three given points (see Figure 4-1). Figure 4-2 shows an example form for the application. The form, when activated, allows users to enter x1, y1, x2, y2, x3, and y3. Then the users can click the **Calculate** button. The area and perimeter enclosed by the three given points will be calculated and displayed at the **Area** and **Perimeter** textboxes. When users click the **Clear** button, the textboxes will be empty. When users click the **Cancel** button, the program terminates normally.

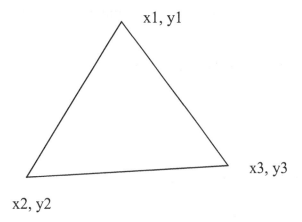

Figure 4-1   Area and Perimeter of Three Given Points

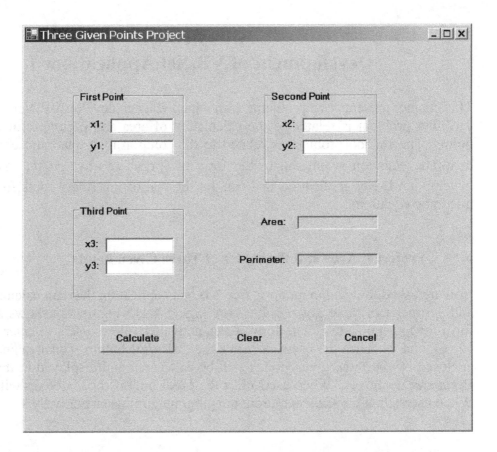

Figure 4-2   An Example Form for the Project

The formula used to calculate the area of three given points is

Area = 0.5 * |(x2*y3 − y2*x3) + (x1*y2 − y1*x2) + (y1*x3 − x1*y3)|

Or

Heron's formula:

$$S = \sqrt{s(s-a)(s-b)(s-c)}$$

Where s = ½ $(a + b + c)$ is the **semi-perimeter**, or one half of the triangle's perimeter.

    a   = distance between point (x1,y1) and point (x2, y2)
    b   = distance between point (x2,y2) and point (x3, y3)
    c   = distance between point (x1,y1) and point (x3, y3)

The distance between two given points can be calculated using the below formula:

$$D = \sqrt{|x1 - x2|^2 + |y1 - y2|^2}$$

4.2   Project II: Roots for a Quadratic Equation

You are asked to develop a Visual Basic.Net application that can determine roots of a quadratic equation. The functional requirements of this project are as follows:

1)   Design a form to allow users to define a quadratic equation. The form should have a textbox control created from the textbox control template (see Figure 4-3). This textbox control will allow users to enter a quadratic expression. For example, if we want to determine the roots for

$$x^2 + 2x + 1 = 0$$

The textbox control should allow users to enter in the quadratic expression in it:

$$1x^2 + 2x + 1$$

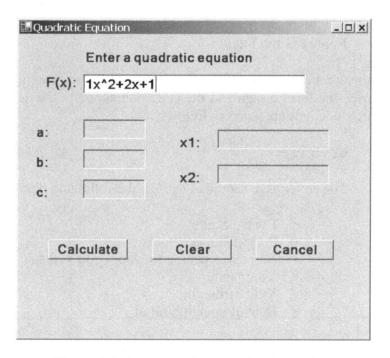

Figure 4-3 An Example Form for the Project

2)   When a quadratic equation is entered in the textbox, the parameters (*a, b, and c*) of the expression should be extracted when users enter the Enter key. The extracted parameters are then displayed in the textboxes for them, respectively. Hint: You need to use the **KeyPress** event to respond to the

textbox for the quadratic equation. For example, when the textbox is named *Func*, the event procedure to respond to the *KeyPress* event will be as follow:

```
Private Sub Func_KeyPress(ByVal sender As Object,      _
    ByVal e As System.Windows.Forms.KeyPressEventArgs) _
    Handles Func.KeyPress

End Sub
```

More information about how to respond to the *KeyPress* event is provided in Chapter 5. When you are working on this project, you should read Chapter 5 to get a better understanding of VB.Net statements that are related to this project.

3)   Once the parameters a, b, and c are extracted from the quadratic equation and displayed in the three designated textboxes, you are asked to calculate the roots and display them on the form.

4)   The VB.Net application should have extensive checking capabilities to ensure the roots are calculated accurately. The application should be able to determine both real and imaginary roots.

4.3   Report Guidelines

A project report is required for the above two VB.Net applications. The report should describe the form design and the code that supports the determination of roots. The report guidelines are listed as follows:

- Cover Page

  The cover page should consist of the following items:

  - ✓ Course Name
  - ✓ Project Name
  - ✓ Name of a person to whom you will submit
  - ✓ Your name
  - ✓ Your affiliation
  - ✓ Date of your submittal

  Remember the cover page is the face of the report. Prepare your report with a professional looking face.
- Project Objectives

  In this section objectives of the application should be provided so that users can understand what the project is supposed to do.

- GUI Interface Design

  The form designed to implement the logic of the VB.Net application should be documented. A table that explains the control names defined in the form should be included so that developers and programmers can understand how the project is developed.

- Source Code

  All the source code should be provided in this section. Your code should have a rich set of comments so that the project logic can be easily understood.

- Running Results

  Detailed running steps should be documented. This section should have a lot of pictures that snap the course of execution of the program. If you do not know how to do screen snap, below are the steps for that:

  Step 1:   Run the program and make the project running window active.

  Step 2:   Press *Alt* and ***Print Screen*** keys at same time. This step will snap your screen as an image and save it in the ***Clipboard.***

  Step 3:   Press *Ctrl* and *V* keys together to retrieve the image and insert into the word or power point for your report.

- Conclusions and Suggestions

Chapter 5
More VB.Net Statements

In the first four chapters of this book, we have discussed that a VB.Net application is made of a set of event procedures that support the logic of the application. Also, we have discussed that an event procedure is made of a series of VB.Net statements that are executed one by one from top to bottom, from left to right. As you see in Chapter 3, a number of statements such as Dim statements, Assignment statements, If-Then and If-Then-Else statements are introduced.

In this chapter we will introduce you more statements that are often used in the development of VB.Net applications. We first have an overview of all the statements for application development. Then we will concentrate on decision-making and loop statements.

5.1   Overview of VB.Net Statements

VB.Net provides a set of statements that can be used in various event procedures. Table 5-1 lists these statements in alphabetical order. As you can see, there are a total of 49 statements available in the VB.Net Integrated Development Environment (IDE) for application development.

A VB.Net statement is described by its function, syntax and descriptions of its arguments. You need to pay attention to the descriptions of its arguments.

This book cannot discuss all the statements listed in Table 5-1 in great detail. The focus of this book is to introduce the statements that will be often used in solving problems in later chapters. The statements to be discussed in this chapter consist of Select Case, Do-Loop, While – End While, and For Next statements.

The If-Then-Else statement discussed in the previous chapters involves a decision that controls the program execution path. When the logical condition within an If-Then-Else statement is *True*, the VB.Net statements in the Then part should be executed. Otherwise, the VB.Net statements in the Else part should be executed. The Select Case statement shows another way of making decisions on which part of VB.Net statements to be executed. The loop statements repeat a group of operations until a logical condition is satisfied.

Table 5-1   List of VB.Net Statements

Statement Name	Description
AddHandler	Associate an even with a handler. `AddHandler Event, Addressof Handler`
Call	Transfers control to a Sub procedure or Function procedure. `Call ProcedureName <Argument List>`
Class	Declares the name of a class, as well as a definition of the variables, properties, events, and methods that comprise the class. `See Help to find its syntax and an example use of it.`
Const	Used at module, class, structure, procedure, or block level to declare constants for use in place of literal values. `Example: Const PI as Double = 3.14259265`
Declare	Used at module level to declare references to external procedures. `See Help to find its syntax and an example use of it.`
Declare	Used to declare a delegate. Delegates are a reference type that refers to a Shared method of a type or to an instance method of an object. `See Help to find its syntax and an example use of it.`
Dim	Used at module, class, structure, procedure, or block level to declare and allocate storage space for variables. `See its discussion in Chapter 3.`
Do Loop	Repeats a block of statements while a Boolean condition is True or until the condition becomes True. `More discussion in this chapter.`
End	Terminate execution immediately. `End`
Enum	Used at module, class, or structure level to declare an enumeration and define the values of its members. `See Help to find its syntax and an example use of it.`
Erase	Used to release array variables and de-allocate the memory used for their elements. `Erase <ArrayList>`
Error	Simulate the occurrence of an error `Error <ErrorNumbe>`
Event	Declares a user-defined event. `See Help to find its syntax and an example use of it.`
Exit	Exits a procedure or block and transfers control immediately to the statement following the procedure call or the block definition. `Exit { Do	For	Function	Property	Select	Sub	Try	While }`
For Each ...Next	Repeats a group of statements for each element in an array or collection. `More discussion will be provided in this chapter.`
For ... Next	Repeats the execution of a group of statements a specified number of times. `More discussion will be provided in this chapter.`
Function	Declares the name, arguments, and code that define a Function procedure. `More discussion will be provided in later chapters.`

Table 5-1   List of VB.Net Statements (Cont'd)

Statement Name	Description
Get	Declares a Get property procedure used to assign a value to a property. `See Help to find its syntax and an example use of it.`
GoTo	Branches unconditionally to a specified line within a procedure. `GoTo line`
If-Then-Else	Conditionally executes a group of statements, depending on the value of an expression. `See its discussion in Chapter 3.`
Implements	Specifies one or more interfaces, or interface members for class or structure definition. `See Help to find its syntax and an example use of it.`
Imports	Imports namespace names from referenced projects and assemblies. `See Help to find its syntax and an example use of it.`
Inherits	Causes the current class or interface to inherit the attributes, fields, properties, methods, and events from another class or interface. `Inherits typename`
Interface	Declares the name of an interface, as well as the properties, methods and events that comprise the interface. `See Help to find its syntax and an example use of it.`
Mid	Replaces a specified number of characters in a **String** variable with characters from another string. `See Help to find its syntax and an example use of it. Also see its difference from Mid function.`

Module	Declares a module block.
	`    Public Module Module1`
	`        ' Add classes, properties, methods, fields,`
	`        ' and events for this module.`
	`    End Module`

Namespace	Declares the name of a namespace. `See Help to find its syntax and an example use of it. Also see Imports statement.`
On Error	Enables an error-handling routine and specifies the location of the routine within a procedure. `Its discussion will be provided in later chapters.`
Option Compare	Used at file level to declare the default comparison method to use when string data is compared. `See Help to find its syntax and an example use of it.`
Option Explicit	Used at file level to force explicit declaration of all variables in that file. `Option Explicit { On	Off }`
Option Restrict	Implicit data type conversions are restricted to *widening* conversions only. `Option Strict { On	Off }`
Property	Declares the name of a property, and the property procedures used to store and retrieve the value of the property. `See its discussion in later Chapter.`

Table 5-1   List of VB.Net Statements (Cont'd)

Statement Name	Description
RaiseEvent	Triggers an event declared at module level within a class, form, or document. `See Help to find its syntax and an example use of it.`

Randomize	Initializes the random-number generator.
	`Randomize [ number ]`
	`See its discussion in this chapter.`

ReDim	Used at procedure level to re-allocate storage space for an array variable. `ReDim [Preserve ] name[(boundlist)].` `See also its discussion in later chapter.`

REM	Used to include explanatory remarks in a program
	`REM comment`
	`' comment`

RemoveHandler	Removes the association between an event and an event handler. `RemoveHandler event, AddressOf eventhandler`
Resume	Resumes execution after an error-handling routine is finished. `Resume [Next	line]`
Return	Returns control to the code that called a Sub, Function, or Property procedure. `Return  -or-  Return expr`
Select Case	Executes one of several groups of statements, depending on the value of an expression. `See its discussion in this chapter.`
Set	Declares a Set property procedure used to assign a value to a property. `See its discussion in later chapters.`
Stop	Suspends execution.
Structure	Used at module or class level to declare a structure and define the characteristics of its members. `See its discussion in later Chapter.`
Sub	Declares the name, arguments, and code that define a Sub procedure. `See its discussion in previous chapters.`
Synclock	Allows statements to be synchronized on a single expression. `See Help to find its syntax and an example use of it.`
Throw	Creates an exception within a procedure. `Throw expression`
Try .. Catch... Finally	Provides a way to handle some or all possible errors that may occur in a given block of code, while still running code. `See Help to find its syntax and an example use of it.`
While ... End While	Executes a series of statements as long as a given condition is True. `See more discussion in this chapter.`
With ... End With	Executes a series of statements making repeated reference to a single object or structure. `See more discussion in later chapters.`

5.2   Select Case Statement

A Select Case statement is an efficient decision-making VB.Net statement that deals with more than two branches of execution flows. It executes one of several groups of VB.Net statements, depending on the value of an expression. The expression can be either numeric expression or string expression.

The syntax of a Select Case statement is as follows:

```
Select Case Expression

    Case Condition
        VB.Net Statements 1

    Case Condition
        VB.Net  Statements 2

        ...

    Case Else
        VB.Net Statements n
End Select
```

Select Case statements are often used to replace nested If-Then statements. Suppose you have a nested If-Then-Else statement that looks like:

```
IF Scores >= 90 Then
      Grade = "A"
Else
      If Scores >= 80 and Scores < 90 then
            Grade = "B"
      Else
            If Scores >= 70 and Scores < 80 then
                  Grade = "C"
            Else
                  If Scores >= 69 and Scores < 70 then
                        Grade = "D"
                  Else
                        Grade = "F"
                  End If
            End If
      End If
End If
```

You feel that the logic of the code is not easy to follow since it involves four If-Then-Else statements. To simplify the code, we can use a Select Case statement to replace it.

```
Select Case Scores

        Case Is >= 90
                Grade = "A"
        Case Is >= 80
                Grade = "B"
        Case Is >= 70
                Grade = "C"
        Case Is >= 60
                Grade = "D"
        Case else
                Grade = "F"
    End Select
```

In this example, you can see that the Select Case statement has three parameters listed in Table 5-2. Note that when the Select Case statement is executed, the program first checks if the expression (or the variable "Scores" for the above example) matches any Case condition expression. If it matches one of the case condition expressions, the statements in that Case clause are executed up to the next Case clause, or, for the last clause, up to End Select.

The Case Else clause will be executed if no match is found between the expression and any case condition. The Case Else clause is optional that often handles unexpected conditions.

The execution flow for the example Select Case statement is shown in Figure 5-1.

Table 5-2 Syntax of the Select Case Statement

Parameters	Description
Expression	Required. A numeric expression or a string expression.

Case Condition	Required. It can be in one or more of the following forms:
	
	 `expression`
	 `expression To expression`
	 `Is expression.`

VB.Net statements	Optional. These statements will be executed if the expression matches their case condition expression.
Else statements	Optional. These statements will be executed if the condition doesn't match any Case conditions.

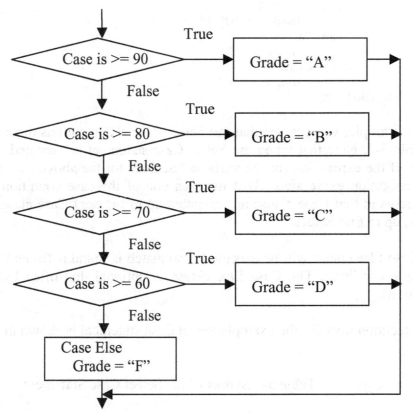

Figure 5-1 Execution Flow of the Select Case Statement

EXAMPLE 5-1 for Select Case Statement

You are asked to design a form in VB.IDE. The properties of the key controls are shown in Figure 5-2.   When this form is executed, users will click the button on the form. The *Case Selection Example* window will appear. It lets users enter the exam scores for a student in the *ScoresVal* textbox, the program then tells which grade the student will get in the *GradeVal* textbox.

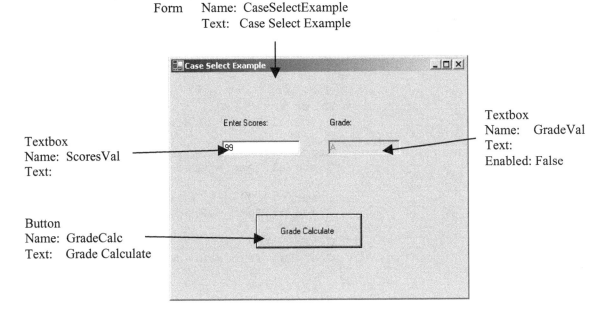

Form   Name: CaseSelectExample
        Text: Case Select Example

Textbox
Name: ScoresVal
Text:

Textbox
Name: GradeVal
Text:
Enabled: False

Button
Name: GradeCalc
Text: Grade Calculate

Figure 5-2   Form used in the Select Case Example

The code for the Select Case example is as follows:

```
Public Class DoWhileExample
    Inherits System.Windows.Forms.Form


        | Windows Form Designer generated code |


Private Sub GradeCalc_Click(ByVal sender As System.Object,  _
        ByVal e As System.EventArgs)                        _
        Handles GradeCalc.Click

    Dim scores As Integer, Grade As String
    ' Before Any calculation is performed, a check is
    ' required to ensure that the value entered in the
    ' ScroesVal textbox is a numeric value. If it is not,
    ' the program will exit this event procedure.

    If Not IsNumeric(ScoresVal.Text) Then
        MessageBox.Show("Enter a numeric value ... ")
        Exit Sub
    End If


    '  To get a numeric value from the ScoresVal Textbox and
    '  Assign the value to a variable called scores.

     scores = Val(ScoresVal.Text)
```

```
' The below Select Case statement checks which
' category the value stored in the variable scores
' belongs to and executes the VB.Net statement within
' that category.

  Select Case scores

            Case Is >= 90
                Grade = "A"
                GradeVal.Text = Grade
            Case Is >= 80
                Grade = "B"
                GradeVal.Text = Grade
            Case Is >= 70
                Grade = "C"
                GradeVal.Text = Grade
            Case Is >= 60
                Grade = "D"
                GradeVal.Text = Grade
            Case Else
                Grade = "F"
                GradeVal.Text = Grade
      End Select

  End Sub

End Class
```

5.3   Indeterminate Loop Statements

There are four types of indeterminate loop statements that repeat a group of operations until a certain condition is reached. The number of repetitions is not known in advance. These types of statements are:

1)   Do Until < Logical Condition >

          VB.Net Statements
     Loop

2)   Do While <Logical Condition >

          VB.Net Statements
     Loop

3)   DO
          VB.Net Statements

     Loop Until   <Logical Condition>

4)   Do
                VB.Net Statements

        Loop While <Logical Condition>

The first two loop statements test the logical condition before the VB.Net statements are executed. We call them as pre-check statements. The last two loop statements execute the VB.Net statements first and then check the logical condition to decide if further execution should continue. Because the logical condition is checked after an execution of the VB.Net statements, we call them the post-check statements.

We will discuss the statements 2) and 3 in this chapter because they are commonly used in the development of VB.Net applications. The statements 1) and 4) remain to be your assignments.

5.3.1   Do While Statement

Do While statements are used to repeat a block of statements while its logical condition is **True**. Its syntax is as follows:

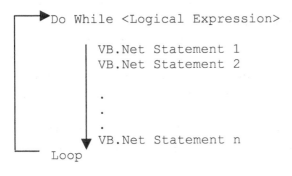

```
Do While <Logical Expression>

     VB.Net Statement 1
     VB.Net Statement 2
          .
          .
          .
     VB.Net Statement n
Loop

Next VB.Net Statement
```

When a Do While statement is executed, the program first calculates the value of the logical expression and checks if it is *True*. If the value is *True*, the VB.Net statements inside the loop will be executed. When the execution reaches the Loop keyword, the program will go back to calculate the logical expression again. It continues the execution until the logical expression becomes *False*. Figure 5-3 shows the execution flow chart of the Do While statement.

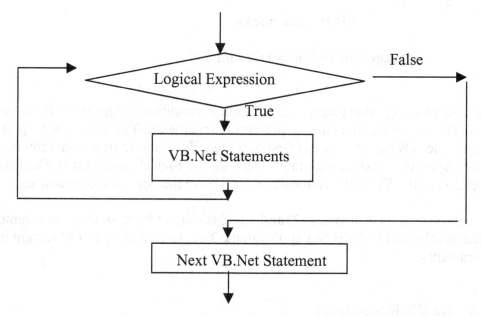

Figure 5-3 Execution Flow Chart of Do While Statement

EXAMPLE 5-2 for Do While Statement

The below example of the Do While statement is used to show the definition of ASCII code and the KeyPress event of a textbox. Figure 5-4 shows the form for this example.

In this form, there are five controls: one form control, one textbox control, one list box control, and two label controls. Table 5-3 shows the names of the controls.

Table 5-3 Control Names for the Do While Example

Control	Type	Property		Comments
1	Label	Text:	Letters:	Not used in code
		Name:	Label1	
2	Label	Text:	ASCII Code:	Not used in code
		Name:	Label2	
3	Textbox	Text:		Used in the code to get a series of letters
		Name:	Letters	
4	Listbox	Name:	ASCIIList	Used in the code to show the ASCII code of the entered letters
5	Form	Title:	Do While Example	Not used in code
		Name:	DoWhileExample	

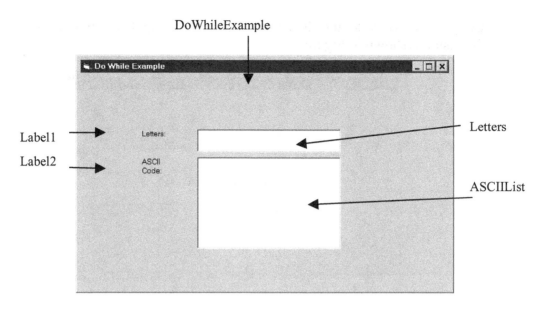

Figure 5-4 Form for the Do While Example

The code for the Do While Example is as follows:

```
Public Class DoWhileExample
    Inherits System.Windows.Forms.Form

    Windows Form Designer generated code

    Private Sub Letters_KeyPress(ByVal sender As Object,      _
        ByVal e As System.Windows.Forms.KeyPressEventArgs)   _
        Handles Letters.KeyPress

        Dim ALetter As String
        Dim ASCIICodeforLetter As Integer
        Dim i As Integer
        If Asc(e.KeyChar) = 13 Then

            ASCIIList.Items.Clear()
            ASCIIList.Items.Add("Entered Letter" + vbTab +    _
                    "ASCII Code")
            ALetter = Mid(Letters.Text, 1, 1)
            i = 1
            Do While i <= Len(Letters.Text)
                ASCIICodeforLetter = Asc(ALetter)
                ASCIIList.Items.Add(ALetter + vbTab + vbTab   _
                                + Str(ASCIICodeforLetter))
                i = i + 1
                ALetter = Mid(Letters.Text, i, 1)
            Loop
        End If
    End Sub
End Class
```

Copy the above code into the code window of the application and run it. You will see the result as shown in Figure 5-5.

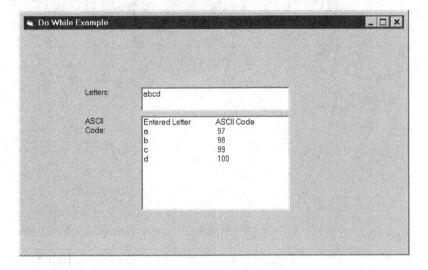

Figure 5-5   Running Results of the Example Code

Note that the example involves a number of new terms and concepts. Before we discuss the Do While statement, let us discuss these terms and concepts first.

1)   *KeyPress* Event

The *KeyPress* event is an event that indicates a user's key action. When a user presses and then releases a key, the *KeyPress* event is activated. Normally the *KeyPress* event procedure that supports the *KeyPress* action is as follows:

```
Private Sub ControlName_KeyPress(ByVal sender As Object,     _
    ByVal e As System.Windows.Forms.KeyPressEventArgs)       _
    Handles ControlName.KeyPress
End Sub
```

Inside the parentheses there are two objects: *Sender* and *e*. The *e* object stores a list of arguments related to the *KeyPress* action. One of the arguments is the property called *KeyChar*. The *KeyChar* property records the key pressed by the user. Assume the user presses the "A" key, the computer will have the "A" key stored in the *e.KeyChar*.

A key on the keyboard is linked to a code called *ASCII* code as shown in Table 5-4. ASCII stands for American Standard Code for Information Interchange. An ASCII code is a code used for representing English characters as numbers, with each letter assigned a number from 0 to 127. For example, the ASCII code for uppercase *A* is 65. Most computers use ASCII codes to represent text, which makes it possible to transfer data from one computer to another.

Table 5-4 ASCII Table

ASCII	Symbol	ASCII	Symbol	ASCII	Symbol	ASCII	Symbol
0	NUL	16	DLE	32	(space)	48	0
1	SOH	17	DC1	33	!	49	1
2	STX	18	DC2	34	"	50	2
3	ETX	19	DC3	35	#	51	3
4	EOT	20	DC4	36	$	52	4
5	ENQ	21	NAK	37	%	53	5
6	ACK	22	SYN	38	&	54	6
7	BEL	23	ETB	39	'	55	7
8	BS	24	CAN	40	(	56	8
9	TAB	25	EM	41	)	57	9
10	LF	26	SUB	42	*	58	:
11	VT	27	ESC	43	+	59	;
12	FF	28	FS	44	,	60	<
13	CR	29	GS	45	–	61	=
14	SO	30	RS	46	.	62	>
15	SI	31	US	47	/	63	?
ASCII	**Symbol**	**ASCII**	**Symbol**	**ASCII**	**Symbol**	**ASCII**	**Symbol**
64	@	80	P	96	`	112	p
65	A	81	Q	97	a	113	q
66	B	82	R	98	b	114	r
67	C	83	S	99	c	115	s
68	D	84	T	100	d	116	t
69	E	85	U	101	e	117	u
70	F	86	V	102	f	118	v
71	G	87	W	103	g	119	w
72	H	88	X	104	h	120	x
73	I	89	Y	105	i	121	y
74	J	90	Z	106	j	122	z
75	K	91	[	107	k	123	{
76	L	92	\	108	l	124	|
77	M	93	]	109	m	125	}
78	N	94	^	110	n	126	⌂
79	O	95	_	111	o	127	

The *e.KeyChar* property stores the key last entered by users. When users press an 'a' key, the ASCII code (97) that corresponds to the key is stored. Similarly, when the user presses the *Enter key* (or the *Carriage Return* key), the ASCII code 13 is stored.

The meaning of ByVal will be discussed in later chapters. Right now, we just skip the byVal term in our explanation of the *KeyPress* event.

2)   *ListBox* Control Template

This example introduces a *Listbox* control derived from the ListBox control template. The *ListBox* control displays a list of items from which the user can select one or more. If the number of items exceeds the number that can be displayed, a scroll bar is automatically added to the *ListBox* control.

To remove all the elements in the list, use the *Items.Clear* method. To add or delete items in a *ListBox* control, use the *Items.Add* or *Items.Remove* method. As you can see in the example, the *Items.Add* method requires a string as its argument. The string is concatenated from three strings such as "Entered Letters", VBTab, and "ASCII Code" (see Figure 5-5.) VBTab is a reserved string constant that represents the Tab key. Detailed descriptions of *ListBox* control's properties and methods will be provided in later chapters.

3)   *Len()* function

The *Len()* function returns a *Long*-type numerical value that records the number of characters in a string. Its syntax is *Len(string)*. For example, *Len("ABCD")* returns 4 because there are four letters in the string.

4)   *Asc()* Function

The *ASC()* function returns an Integer that represents the ASCII code of the first letter in a string. Its syntax is *Asc(string)*. The return value is ranged 0-127 because there are only 127 ASCII codes in the ASCII table. For example, ASC("A") returns 65. ASC("a") returns 97 . ASC("DO While Example") returns 68.

5)   *Do While* Statement

With the knowledge about the *Keypress* event, *ListBox* control, and several string manipulation functions, we can explore the Do While statement in the example.

```
Do While i <= Len(Letters.Text)
      ASCIICodeforLetter = Asc(ALetter)
      ASCIIList.Items.Add(ALetter + vbTab + vbTab      _
          + Str(ASCIICodeforLetter))
      i = i + 1
      ALetter = Mid(Letters.Text, i, 1)
   Loop
```

In this Do-While statement, the logical expression is

```
        I <= len(letters.text)
```

The variable I is a counter or position pointer. It increases in the loop that indicates the move from the first letter to the last one of the entered string. There are four VB.Net statements in the loop. The first statement gets the ASCII code for the current letter extracted out from the *Letters* textbox. The second statement adds a letter and its associated ASCII code in the *ASCIIList* listbox. The third increases the counter. The last one moves the pointer to the next letter in the string and extracts the letter out for the next iteration.

How many times does the *KeyPress* event procedure run? How many times does the Do While statement run? How many times do the three loop statements run? A hint to answer the above questions is that whenever a key is pressed, the *KeyPress* event procedure should be activated to respond to the event. As five keys ('Key a', 'Key b', 'Key c', 'Key d' and Enter key) are entered in the *Letters* textbox, therefore, there are five times that the *KeyPress* event procedure is executed. Since the Do While loop is inside the following statement:

```
If Asc(e.KeyChar) = 13 Then


End If
```

Therefore, the statement is executed only one time. As to the third question, since there are four letters in the entered string, therefore the loop statements are executed four times.

5.3.2   Do Loop Until Statement

Do Loop Until statements are used to repeat a block of statements until a logical condition becomes *True*. Its syntax is as follows:

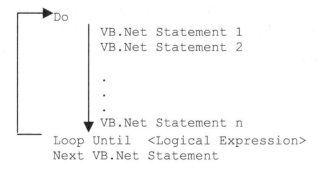

```
    Do
          VB.Net Statement 1
          VB.Net Statement 2

          .
          .
          .
          VB.Net Statement n
    Loop Until  <Logical Expression>
    Next VB.Net Statement
```

When a Do Loop Until statement is executed, the program first executes the VB.Net statements inside the loop. After that, it calculates the value of the logical expression and checks if it is *True*. If the value is True, the program moves out of the loop and goes to the next VB.Net statement. If the value is False, the program continues its execution of the VB.Net statements in the loop until the logical expression becomes True. Figure 5-6 shows the execution flow chart of a Do Loop Until statement.

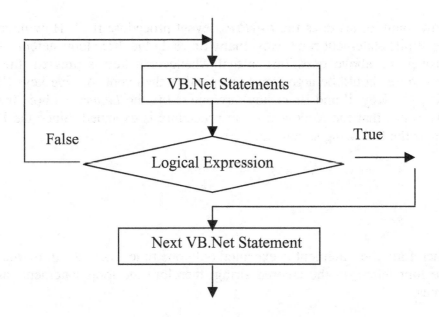

Figure 5-6 Execution Flow Chart of Do Loop Until Statement

AMPLE 5-3 for Do Loop Until Statement

Assume you are asked to write a VB.Net application. This application has one form on which there is one button called **Button1** (see Figure 5-7). When the application is run and the form appears on the computer screen, users can click the **Button1** button and the below event procedure will be executed.

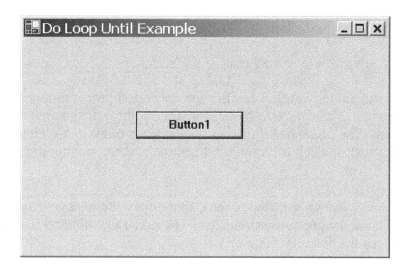

Figure 5-7 Do Loop Until Example

```
Public Class DoLoopUntilExample
    Inherits System.Windows.Forms.Form

    Windows Form Designer generated code


    Private Sub Button1_Click(ByVal sender As
            System.Object, ByVal e As System.EventArgs)
            Handles Button1.Click

        DIM UserInput as String
        DIM Message as String
        DIM Title as String
        DIM Default1 as string
        DIM sum as Integer, aValue as Integer

        Message = "Enter a value between 1 and 100"
        Title = "DO While and InputBox Example"
        Default1 = "1"

        Sum  = 0
        aValue = 0
        Do
                Sum = Sum + aValue
                UserInput = InputBox(Message, Title, Default1)
                Avalue = val(UserInput)
        Loop Until aValue < 1 or aValue > 100
        Console.WriteLine Sum
        Console.WriteLine(aValue < 1 Or aValue > 100)
    End Sub
End Class
```

The logical expression in the Do Loop Until statement is

```
aValue < 1 or aValue > 100
```

Its logical value is evaluated after the execution process moves into the loop. Its value of *True* or *False* is totally dependent on the value received from the *Inputbox()* function. The *inputbox()* function displays a prompt in a dialog box, waits for users to input a text or click a button, and returns a string containing the contents of the text box.

Figure 5-8 shows the dialog box that takes the message, title and default1 value specified in the previous statements. The user can enter any number between 1 and 100 to replace the default1 value of 1.

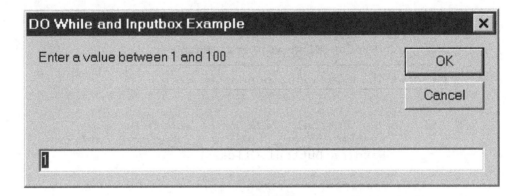

Figure 5-8 Inputbox Dialog Box

Note that the return value from the *inputbox()* function is a string. It should be converted into a numerical value using the *val()* function before we add it to variable *sum*.

Also note that the Do Loop Until statement has three VB.Net statements within the loop. The statement that contains the *inputbox ()* function keeps asking users for input. If users enter a number less than 1 and greater than 100, the logical expression will be *True*. The execution process will exit from the loop and go to the next VB.Net statement.

There are two *Console.WriteLine* statements after the Do Loop Until statement. These two statements are used to display the value of *Sum* and the result of the logical expression, after the execution process exits from the loop. The value of *Sum* and the result of the logical expression are displayed in the *Output* window. If you cannot see the *Output* window, you can enable it through the following steps in the VB.Net IDE:

1)   Go to *View -> Other Windows -> Output* or Type *Ctrl+Alt+O*

2)   Place the *Output* window in a place so that you can see the results from *Console.WriteLine* statements.

A VB.Net statement called *Exit Do* may be used to force the execution process to be out of the loop. You can learn the *Exit Do* statement by using the VB.Net help utility.

In summary, Do Loop Until statements terminate a group of operations on *True* condition.

Now let's check your understanding of this Do Loop Until Example application. When you run the application, you go through the following steps:

1)   Run the application, the below *Inputbox* window appears and you enter 2 in the textbox (see Figure5-9).

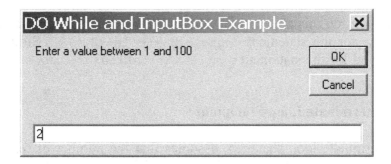

Figure 5-9 Inputbox Window with 2 Entered

2)   The *Inputbox* appears again, you enter 3 in the textbox as shown in Figure 5-10.

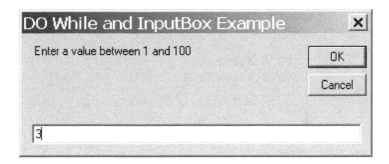

Figure 5-10 Inputbox Window with 3 Entered

3)   The *Inputbox* appears again. You enter -1 in the textbox as shown in Figure 5-11.

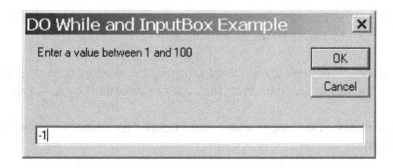

Figure 5-11 Inputbox Window with -1 Entered

4)   The application is terminated.

After you run this application, do you know what is the value displayed in the *Output* window for the statement `Console.WriteLine(Sum)`?   Similarly, what is the value displayed for the statement `Console.WriteLine(Not aValue >= 1 And aValue <= 100)`?

5.4 Determinate Loop Statement

A determinate loop statement assumes that the number of repetitions of operations is known in advance. In this section, we will introduce the For-Next loop statement. This statement is often used in handling matrices and arrays in later chapters.

The syntax of a For-Next loop statement is as follows:

```
For variable = <initiate-value> To <end-value> Step      _
<change-interval>

        VB Statement 1
        VB Statement 2
        .
        .
        .
        VB Statement n
Next Variable
```

The variable in the syntax is the counter variable in the loop. The <initiate-value> is the placeholder that can be filled with a numerical expression representing the starting value of the counter variable. The <end-value> is also the placeholder for a numerical expression whose value is the ending value of the counter variable. The placeholder <change-interval> provides the interval the counter variable changes each time in the loop. If the change interval is 1, the *Step* keyword can be omitted.

An example of the For-Next loop statement is as follows:

```
FOR I = 1 TO 10 STEP 1
        ListBox1.Items.Add Str(I)
NEXT I
```

Note that the variable after the keyword *Next* is the same as that after *For* keyword. Figure 5-12 is the flow chart for the above example of the For-Next Loop statement.

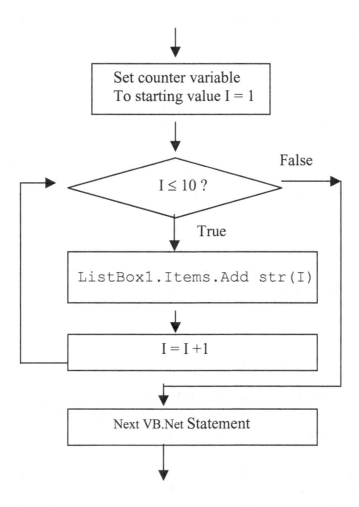

Figure 5-12 Execution Flow Chart of the Example For-Next Statement

As shown in Figure 5-12, the execution process is as follows:

1)   The program first sets the counter variable as the starting value. In this example, variable I is set with 1.

2)   The program then checks if the variable value is greater than the ending value. In the example I ≤ 10.

3)   If the value is less than or equal to the ending value, the program goes into the loop and executes the VB.Net statements in the loop. After that it moves onto the keyword *Next*.

4)   After the loop statements are executed, the counter variable is increased by an interval (1 as shown in the example) and goes back to Step 2).

5)   The program continues the loop until the value in the counter variable is greater than the ending value and moves onto the next VB.Net statement.

EXAMPLE 5-4 for For-Next Statement

You are asked to develop a VB.Net application that can have a number of operations for a *ListBox* control. Figure 5-13 shows the form in the application. As you can see, the form contains eight command buttons, a ListBox control, a Label control, and a TextBox control.

Table 5-5 lists the key control names used in this form. Note that the *Add1*, not *Add,* is used to be the name of the *Add* button since *Add* is the reserved word in VB.Net IDE. For the same reason, *Remove1* (instead of *Remove*) and *Update1* (instead of *Update*) are used to be the name for *Remove* and *Update* buttons.

The logic of this application is as follows:

1)   When this application is run and this form is prompted to users. Users can type a numeric value and click the *Add* button. The numeric value in the *NumVal* textbox is then added into the *List1* list.

2)   When a user wants to insert a numeric value before a specified item in the list, he or she can highlight the item in the Listbox, enter the numeric value to be inserted, and click the *Insert* button. The numeric value is then inserted into the Listbox.

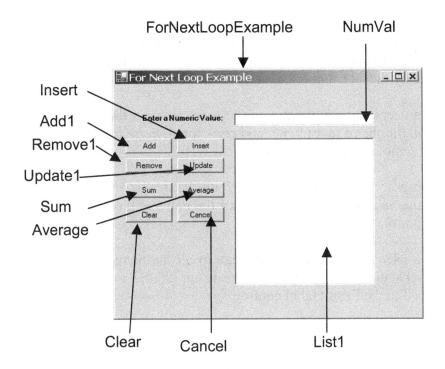

Figure 5-13 Form for the For-Next Loop Example

Table 5-5 Control Names for the For-Next Example

Control	Type	Property		
1	Label	Name:	Label1	
		Text:	Enter a Numeric value	
2	Textbox	Name:	NumVal Text:	
3	Button	Name:	Add1 Text:	Add
4	Button	Name:	Insert Text:	Insert
5	Button	Name:	Remove1 Text:	Remove
6	Button	Name:	Update1 Text:	Update
7	Button	Name:	Sum Text:	Sum
8	Button	Name:	Average Text:	Average
9	Button	Name:	Clear Text:	Clear
10	Button	Name:	Cancel Text:	Cancel
11	ListBox	Name:	List1	
		SelectionMode: MultiSimple		
12	Form	Name:	ForNextLoopExample	
		Title:	For Next Loop Example	

3)   When a user wants to update an item in the Listbox by a new one, the user needs to highlight the item to be updated, and enter the replacing numeric value in the textbox, and click the *Update* button. The item in the Listbox will be updated by the new numerical value.

4)   When a user wants to remove one or more items in the Listbox, the user needs to highlight one or more items and click the *Remove* button. The selected items will be removed from the Listbox.

5)   When a user wants to get the sum of all the items in the Listbox, the user just clicks the *Sum* button. The sum of all the items will be displayed in the *Result* label control.

6)   When a user wants to get the average of all the items in the Listbox, the user just clicks the *Average* button. The result of the average operation will be displayed in the Result label control.

The code for this application is listed as follows:

```
Public Class ForNextLoop
        Inherits System.Windows.Forms.Form

        ┌────────────────────────────────────────┐
        │  Windows Form Designer generated code  │
        └────────────────────────────────────────┘


        Private Sub Cancel_Click(ByVal sender As       _
                System.Object, ByVal e As              _
                System.EventArgs)                      _
                Handles Cancel.Click
            End
        End Sub



        Private Sub Clear_Click(ByVal sender As         _
                System.Object, ByVal e As               _
                System.EventArgs)                       _
                Handles Clear.Click
            NumVal.Text = ""
            List1.Items.Clear()
        End Sub
```

```
Private Sub Add1_Click(ByVal sender As              _
            System.Object, ByVal e As              _
            System.EventArgs)                      _
            Handles Add1.Click
    Dim aNumericValue As Double

    ' Check if a numeric value is entered in
    ' the textbox. If the value is a numeric value,
    ' convert the value as a numeric value
    ' and insert it in the list. Otherisw, display
    ' a message and exit the procedure.

    If IsNumeric(NumVal.Text) Then
        aNumericValue = Val(NumVal.Text)
        List1.Items.Add(aNumericValue)
    Else
        MessageBox.Show("Enter a Numeric Number")
        Exit Sub
    End If
End Sub

 Private Sub Insert_Click(ByVal sender As           _
            System.Object, ByVal e As              _
            System.EventArgs)                      _
            Handles Insert.Click

 Dim aNumericValue As Double
 Dim SelectedItemPos As Integer
 SelectedItemPos = List1.SelectedIndex

 ' Check if an item in the list is highlighted.
 ' If no item is selected, display a message and
 ` exit the procedure.

 If SelectedItemPos < 0 Then
     MessageBox.Show(                              _
            "Specify a position to insert the number ...")
     Exit Sub
 End If

 ' Check if a numeric value is entered in the textbox.
 ' If the value is a numeric value, convert the
 ' value as a numeric value and insert it in the list.
 ' Otherwise, display a message and exit the
 ' procedure.

 If Not IsNumeric(NumVal.Text) Then
     MessageBox.Show("Enter a Numeric Number")
     Exit Sub
 End If
```

```
        aNumericValue = Val(NumVal.Text)




        ' Insert the numeric value in the textbox into
        ' the list.

        ' The inserted value will be placed before
        ' the highlighted item.

        List1.Items.Insert(SelectedItemPos, aNumericValue)

End Sub

Private Sub Update1_Click(ByVal sender As
            System.Object, ByVal e As
            System.EventArgs) Handles Update1.Click

    Dim aNumericValue As Double
    Dim SelectedItemPos As Integer
    SelectedItemPos = List1.SelectedIndex

    ' Check if an item in the list is highlighted.
    ' If no item is selected, display a message and
    ' exit the procedure.

    If SelectedItemPos < 0 Then
        MessageBox.Show(
"Specify a position to update the number ...")
        Exit Sub
    End If

    ' Check if a numeric value is entered in the textbox.
    ' If the value is a numeric value, convert the value
    ' as a numeric value and insert it in the list.
    ' Otherwise, display a message and exit the
    ' procedure.

    If Not IsNumeric(NumVal.Text) Then
        MessageBox.Show("Enter a Numeric Number")
        Exit Sub
    End If

    aNumericValue = Val(NumVal.Text)

    ' Insert the numeric value in the textbox into
    ' the list.
    ' The inserted value will be placed before the
    ' highlighted item.

    List1.Items.RemoveAt(SelectedItemPos)
    List1.Items.Insert(SelectedItemPos, aNumericValue)


End Sub
```

```
Private Sub Remove1_Click(ByVal sender As
        System.Object, ByVal e As System.EventArgs) _
        Handles Remove1.Click

    Dim I As Integer, count As Integer
    Dim anObject As Object
    Dim SelectedItems As ListBox.SelectedObjectCollection
    SelectedItems = List1.SelectedItems
    Do While SelectedItems.Count > 0
        anObject = List1.SelectedItems.Item(0)
        List1.Items.Remove(anObject)
    Loop
End Sub


Private Sub Sum_Click(ByVal sender As
        System.Object, ByVal e As System.EventArgs) _
        Handles Sum.Click

    Dim i As Integer
    Dim sum As Double
    sum = 0
    For i = 0 To List1.Items.Count - 1
        sum = sum + List1.Items.Item(i)
    Next i
    Result.Text = "Sum is     " & Str(sum)

End Sub

Private Sub Average_Click(ByVal sender As
        System.Object, ByVal e As System.EventArgs) _
        Handles Average.Click
    Dim i As Integer
    Dim sum As Double
    Dim ResultString as String
    sum = 0
    For i = 0 To List1.Items.Count - 1
        sum = sum + List1.Items.Item(i)
    Next i
    ResultString = Str(Sum/List1.Items.Count)
    Result.Text = "Average is :  " & ResultString
End Sub

End Class
```

Note that the following For-Next loop statement is used within the *Sum_Click* and *Average_Click* event procedures:

```
For i = 0 To List1.Items.Count - 1
    sum = sum + List1.Items.Item(i)
Next i
```

This statement browses the *List1* Listbox and adds each item (or a numeric value) into the *Sum* variable. The `List1.Items.Count` method is used here to get the total number of items within the *List1* Listbox. Given the *List1* Listbox shown in Figure 5-14, the return of this method is 4.

Besides the use of For-Next loop statement, this application also introduces a set of methods for the operations of the *List1* Listbox. For example, the statement `List1.Items.Clear()` is used in the `Clear_Click` event procedure. This statement clears the *List1* Listbox. The statement `List1.Items.Add(aNumericValue)` is used in the *Add1_Click* event procedure to add a numeric value into the *List1* Listbox.

The two below statements are used in the ***Insert_Click*** event procedure.

```
SelectedItemPos = List1.SelectedIndex
List1.Items.Insert(SelectedItemPos, aNumericValue)
```

The *SelectedIndex* method within the *List1* Listbox returns the index of the item highlighted in the *List1* Listbox. For Example, if you highlight 303 within the below *List1* Listbox, the *SelectedIndex* method will returns 2 (see Figure 5-14). Note that the index of a Listbox control always starts from 0.

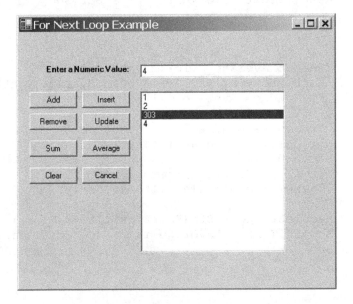

Figure 5-14 Example of the SelectedIndex Method in the List1 Listbox

The `List1.Item.Insert ()` requires two arguments in order to insert a numeric value into the *List1* Lisbox. The first argument is the index that specifies the location where the numeric value should be inserted. The second argument is the numeric value to be inserted.

The *Remove1_Click* event procedure allows users to select a group of items and delete them. Within this procedure, the variable *SelectedItems* is defined to be the *Listbox.SelectedObjectCollection* date type. The *SelectedItems* method is used in this procedure to return a collection of selected objects or items. The returned collection of items is assigned to the *SelectedItems* variable.

A Do-While loop statement is used in this procedure to delete the items within the collection one by one. The statement `anObject = List1.SelectedItems.Item(0)` in the loop uses the Object-type variable *anObject* to point to the first item within the collection, then the statement `List1.Items.Remove(anObject) is used to` delete the item. Once the item is removed from the collection, it is not in the collection and the *List1* Listbox anymore. The Do While statement exits the loop when there are not any items left in the collection.

5.5   Nested Loop Statements

We have learned a lot about the loop statements. Within the loop part of these statements, you are allowed to have other loop statements. For example, a For Column-Next Column statement listed below can be contained inside the For Row -Next Row statement.

```
FOR Row = 1 TO 10
      FOR Column = 1 TO 10
            Console.WriteLine (Row, Column)
      NEXT Column
FOR Row
```

The statement of `Console.WriteLine (Row, Column)` writes the values of row and column onto the *Output* window in the VB.Net Integrated Development Environment (IDE).

We call the above statement the nested For-Next statement. Similarly, a Do-While loop statement can be inside another DO-While statement. We call this Do-While statement the nested Do-While statement. Figure 5-15 shows the structures for several examples of nested loop statements.

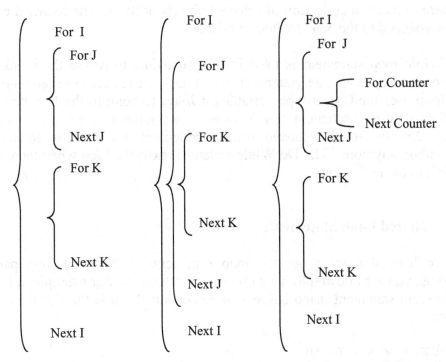

Figure 5-14a   Structures of Nested FOR-NEXT Loop Statements

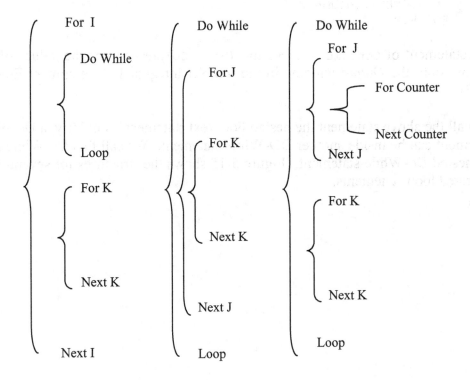

Figure 5-14b   Structures of Nested Loop Statements

5.6   Questions

Q1.   Write a program that uses a loop statement (DO While, Do Loop Until, or For-Next) to calculate the following:

$$\text{Result} = \quad 1^2 + 2^2 + 3^2 + \dots + n^2$$

The value n is provided in a textbox of the user graphical interface (GUI).

Q2.   Draw an execution flow chart for the following statements and calculate the result of Sum and Counter after the loop:

a)
```
Sum = 0
Counter = 1
Do While counter <= 100
        Sum = Sum + Counter
        Counter = Counter + 1
Loop
Messagebox.Show "Sum =" & Sum
Mesaagebox.Show "Counter =" & Counter
```

b)
```
Sum = 0
Counter = 0
Do
        Counter = Counter + 1
        Sum = Sum + Counter
Loop Until Counter > 100
Messagebox.Show "Sum =" & Sum
Mesaagebox.Show "Counter =" & Counter
```

c)
```
Sum = 0
For Counter = 1 TO 100
        Sum = Sum + Counter
Next Counter
Messagebox.Show "Sum =" & Sum
Mesaagebox.Show "Counter =" & Counter
```

Q3.   Write a VB.Net application to computer n!, where n is provided in a textbox.

$$n! = n*(n-1)*(n-2)\dots3*2*1$$

Q4.   Suppose you need to develop a VB.Net application with a form that has a textbox, a label control, a listbox, and two command buttons *add* and *average*. When the user clicks the *add* button, the value inside the textbox will be inserted into the listbox. If no value is inside the textbox when the *add* button is clicked, a warning message is prompted to let the user know that the textbox is empty. When the user clicks the *average* button, the program should get the average of all the values listed in the listbox and display the average in the caption of the label control. If there is no element in the listbox when the user clicks the *average* button, the program should prompt a message box indicating no element in the listbox.

Q5.   Answer the following questions based on the given event procedure

a) What control does this procedure respond to?

b) If you enter 120022331211 into the text box with control name: text1, What is Value of text1.Text? What are values of total_0, total_1, and total_2?

```
Private Sub Text1_KeyPress(ByVal sender As Object,        _
    ByVal e As System.Windows.Forms.KeyPressEventArgs) _ Handles
    Text1.KeyPress

    Dim Total_0 as Integer
    Dim Total_1 as Integer
    Dim Total_2 as integer
    Select Case KeyAscii
            Case  Asc("0")
                    Total_0 = Total_0 + 1
            Case Asc("1")
                    Total_1 = total_1 + 1
            Case Asc("2")
                    Total_2 = total_2 + 2
    End Select

End Sub
```

```
+------------------------------------+
|   +----------------------------+   |
|   | Control Name:              |   |
|   | Text1                      |   |
|   +----------------------------+   |
|                                    |
|   +----------------------------+   |
|   | Control Name:              |   |
|   | Text2                      |   |
|   +----------------------------+   |
|                                    |
+------------------------------------+
```

Chapter 6
Arrays

Arrays consist of related data items that share the same data type and name in a group of contiguous memory cells. They support the implementation and manipulation of matrices as well as the determination of linear equations. In this chapter we will discuss how to define and use various types of arrays. In later chapters we will discuss how to use arrays in EXCEL, MatLab, and VB.Net to determine roots of equations, perform matrix operations, and solve problems that can be formulated as a system of linear equations.

Similar to a variable to which a value is assigned, an array is a group of memory locations or cells. Each cell is considered an element in the array. Values are assigned to elements based on their index or relative position in the array.

They are two types of arrays often used in VB.Net applications: one-dimensional arrays and two-dimensional arrays. We discuss these two types of arrays in the following sections.

6.1   One-Dimensional Arrays

Figure 6-1 shows the definition of a dimensional array and its relationship with variables and VB.Net applications. Four applications illustrated in Figure 6-1 run at the same time. Each of them is taking a certain amount of memory locations. Application 1 has five variables (a1, a2, a3, a4, and a5) and a one-dimensional array (Array B). The variables are scattered in the memory, while the Array B is allocated with five continuous memory cells. Application 2 takes an array (Array C) of five continuous memory cells. Application 3 uses three variables (or x1, y1, z1) and an array (Array D) of 10 continuous memory cells. Application 4 takes only one variable (xyz).

When we zoom in Array B in Figure 6-1, we will see that the Array B looks like:

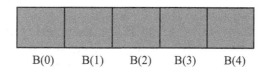

B(0)   B(1)   B(2)   B(3)   B(4)

The one-dimensional array has five elements. Each of them is referenced by an index. The first array element has its index of 0. The last element has its index of 4. The values stored in these five elements should be of same data type.

A challenging question you may have right now is how to define an array in a VB.Net application? The answer is to use a Dim statement.

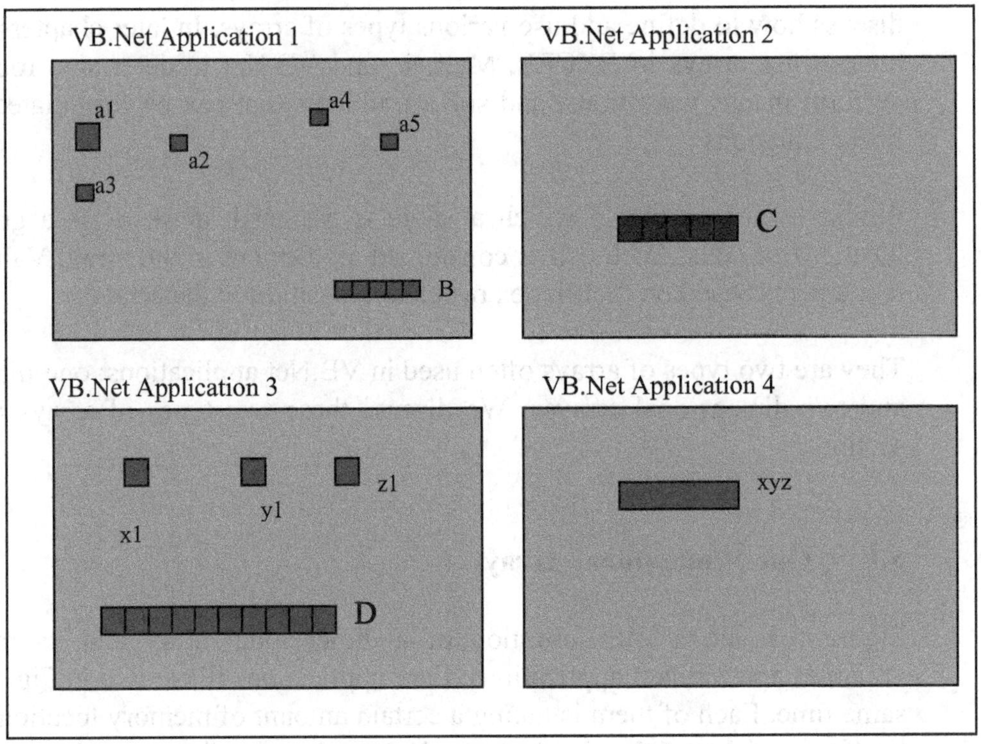

Computer Memory

Figure 6-1 Arrays in VB.Net Applications

As you have already known, the Dim statement is used to declare a variable in a VB.Net application. We can also use a Dim statement to define a one-dimensional array. Suppose we want to create Array B, the one used in the above Application 2, the Dim statement should be as follows:

```
Dim B(4) as Integer
```

Note that all the elements in Array B are assumed to be the Integer data type. This statement tells the computer to allocate a group of continuous 5 memory cells for Array B. The size of each memory cell in Array B is 2 bytes because each cell in the array is defined by the Integer data type. The starting index of the array is 0 and the ending index is 4.

The syntax for an array declaration is as follows:

```
Dim ArrayName (NumberofElement - 1) as DataType
```

The `ArrayName` can be any name that follows the VB.Net naming convention. The `NumberofElement` is an Integer number. Its value normally is determined based on logic of the application. The `DataType` can be any type such as Integer, Double, and String.

Once an array is declared in the memory, values can be assigned to each individual element in the array. Normally we use an assignment statement to assign a value to an element in an array. For example, if we work with an Integer array (or Array A) with 101 elements and want to assign 89 to the element with the index of 10, we can have the following statement:

```
A(10) = 89
```

What do we do if we want to assign all the elements with 0? We can use the following For-Next loop statement to implement it:

```
DIM I as Integer
For I = 0 to 100
     A(I) = 0
Next I
```

The above statement can also be refined as follows:

```
DIM I as Integer
For I = Lbound(A) to Ubound(A)
     A(I) = 0
Next I
```

`Lbound(A)` and `Ubound(A)` are the two VB.Net built-in functions whose returned values are the beginning (or the lowest) and the ending (or the highest) indices of the array A, respectively. In this case, the returned value of `Lbound(A)` is 0 and the returned value of `Ubound(A)` is 100.

A question to you is how to assign the above array with the following values:

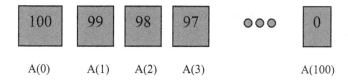

The first element is assigned with 100, the second 99, and the third 98. The assignment keeps the same pattern until the last one is assigned with 0.

The statement to solve the above problem is as follows:

```
DIM I as integer
For I = 0 to 100
      A(I) = 100 - I
Next I
```

Note that when an array is created, its lowest index is 0 by default.

Example 6-1   Use of Rnd() Function

You are asked to write a VB.Net application that uses one-dimensional array and the built-in function called Rnd() to generate random numbers whose range is 0-10. As you may know, Rnd () is a powerful tool useful for computer simulation, computer game, and computer programs where probability and statistics are involved. The Rnd () function can generate random numbers that follow different probability distributions. For example, if we want to create random numbers that follow uniform distribution between 0 and 10, we can use the following expression in VB.Net to implement it:

```
Int (Rnd * 10)
```

Let us write a VB.Net application to verify if the Rnd () function can generate random numbers uniformly from 0 to 10. Figure 6-2 shows the form layout of the application for this purpose. When the application is running, its execution logic is as follow:

1)   When a number is entered to specify the total times of execution of the Rnd () function, the user can click the *Frequency* button. Random numbers that fall into the intervals of 0-1, 1-2, 2-3, 3-4, 4-5, 5-6, 6-7, 7-8, 8-9, and 9-10 are then summarized in the list.

2)   When the user clicks the *Clear* button, the program will clear out the items in the list and the textbox.

3)   When the user clicks the *Cancel* button, the program terminates the application.

Figure 6-2 shows the definition of key control names used in the application. Table 6-1 lists these control names shown in Figure 6-2.

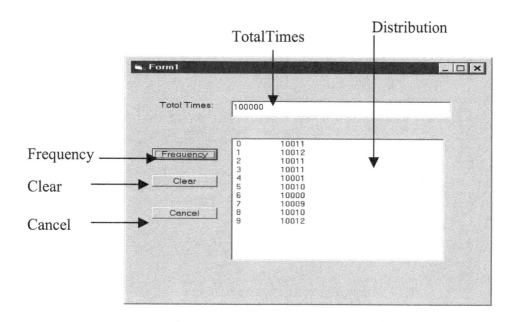

Figure 6-2   Key Control Names for the Example Application

Table 6-1   List of Control Names for the Example Application

Control	Properties	Comments
Textbox	Name: TotalTimes Text:	Used to enter a number. The number indicates the number of times of executing the Rnd() function for generating random numbers
ListBox	Name: Distribution List: {}	Frequency distribution of random numbers in the intervals of 0-1, 1-2, … , and 9-10
Button	Name: Frequency Text: Frequency	Used for generating random numbers
Button	Name: Clear Text: Clear	Used for clear the Listbox and Textbox
Button	Name: Cancel Text: Cancel	Terminates the program

Below is the code for the example application:

```
Public Class Example6_1
    Inherits System.Windows.Forms.Form

    Windows Form Designer Generated Code
```

```
Dim A(10) As Long
Private Sub Frequency_Click(ByVal sender As
     System.Object, ByVal e As System.EventArgs)
     Handles Frequency.Click

  Dim i As Long
  Dim RandomNumber As Single
  Dim category As Integer
  Dim TotalNumberofSimulation As Long

  '
  ' Check if the entered value is a numeric value.
  ' If it is not a numeric value, send a message
  ' out and stop the execution of the procedure.
  '
  ' Also Check if the TotalTimes Textbox is empty.
  ' If it is, send a message out and stop the
  ' execution of the procedure.

  If Not IsNumeric(TotalTimes.Text) Or
          TotalTimes.Text = "" Then
     MessageBox.Show("Enter a Numeric Value ... ")
     Exit Sub
  End If

  '
  '  To reset the value in each element of
  '  Array A to be 0
  '
  For i = 0 To 9
     A(i) = 0
  Next

  TotalNumberofSimulation = Val(TotalTimes.Text)

  '
  ' Get a random number using RND() function
  ' Determine which category the random number
  ' will belong to Add 1 to its corresponding category
  '
  For i = 1 To TotalNumberofSimulation
     RandomNumber = Rnd()
     category = Int(RandomNumber * 10)
     A(category) = A(category) + 1
  Next i


  '
  ' Clear the listbox before the distribution is
  ' inserted in it.
  '
  Distribution.Items.Clear()

  '
  ' Insert the distribution into the Listbox
  '
```

```
      For i = 0 To 9
         Distribution.Items.Add(Str(i) + vbTab +       _
                                   Str(A(i)))
      Next i

   End Sub



   Private Sub Clear_Click(ByVal sender As             _
         System.Object,ByVal e As System.EventArgs)    _
         Handles Clear.Click

      Dim i As Integer
      TotalTimes.Text = ""

      Distribution.Items.Clear()

      For i = 0 To 9
         A(i) = 0
      Next i

   End Sub



   Private Sub Cancel_Click(ByVal sender As            _
         System.Object, ByVal e As System.EventArgs)   _
         Handles Cancel.Click

      End

   End Sub

End Class
```

Note that there are three event procedures that respond to the three actions for the application. Also note that a form-level array called A(10) is declared outside of any event procedures. The array A(10) is sized of 11 elements, each of which is declared with Long Integer data type. Note that the starting index of the array is 0 and the ending index is 10.

Inside the *Frequency_Click* event procedure, the index for the array A is the random number generated by the Rnd () function. The built-in function Int() is used to round off the random number generated from the Rnd ( ) function. For example, int(5.4) yields 5 and int(7.999) will be 7.

Figure 6-2 shows the running result of the application when the total times to generate random numbers are 100,000. The frequency of random numbers falling into the intervals of 0-1, 1-2, 2-3, 3-4, 4-5, 5-6, 6-7, 7-8, 8-9, and 9-10 is approximately evenly distributed. The running results confirms that the Rnd () function can be used to generate a uniform distribution of random numbers.

Example 6-2   ListBox and Array

You are asked to write a VB.Net application that has the form as shown in Figure 6-3. Table 6-2 shows the key controls used in the application.

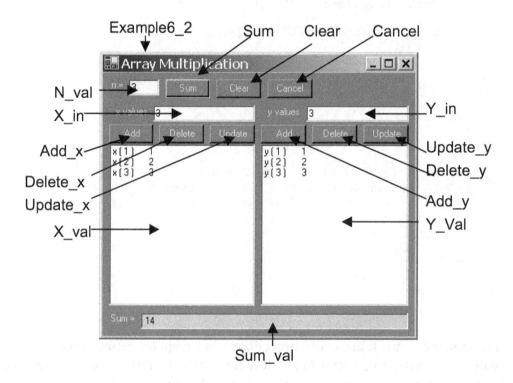

Figure 6-3   Second Example for One-Dimensional Array

The form has a set of controls that enables a user to do the following:

1)   When this application is executed, this form will appear and wait for the user to play with it.

2)   The user can enter a numeric value in the *X_in* Textbox. When the user clicks the *Add_x* Button or presses the *Enter key*, the entered value is inserted into the *X_Val* Listbox. For example, when the user enter 1 in the *X_in* Textbox and

Click the *Add_x* Button, the value of   "X(1)   1" is inserted in the *X_Val* Listbox.

Table 6-2   List of Control Names for the Example Application

Control	Properties	
Textbox	Name: Text:	NVal
Textbox	Name: Text:	X_in
Textbox	Name: Text:	Y_in
Textbox	Name: Text:	Sum_Val
ListBox	Name: List:	X_Val {}
ListBox	Name: List:	Y_Val {}
Button	Name: Text:	Add_X Add
Button	Name: Text:	Delete_X Delete
Button	Name: Text:	Update_X Update
Button	Name: Text:	Add_Y Add
Button	Name: Text:	Delete_Y Delete
Button	Name: Text:	Update_Y Update
Button	Name: Text:	Clear Clear
Button	Name: Text:	Cancel Cancel
Button	Name: Text:	Sum Sum

3)   The user can keep adding a series of numeric values into the *X_Val* Listbox.

4)   The user can follow the same method to add a series of numerical values into the *Y_val* Listbox. For example, the user can enter 1 in the *Y_in* Textbox and Click the *Add_y* Button, the value of   "Y(1)   1" is inserted in the *Y_val* Listbox.

5)   The user can highlight a numeric value in either *X_Val* or *Y_Val* Listbox and clicks the *Update* button above the *X_Val* or *Y_Val* Listbox. The application will prompt a window and ask the user to enter the replacing numeric value within the window. Once the numeric value is entered, it will replace the highlighted numeric value in the Listbox below the *Update* button you clicked.

6)   The user can highlight a numeric value in either *X_Val* or *Y_Val* Listbox and clicks the *Delete* button above it. The highlighted numeric value will be removed.

7)   Once a series of X and Y values are added into the X_Val and Y_val Listboxes. The user can implement the below formula:

$$\text{Result} = x_1*y_1 + x_2*y_2 + \ldots + x_n*y_n$$

The user can enter a number in the *N_val* Textbox to specify the N value used in the above formula.

If the N value entered in the N_Val Textbox is greater than the total number of items in *X_Val* or *Y_Val* Litsbox, a message will prompt to the user.

8)   The user can clear all the numberic values in *X_Val* and *Y_Val* Listboxes when he or she clicks the *Clear* button.

9)   When the user clicks the *Cancel* button, the application terminates.

The code for this application is listed below:

```
Public Class Example6_2
    Inherits System.Windows.Forms.Form

    ┌─────────────────────────────────────────────┐
    │ Windows Form Designer generated code        │
    └─────────────────────────────────────────────┘

    Private Sub add_x_Click(ByVal sender As System.Object,  _
            ByVal e As System.EventArgs)                    _
            Handles add_x.Click

    ' Check if the value to be added in X_Val Listbox is
    ' a numeric value or not. It is not, exit the
    ' procedure.

        If Not IsNumeric(x_in.Text) Then
            MessageBox.Show("Please enter numeric values.")
            Exit Sub
        End If

    ' The below statement is to format a string and add
    ' the string into the X_Val Listbox. For example,
    ' If the users enter the first numeric value such as
    ' 1, the string to be formatted is "X (1) 1"
    ' The string is then added into the X_Val Listbox.
```

```
      x_val.Items.Add("x (" + Str(x_val.Items.Count + 1)   _
                     + " )" + vbTab + x_in.Text)
End Sub

Private Sub add_y_Click(ByVal sender As System.Object,   _
        ByVal e As System.EventArgs)                     _
            Handles add_y.Click

   ' Check if the value to be added in Y_Val Listbox is
   ' a numeric value or not. It is not, exit the
   ' procedure.

      If Not IsNumeric(y_in.Text) Then
          MessageBox.Show("Please enter numeric values.")
          Exit Sub
      End If


   ' The below statement is to format a string and add
   ' the string into the Y_Val Listbox. For example,
   ' If the users enter the first numeric value such as
   ' 1, the string to be formatted is "Y (1) 1"
   ' The string is then added into the Y_Val Listbox.

     y_val.Items.Add("y (" + Str(y_val.Items.Count + 1)   _
                     + " )" + vbTab + y_in.Text)
End Sub

Private Sub clear_Click(ByVal sender As System.Object,   _
        ByVal e As System.EventArgs)                     _
            Handles clear.Click
     x_val.Items.Clear()
     y_val.Items.Clear()
     x_in.Text = ""
     y_in.Text = ""
     n_val.Text = ""
     sum_val.Text = ""
End Sub

Private Sub cancel_Click(ByVal sender As System.Object, _
        ByVal e As System.EventArgs)                     _
            Handles cancel.Click
     End
End Sub


Private Sub sum_Click(ByVal sender As System.Object,     _
        ByVal e As System.EventArgs)                     _
            Handles sum.Click

   ' Check the value enterd in the N_val is a
   ' numeric value or not. If it is not, exit the
   ' procedure

      If Not IsNumeric(n_val.Text) Then
          MessageBox.Show("Please enter numeric values.")
          Exit Sub
```

```
        End If

' Check if the N value is greater than the number of
' items in two Listboxes. If the check gives a TRUE
' condition, exit the procedure.

    If  x_val.Items.Count < Val(n_val.Text) Or          _
        y_val.Items.Count < Val(n_val.Text) Then

        MessageBox.Show("Insufficient X or Y values.")
        Exit Sub
    End If

    Dim n As Integer
    n = val(n_val.Text)

' This is a new way to define an array. We can get a
' the n value first from the N_Val Textbox, and use it
' to define the size of an array.

    Dim x(n) As Double
    Dim y(n) As Double
    Dim i As Integer

    Dim sum As Double
    sum = 0

    For I = 0 to n - 1

' Get the X and Y values from the two Listboxes

        x(i) = Val(Mid(x_val.Items(i), 9))
        y(i) = Val(Mid(y_val.Items(i), 9))
        sum = sum + x(i) * y(i)

    Loop
    sum_val.Text = Str(sum)
End Sub

Private Sub x_in_KeyPress(ByVal sender As             _
        System.Object, ByVal e As                    _
        System.Windows.Forms.KeyPressEventArgs)      _
        Handles x_in.KeyPress

' If the Enter key is entered, the procedure will add
' the value in the X_in Textbox into the X_Val Listbox.

    If Asc(e.KeyChar) = 13 Then
        If Not IsNumeric(x_in.Text) Then
            MessageBox.Show("Enter numeric values.")
            Exit Sub
        End If
        x_val.Items.Add("x (" + Str(x_val.Items.Count + _
                    1) + " )" + vbTab + x_in.Text)
        x_in.Text = ""
    End If
End Sub
```

```
Private Sub y_in_KeyPress(ByVal sender As
        System.Object, ByVal e As                          _
        System.Windows.Forms.KeyPressEventArgs)            _
        Handles y_in.KeyPress                              _


' If the Enter key is entered, the procedure will add
' the value in the Y_in Textbox into the Y_Val Listbox.

    If Asc(e.KeyChar) = 13 Then
        If Not IsNumeric(y_in.Text) Then
            MessageBox.Show("Enter numeric values.")
            Exit Sub
        End If
        y_val.Items.Add("y (" + Str(y_val.Items.Count + _
            1) + " )" + vbTab + y_in.Text)
        y_in.Text = ""
    End If
End Sub




Private Sub delete_x_Click(ByVal sender As
        System.Object, ByVal e As System.EventArgs)        _
        Handles delete_x.Click                             _

' This DIM statement defines a variable called anIndex and
' assigns the index of the selected item in the X_Val Listbox
' to it.

    Dim anIndex As Integer = x_val.SelectedIndex

    x_val.Items.Remove(x_val.SelectedItem)

End Sub

Private Sub delete_y_Click(ByVal sender As
        System.Object, ByVal e As System.EventArgs)        _
        Handles delete_y.Click                             _

' This DIM statement defines a variable called anIndex and
' assigns the index of the selected item in the Y_Val Listbox
' to it.

    Dim anIndex As Integer = y_val.SelectedIndex
    y_val.Items.Remove(y_val.SelectedItem)
End Sub




Private Sub update_x_Click(ByVal sender As
        System.Object, ByVal e As System.EventArgs)        _
        Handles    update_x.Click                          _
    Dim anIndex As Integer = x_val.SelectedIndex
    Dim replace_val As Double

    If anIndex = -1 Then
```

```
                MessageBox.Show("Select a value to replace.")
                Exit Sub
        Else
                replace_val = Val(InputBox(                        _
                  "Enter the replacing value.", "Update Value"))

' This statement overwrites a string into the X_Val Listbox.

                x_val.Items(anIndex) = "x (" + Str(anIndex + 1) _
                        + " )" + vbTab + Str(replace_val)

        End If
    End Sub


    Private Sub update_y_Click(ByVal sender As              _
            System.Object, ByVal e As System.EventArgs)     _
            Handles update_y.Click

        Dim anIndex As Integer = y_val.SelectedIndex
        Dim replace_val As Double
        If anIndex = -1 Then
            MessageBox.Show("Select a value to replace.")
            Exit Sub
        Else

            replace_val = Val(InputBox(                        _
              "Enter the replacing value.", "Update Value"))

            y_val.Items(anIndex) = "y (" + Str(anIndex + 1) _
                    + " )" + vbTab + Str(replace_val)
        End If
    End Sub

End Class
```

Copy all these event procedures into the code window of the application and run them.

6.2   Two-Dimensional Arrays

Arrays can have more than one dimension. Two-dimensional arrays are often used in VB.Net to represent table-like values arranged in rows and columns. Figure 6-4 shows a two-dimensional array in a VB.Net application.

Note that the VB.Net application 3 in Figure 6-4 has a two-dimensional array. This array has 5 elements in each row and 20 elements in total. The array row index starts from 0 to 3 and its column index from 0 to 4. Any element inside the array is positioned by two indices. The first one is used to identify the element's row and the second is used to identify the element's column.

A DIM statement is used to declare a two-dimensional array. Suppose we want to create the above two-dimensional array that contains elements of Integer data type, we can have the following statement:

```
DIM A(3, 4) as Integer
```

Let us look at another statement

```
DIM B(9,9) as Integer
```

Computer Memory

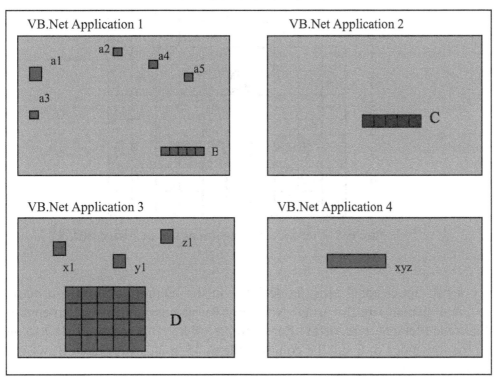

Figure 6-4   Two-Dimensional Array in a VB.Net Application

This statement tells the computer to allocate a group of continuous 100 memory cells for an Integer array called B. The memory locations should be arranged in a table format that has 10 rows and 10 columns. The starting index for rows and columns is 0 and the ending index is 9. Figure 6-5 shows the memory allocation for the above statement. The shaded element is identified by its row index of 4 and its column index of 4.

Generally speaking, the syntax for a two-dimensional array declaration is as follows:

```
DIM ArrayName (Rows, Columns) as DataType
```

The ArrayName can be any name that follows the VB.Net naming convention of a variable. The Rows and Columns are a numerical constant which is often determined based on logic of the application. The DataType can be any type such as Integer, Double, and String. The total elements in the array are (Rows + 1) * (Columns +1).

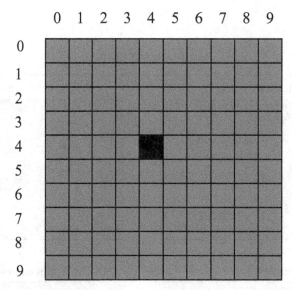

Figure 6-5 Memory Arrangement for an Array B(9, 9)

Once a two-dimensional array is declared in the memory, values can be assigned to individual elements in the array. Normally we use assignment statements to assign a value to an element in an array. For example, if we want to assign 189 to the element with the row index of 6 and the column index of 5 in an array called B, we can have the following statement:

```
B(6, 5) = 189
```

What do we do if we want to assign all the elements with 0? We can use the following nested For-Next loop statement to implement it:

```
DIM A(100, 100) as double
DIM Row as Integer, Column as Integer
For Row = 0 to 100
   For Column = 0 to 100
      A(Row, Column) = 0
   Next Column
Next Row
```

The above statement can also be refined as follows:

```
DIM A(100, 100) as double
DIM Row as Integer, Column as Integer
For Row = Lbound(A) to Ubound(A)
   For Column = Lbound(A, 2) to Ubound(A, 2)
      A(Row, Column) = 0
   Next Column
Next Row
```

Lbound() and Ubound() are the two VB.Net built-in functions that can be used for a two-dimensional array. If only one argument is specified in the Lbound() and Ubound() functions, they imply that their returned values are the beginning (or the lowest) and the ending (or the highest) indices of the array A for the first dimension, respectively. In this case, the first dimension is the row dimension, therefore the returned value of Lbound(A) is 0 and the returned value of Ubound(A) is 100.

When two arguments are specified in the Lbound() and Ubound() functions, the second argument specifies the number of the dimension. For example in the below For-Next statement

```
For Column = Lbound(A, 2) to Ubound(A, 2)
     A(Row, Column) = 0
   Next Column
```

The Lbound() and Ubound() functions return the lower bound and upper bound of the second dimension, that is, the column dimension.

Another statement related to arrays is the REDIM statement. The REDIM statement redefines the size of an existing array. The syntax of a REDIM statement for a two-dimensional array is as follows:

```
Dim ArrayName() as DataType

.
.
.

REDIM  ArrayName(NumberofRows, NumberofColumns)
```

The first DIM statement does not have a range. It indicates that the size of the array will be redefined based on the logic of the application at the run time.

An example of the Dim and REDIM statements is as follows:

```
Dim matrix_temp1() as single

REDIM matrix_temp1(100, 100)
```

Example 6-3   Use of DataGrid Control in Two-Dimensional Array

---

Suppose you are asked to develop a VB.Net application that allows the user to enter two matrices with same number of columns and rows. When the user clicks the *Add* button, the program can add the two matrices together. When the user clicks the *Subtract* button the program subtracts the second matrix from the first one. When the user clicks the *Cancel* button, the program will be terminated (see Figure 6-6).

As you may already know, a matrix is defined as follows:

$$[A] = [a_{ij}] = \begin{bmatrix} a_{11} & a_{12} & \cdots & a_{1j} & \cdots & a_{1n} \\ a_{21} & a_{22} & & & & \vdots \\ \vdots & & \ddots & & & \vdots \\ a_{i1} & & & a_{ij} & & a_{in} \\ \vdots & & & & \ddots & \vdots \\ a_{n1} & \cdots & \cdots & a_{nj} & \cdots & a_{nn} \end{bmatrix}$$

A matrix is a rectangular array of elements arranged in m rows and n columns. The element values of a matrix may be numbers, variables, functions of variables, etc. For example, we can have two matrices as follows:

$$A = \begin{bmatrix} 1 & 1 & 3 \\ 5 & 2 & 1 \\ 2 & 3 & 1 \end{bmatrix}$$

$$B = \begin{bmatrix} 2 & 3 & 5 \\ 3 & 1 & -1 \\ 1 & 3 & 4 \end{bmatrix}$$

Both matrix A and matrix B have an order of 3x3. Elements inside the matrices are numbers.

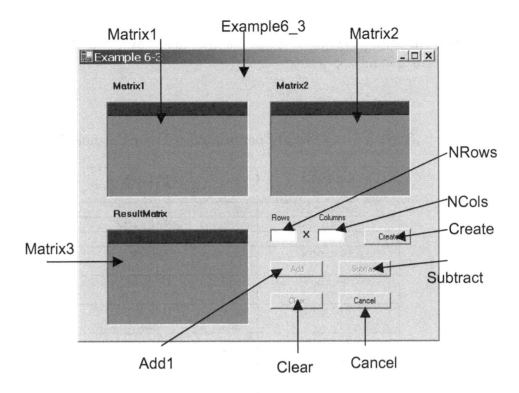

Figure 6-6   Key Control Names for the Above Example

We can add these two matrices together because they have the same order. Also we can subtract B from A.

The add operation of two matrices by definition is to add elements one by one in A with those in B that have the same position. The subtract operation by definition is to subtract elements in B from those elements in A that have the same position.

$A + B =$

$$\begin{bmatrix} 1 & 1 & 3 \\ 5 & 2 & 1 \\ 2 & 3 & 1 \end{bmatrix} + \begin{bmatrix} 2 & 3 & 5 \\ 3 & 1 & -1 \\ 1 & 3 & 4 \end{bmatrix} = \begin{bmatrix} 1+2 & 1+3 & 3+5 \\ 5+3 & 2+1 & 1-1 \\ 2+1 & 3+3 & 1+4 \end{bmatrix} = \begin{bmatrix} 3 & 4 & 8 \\ 8 & 3 & 0 \\ 3 & 6 & 5 \end{bmatrix}$$

$A - B =$

$$\begin{bmatrix} 1 & 1 & 3 \\ 5 & 2 & 1 \\ 2 & 3 & 1 \end{bmatrix} - \begin{bmatrix} 2 & 3 & 5 \\ 3 & 1 & -1 \\ 1 & 3 & 4 \end{bmatrix} = \begin{bmatrix} 1-2 & 1-3 & 3-5 \\ 5-3 & 2-1 & 1+1 \\ 2-1 & 3-3 & 1-4 \end{bmatrix} = \begin{bmatrix} -1 & -2 & -2 \\ 2 & 1 & 2 \\ 1 & 0 & -3 \end{bmatrix}$$

Figure 6-6 shows the form design for the above example. Table 6-3 lists the key controls used in the application.

Table 6-3   List of Control Names for the Example Application

Control	Properties	
DataGrid	Name:	Matrix1
DataGrid	Name:	Matrix2
DataGrid	Name:	Matrix3
Textbox	Name:	NRows
	Text:	
Textbox	Name:	NCols
	Text:	
Button	Name:	Create
	Text:	Create
Button	Name:	Add1
	Text:	Add
Button	Name:	Subtract
	Text:	Subtract
Button	Name:	Clear
	Text:	Clear
Button	Name:	Cancel
	Text:	Cancel

In this application we use a new control template to generate an EXCEL-like spreadsheet. The control template is called *DataGrid*. You can find the *DataGrid* control template within the Toolbox window.

The logic of this application is as follows:

1)   When a user is running this application, the form as shown in Figure 6-6 appears.

2)   The user types the number of rows and the number of columns into the *NRows* and *NCols* textboxes. The user clicks the *Create* button. The application then fills in three table-like data grids.

3)   The user can type in a matrix of numeric values in *Matrix1* control and a matrix in *Matrix2* control. The user can then click the *Add* or *Subtract* button. The result of the matrix operation is displayed in *Matrix3* DataGrid.

The program code for this application is as follows:

```
Public Class Example6_3
    Inherits System.Windows.Forms.Form

    Windows Form Designer Generated Code


    Dim m1_DataView As DataView
    Dim m2_DataView As DataView
    Dim m3_DataView As DataView

    Dim m1_DataTable As DataTable = New DataTable
    Dim m2_DataTable As DataTable = New DataTable
    Dim m3_DataTable As DataTable = New DataTable


    Private Sub Add1_Click(ByVal sender As System.Object,      _
            ByVal e As System.EventArgs)                       _
            Handles Add1.Click

        Dim i, j As Integer
        Dim colname As String
        Dim NumRow as Integer
        Dim NumCol as Integer
        NumRow = Val(NRows.Text)
        NumCol = Val(NCols.Text)

        Dim m1(NumRow, NumCol) As Single
        Dim m2(NumRow, NumCol) As Single
        Dim m3(NumRow, NumCol) As Single

        Dim m1_row As DataRow
        Dim m2_row As DataRow
        Dim m3_row As DataRow

        Dim m1_startindex, m1_endindex As Integer
        Dim m2_startindex, m2_endindex As Integer

        m1_startindex = m1_datatable.Select.GetLowerBound(0)
        m1_endindex = m1_datatable.Select.GetUpperBound(0)
        m2_startindex = m2_datatable.Select.GetLowerBound(0)
        m2_endindex = m2_datatable.Select.GetUpperBound(0)

        If Not m1_startindex = m2_startindex And               _
            Not m1_endindex = m2_endindex Then

            MsgBox("Orders of two matrices are not same.")
            Exit Sub
        End If

        For i = 0 To NumRow - 1

            m1_row = m1_datatable.Rows.Item(i)
            m2_row = m2_datatable.Rows.Item(i)
            m3_row = m3_datatable.Rows.Item(i)
```

```
                For j = 0 To NumCOl - 1
                    colname = "Col" + (j + 1).ToString
                    If Not IsNumeric(m1_row(colname)) And          _
                      Not IsNumeric(m2_row(colname)) Then

                        MsgBox("Cannot Add non-numeric values")
                        Exit Sub
                    End If

                    m1(i, j) = m1_row(colname)
                    m2(i, j) = m2_row(colname)
                    m3(i, j) = m1(i, j) + m2(i, j)
                    m3_row(colname) = m3(i, j)
                Next j
            Next i
      End Sub

      Private Sub Cancel_Click(ByVal sender As System.Object,   _
            ByVal e As System.EventArgs)                          _
            Handles Cancel.Click
          End
      End Sub

      Private Sub Clear_Click(ByVal sender As System.Object,    _
            ByVal e As System.EventArgs)                          _
            Handles Clear.Click

        m1_DataTable.Rows.Clear()
        m2_DataTable.Rows.Clear()
        m3_DataTable.Rows.Clear()

        Add1.Enabled = "False"
        Subtract.Enabled = "False"
        NRows.Text = ""
        NCols.Text = ""

      End Sub


      Private Sub Subtract_Click(ByVal sender As System.Object,  _
            ByVal e As System.EventArgs)                          _
            Handles Subtract.Click

        Dim i, j As Integer
        Dim colname As String

        Dim NumRow as Integer
        Dim NumCol as Integer
        NumRow = Val(NRows.Text)
        NumCol = Val(NCols.Text)

        Dim m1(NumRow, NumCol) As Single
        Dim m2(NumRow, NumCol) As Single
        Dim m3(NumRow, NumCol) As Single
```

```
        Dim m1_row As DataRow
        Dim m2_row As DataRow
        Dim m3_row As DataRow
        Dim m1_startindex, m1_endindex As Integer
        Dim m2_startindex, m2_endindex As Integer

        m1_startindex = m1_datatable.Select.GetLowerBound(0)
        m1_endindex = m1_datatable.Select.GetUpperBound(0)
        m2_startindex = m2_datatable.Select.GetLowerBound(0)
        m2_endindex = m2_datatable.Select.GetUpperBound(0)

        If Not m1_startindex = m2_startindex And Not    _
            m1_endindex = m2_endindex Then
            MsgBox("Orders of two matrices are not same.")
            Exit Sub
        End If

        For i = 0 To NumRow - 1
            m1_row = m1_datatable.Rows.Item(i)
            m2_row = m2_datatable.Rows.Item(i)
            m3_row = m3_datatable.Rows.Item(i)
            For j = 0  To NumCol - 1
                colname = "Col" + (j + 1).ToString
                If Not IsNumeric(m1_row(colname)) And    _
            Not IsNumeric(m2_row(colname)) Then
                    MsgBox("Cannot Subtract non-numeric values")
                    Exit Sub
                End If
                m1(i, j) = m1_row(colname)
                m2(i, j) = m2_row(colname)
                m3(i, j) = m1(i, j) - m2(i, j)
                m3_row(colname) = m3(i, j)
            Next j
        Next i
End Sub


Private Sub Create_Click(ByVal sender As System.Object,   _
        ByVal e As System.EventArgs)                       _
        Handles Create.Click

    ' Define three variables to be of the data
    ' type of DataColumn
    Dim m1_column, m2_column, m3_column As DataColumn

    ' Define a variable to be of the data type of
    ' DataRow

    Dim myrow As DataRow
    Dim i, j As Integer
    Dim columnname As String

    'Check if the entered value in the NRows textbox
    ' is a numeric value. If it is not, exit
    ' the procedure.

    If Not IsNumeric(NRows.Text) Then
```

```
            MsgBox("Enter a numerix value for rows ...")
            Exit Sub
    End If

    'Check if the entered value in the NCols textbox
    ' is a numeric value. If it is not, exit
    ' the procedure.

    If Not IsNumeric(NCols.Text) Then
            MsgBox("Enter a numerix value for columns ...")
            Exit Sub
    End If

    If Val(NRows.Text) <= 0 Or Val(NCols.Text) <= 0 Then
            MsgBox("Cols or Rows > 0 ")
            Exit Sub
    End If
    'Reset three DataTables used in this event procedure.

    m1_DataTable.Reset()
    m2_DataTable.Reset()
    m3_DataTable.Reset()

    ' This For Next loop sets up three Datatables with
    ' a number of columns. Each column is with type of
    ' String. The Column name is Colo, COl1, Col2, ...

    For i = 1 To Val(NCols.Text)

        m1_column = New DataColumn
        m1_column.DataType = Type.GetType("System.String")
        m1_column.ColumnName = "Col" + i.ToString
        m1_DataTable.Columns.Add(m1_column)

        m2_column = New DataColumn
        m2_column.DataType = Type.GetType("System.String")
        m2_column.ColumnName = "Col" + i.ToString
        m2_DataTable.Columns.Add(m2_column)

        m3_column = New DataColumn
        m3_column.DataType = Type.GetType("System.String")
        m3_column.ColumnName = "Col" + i.ToString
        m3_DataTable.Columns.Add(m3_column)
    Next i

    ' This For Next Loop creates a number of rows for
    ' M1_DataTable and sets each column in the
    ' rows to be ""

    For i = 1 To Val(NRows.Text)
        myrow = m1_DataTable.NewRow
        For j = 1 To Val(NCols.Text)

            columnname = "Col" + j.ToString
            myrow(columnname) = ""
        Next j
        m1_DataTable.Rows.Add(myrow)
```

```
        Next i

        ' This For Next Loop creates a number of rows for
        ' M2_DataTable and sets each column in the
        ' rows to be ""

        For i = 1 To Val(NRows.Text)
            myrow = m2_DataTable.NewRow
            For j = 1 To Val(NCols.Text)
                columnname = "Col" + j.ToString
                myrow(columnname) = ""
            Next j
            m2_DataTable.Rows.Add(myrow)
        Next i

        ' This For Next Loop creates a number of rows for
        ' M3_DataTable and sets each column in the
        ' rows to be ""

        For i = 1 To Val(NRows.Text)
            myrow = m3_DataTable.NewRow
            For j = 1 To Val(NCols.Text)
                columnname = "Col" + j.ToString
                myrow(columnname) = ""
            Next j
            m3_DataTable.Rows.Add(myrow)
        Next i

        ' Create a DataView for each DataTable.
        ' Each DataView is a view window of the DataTable.

        m1_DataView = New DataView(m1_DataTable)
        m2_DataView = New DataView(m2_DataTable)
        m3_DataView = New DataView(m3_DataTable)

        ' Assign the window views to the Matrix1, Matrix2,
        ' and Matrix3 so that the three DataGrid objects
        ' can see the contents within the DataTables through
        ' the view windows.

        Matrix1.DataSource() = m1_DataView
        Matrix2.DataSource() = m2_DataView
        Matrix3.DataSource() = m3_DataView

        Add1.Enabled = "True"
        Subtract.Enabled = "True"
        Clear.Enabled = "True"
    End Sub

    Private Sub Form1_Load(ByVal sender As Object,         _
            ByVal e As System.EventArgs)                   _
            Handles MyBase.Load

        Add1.Enabled = "False"
        Subtract.Enabled = "False"
        Clear.Enabled = "False"
    End Sub
```

```
End Class
```

Figure 6-7 shows the running result of the application. Note that the two matrices are

$$A = \begin{bmatrix} 3 & 12 & 1 \\ 4 & 5 & 5 \end{bmatrix} \qquad\qquad B = \begin{bmatrix} 11 & 2 & 2 \\ 1 & 1 & 2 \end{bmatrix}$$

The result is:

$$A + B = \begin{bmatrix} 14 & 14 & 3 \\ 5 & 6 & 7 \end{bmatrix}$$

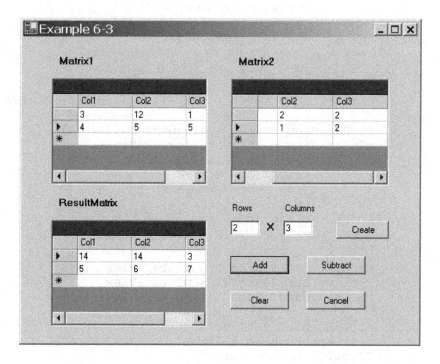

Figure 6-7   Results of the Addition of Two Matrices

6-3   Questions

Q1.   Develop flow charts for all the event procedures in the matrix add and subtract application.

Q2.   Illustrate the memory positions allocated by the following statements:

```
a)      DIM A(10) As Single
b)      DIM A2(4, 5) as Integer
```

Q3.   Write a VB.Net application that can calculate the result based on the following formula:

$$Result = x_1*y_1*z_1 + x_2*y_2*z_2 + \ldots + x_n*y_n*z_n$$

The value n and two arrays should be entered through the form.

Q4.   Explore the properties available in the DataGrid control template.

Q5.   Use the RND Function to generate 1000 random numbers that are ranged in 0-100.

Q6.   Write a VB.Net application that can allow users to use the Rnd () function to create random numbers that follow normal distribution. [Hint: Check a textbook on Probability and Statistics]

Q7.   Assume you have the following statements. Illustrate the computer memory cells used for the Array A.

```
Dim AValue as Integer
AValue = Inputbox ("Enter a numeric value")
Dim A(Avalue)
```

Chapter 7
Procedures, Functions, and Modules

We have learned a number of VB.Net statements in the previous chapters and applied the looping statements and arrays in solving problems that involve repetitions. This chapter continues the discussion of Visual Basic.Net with focus on procedures, functions, and modules. A VB.Net program with elements such as procedures, functions, and modules expands its flexibility and functionality.

7.1   VB.Net Procedures

There are two types of VB.Net procedures in an application: event-driven procedures and user-defined procedures. The event-driven procedures, as you have seen in previous chapters, are structured with the following template:

```
Private Sub ControlName_EventName (ParameterList      )
          Handles ControlName.EventName

      VB Statement 1
      VB Statement 2
      VB Statement 3

         .
         .
         .

      VB Statement n


   End Sub
```

An event procedure uses the *EventName* and *ControlName* linked with "_" to tell which event and control the procedure should respond to. Note that every event-driven procedure begins with a keyword ***Private***, which indicates that the procedure resides only in the form it belongs to and its scope is within the environment of the form. One and only one event and control in the hosting form can invoke the procedure. Events and controls in other forms, even they share the same name, cannot invoke the procedure. Clearly the keyword ***Private*** means "no share" with other forms.

User-defined procedures are any procedures other than even-driven procedures. A user-defined procedure is normally defined inside the ***General Section*** of a form class and is then invoked by any places in the hosting form. The ***General Section*** of a form class is any places outside procedures. For example, the example listed in Chapter 3 can be revised with two procedures:

```
Private Sub QuadraticRtChk (    ByVal   a1 as integer,      _
                                ByVal   b1 as integer,      _
                                ByVal   c1 as integer)
        Dim chk as Long
        Chk = b1^2 - 4*a1*c1
        If chk <  0 then
           Msgbox ("No real roots exist")
           Exit Sub
        End If
End Sub



Private Sub Calc_Click (ByVal sender As system.Object,     _
                        ByVal e As System.EventArgs)        _
                        Handles Calculate.Click


    REM This is a comment statement
    REM Below are Variables a, b, c, rt1, rt2 and
    REM chk declared within this procedure

    Dim a as integer
    Dim b as integer
    Dim c as integer
    Dim rt1 as Double
    Dim rt2 as Double
    Dim chk as Long
    Dim response as integer

    ' The below three statements are used to check
    ' if the values of the textboxes are numeric values.
    ' If they are not, send messages out and terminate
    ' the execution of the procedure.

    If Not IsNumeric(Val_a.text) or Val_a.Text = "" then
         Messagebox.Show ("Please enter a numeric value")
         Exit Sub
    End If

    If Not IsNumeric(Val_a.text) or Val_a.Text = "" then
         Messagebox.Show ("Please enter a numeric value")
         Exit Sub
    End If

    If Not IsNumeric(Val_c.text) or Val_c.Text = "" then
         Messagebox.Show ("Please enter a numeric value")
         Exit Sub
    End If

    ' The below three statements get user inputs
    ' of a, b, and c from the textboxes on the
    ' form after the check.

    A = val(val_a.text)
    B = val(val_b.text)
    C = val(val_c.text)
```

```
'

'  Call the user-defined procedure QuadraticRootCheck
'

QuadraticRtChk(a, b, c)

'
' If there are real roots, calculate the roots
' and assign them to two variables called rt1 and rt2.
'

Rt1 = (-b+Math.sqrt(chk))/(2*a)
Rt2 = (-b-Math.sqrt(chk))/(2*a)

' Output the calculated roots onto the two
' textboxes on the form so that users
' can see the roots.

Root1.text = str(rt1)
Root2.text = str(rt2)
End Sub
```

The statement `QuadraticRtChk(a, b , c)` in the *Calc_Click* event procedure calls a user-defined procedure `QuadraticRtChk (a1, b1, c1)`. The *Calc_Click* event procedure is thus called the calling procedure. The user-defined procedure is called the called procedure.

The user-defined procedure *QuadraticRtChk( )* has three placeholders for values that should be filled when it is called. The placeholders are declared with *ByVal*, which means that the variables are "passed by value". A variable that is passed by value remains its original value unchanged in the calling procedure after the called procedure finishes its execution. "Pass by value" is the default type for passing information from a calling procedure to a called procedure.

The calling event procedure has a statement `QuadraticRtChk(a, b, c)` that activates the execution of the procedure *QuadraticRtChk ( )*. The activation involves the following steps:

Step 1: The calling procedure (*Calc_Click*) passes over the execution right to the called procedure (*QuadraticRtChk*).

Step 2: The calling procedure passes the current values to the three placeholders a, b, and c of the called procedure.

Step 3: Execute the VB.Net statements in the called procedure. The VB.Net statements use the values passed down to check if real roots exist. If no real roots exist, terminate the application. Otherwise, go to Step 4.

Step 4: The called procedure returns the execution right back to the calling procedure and the activation is over.

A user-defined procedure has the following structure:

```
Private Sub ProcedureName (Parameter List)

            VB Statement 1
            VB Statement 2
            VB Statement 3
            .
            .
            .
            VB Statement n
End Sub
```

The parameter list consists of a sequence of placeholders that can be declared with *ByVal* ("pass by value"). As shown in Figure 7-1, when the *QuadraticRtChk* procedure is called, three temporary variables a1, b1, and c1 are created in the workspace of the called procedure. The three temporary variables are assigned with the current values of variables a, b, and c in the calling procedure before the called procedure is executed.

Another alternative to pass information from a calling procedure to a called procedure is "Pass by Reference." If we modify the above *QuadraticRtChk* procedure to allow the variables to be passed by reference, we should have the following:

```
Private Sub QuadraticRtChk     (ByRef A1 as integer, _
                                ByRef B1 as integer, _
                                ByRef C1 as integer)

End Sub
```

A variable that is passed by reference is declared with the keyword *ByRef*. When the called procedure is invoked, the computer creates a pointer for each argument in the parameter list. As shown in Figure 7-2, three pointers are created for the three placeholders. These three pointers point to variables a, b, and c in the calling procedure respectively. When the VB.Net statements in the called procedure access to the pointers, they actually access to the variables in the calling procedure. Any operations in the called procedure that are related to the three pointers are actually performed on the variables a, b, and c in the calling procedure.

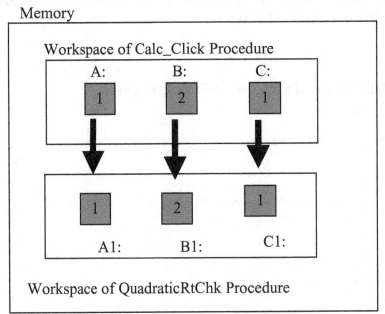

Figure 7-1 "Call by Value" Definition

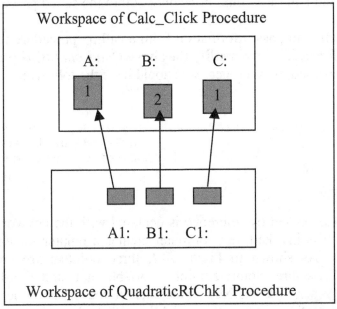

Figure 7-2 "Call by Reference" Definition

Passing information by reference is a little bit difficult to be understood. However it is a powerful mechanism that allows the called procedure to return a series of results back to the calling procedure. Because the called procedure can change things in the calling procedure, it may make VB.Net applications (with errors) difficult to be debugged.

A rule of thumb to use ByVal or ByRef is that if a result needs to be back to the calling procedure, the variable that stores the result should be declared with ByRef. Otherwise, it should be declared with ByVal.

User-defined procedures differ from event-driven procedures in the way that they are not associated with any specific event or control. When a group of code is repeated a number of times in an event-driven procedure, it is better to extract it out and reorganize it by a user-defined procedure. In doing so, the code is simpler and easier to read.

Example 7-1 User-Defined Procedure

Suppose you are asked to develop a VB.Net application that allows a user to insert data into three lists (see Figure 7-1). The user first enters a numerical value into the textbox above the *Insert Option* block. He/she then selects one of the options (List1, List2, or List3) in the *Insert Option* block and clicks the *Insert* button. An event procedure that responds to the *Insert* button will copy the data from a textbox into the selected list.

The user can calculate the average for each of the three lists. When he/she clicks the *Average* button any time, its event procedure is activated and executed. The average of each list is displayed at the bottom of its corresponding list.

Figure 7-3 shows the control names defined for the example application. To make the three option controls (List1, List2, and List3) work together, you need to create a *Group Box* control first. Then you create the three option controls and put them into the *Group Box* control. The name of these three option controls are *Option1, Option2,* and *Option3*, respectively.

You need to create four event-driven procedures for this example application: *Insert_click, Cancel_click, Clear_Click,* and *Average_Click*. The *Insert_Click* procedure responds to the selected option by copying the data from the *InputValue* textbox into the selected list.

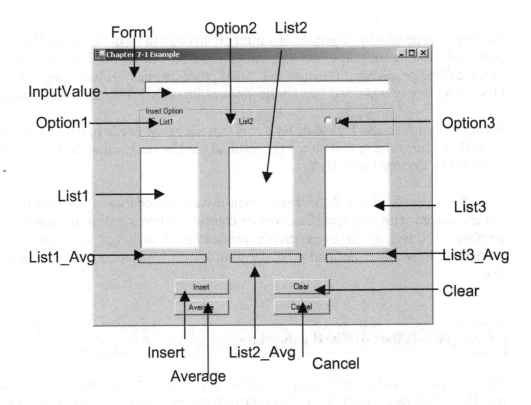

Figure 7-3   Control Names for the Example

```
Private Sub Insert_Click( ByVal sender As Object,      _
                         ByVal e As System.EventArgs)  _
                         Handles Insert.Click


    If Not IsNumeric(InputValue.Text) Then
        MsgBox("Please enter a numeric value ...")
        Exit Sub
    End If
    If Option1.Checked Then
        List1.Items.Add(InputValue.Text)
    End If
    If Option2.Checked Then
        List2.Items.Add(InputValue.Text)
    End If
    If Option3.Checked Then
        List3.Items.Add(InputValue.Text)
    End If

End Sub
```

The *Cancel_Click* procedure terminates the application when the *Cancel* button is clicked.

```
Private Sub Cancel_Click( ByVal sender As Object,             _
              ByVal e As System.EventArgs)                    _
              Handles Cancel.Click
      End
End Sub
```

The *Clear_Click* procedure clears all the list boxes and the *InputValue* textbox when the *Clear* button is clicked.

```
Private Sub Clear_Click(ByVal sender As System.Object,       _
                 ByVal e As System.EventArgs)                _
                 Handles Clear.Click
      List1.Items.Clear()
      List2.Items.Clear()
      List3.Items.Clear()
      InputValue.Text = ""
End Sub
```

The *Average_Click* procedure will calculate the average of all the items in the three lists. If one of the lists is empty, the procedure will do nothing. The procedure will activate when the *Average* button is clicked.

```
Private Sub Average_Click(ByVal sender As System.Object, _
                    ByVal e As System.EventArgs)         _
                    Handles Average.Click
      Dim sum As Long
      Dim counter As Integer

      If List1.Items.Count > 0 Then
          sum = 0
          For counter = 0 To List1.Items.Count - 1
              sum = sum + Val(List1.Items(counter))
          Next counter
          List1_Avg.Text = sum / List1.Items.Count
      End If


      If List2.Items.Count > 0 Then
          sum = 0
          For counter = 0 To List2.Items.Count - 1
              sum = sum + Val(List2.Items(counter))
          Next counter
          List2_Avg.Text = sum / List2.Items.Count
      End If
```

```
     If List3.Items.Count > 0 Then
         sum = 0
         For counter = 0 To List3.Items.Count - 1
             sum = sum + Val(List3.Items(counter))
         Next counter
         List3_Avg.Text = sum / List3.Items.Count
     End If

  End Sub
```

Note that there are three similar groups of code in the *Average_Click* procedure. Imagine the average calculation for 100 list boxes. We could have 100 groups of code. If we do this way, the procedure code is long and tedious.

To solve this problem, we can create a user-defined procedure to replace the three groups to calculate the average for each list. Such improvement simplifies the logic of the code.

The user defined procedure *OneList_Average* takes two arguments. The first one is declared with ByVal and the second one is declared with ByRef. The user defined procedure is called three times in the revised *Average_Click* event procedure listed below.

```
Private Sub Average_Click(ByVal sender As System.Object,    _
         ByVal e As System.EventArgs)                       _
         Handles Average.Click

         OneList_Average(List1, List1_Avg)
         OneList_Average(List2, List2_Avg)
         OneList_Average(List3, List3_Avg)

End Sub



Private Sub OneList_Average(  ByVal ListX As ListBox,        _
                              ByRef Label1 As Label)
         Dim sum As Long
         Dim counter As Integer
         If ListX.Items.Count > 0 Then
             sum = 0
             For counter = 0 To ListX.Items.Count - 1
                 sum = sum + Val(ListX.Items(counter))
             Next counter
             Label1.Text = sum / ListX.Items.Count
         End If

End Sub
```

Replace the old *Average_Click* procedure by the new *Average_Click* procedure and the user defined procedure called *OneList_Average*. Test and debug the application and understand the difference of the two *Average_Click* procedures.

7.2   VB.Net Functions

There are two types of functions available for use in a VB.Net application. These two types are built-in functions and user-defined functions. Built-in functions are provided in VB.Net for string manipulation, data input and output, mathematical calculation, etc. User-defined functions are defined and implemented by users to support the logic of an application. They are used only within the application they reside.

7.2.1   VB.Net Built-In Functions

There are about 165 built-in functions available in VB.Net. Table 7-1 shows a list of primary functions in alphabetical order. Note that a built-in function is often structured with the following template:

```
FunctionName (arg1, arg2, …, argn)
```

Take `Format (Expreesion, FormatTemplate)` as an example. This built-in function has a function name called Format. It has two arguments. The first argument is an expression whose result will be formatted. The second argument is the template by which the result is formatted.

```
' It returns "50,003.40".
Format(50003.4, "##,##0.00")

'It converts all the letters
'in upper case and returns "CE303"

Format("ce303", ">")
```

Note that a number of functions listed in Tables 7-1(a), (b), and (c) are not discussed in the previous chapters. Students need to learn them in later chapters or through other references.

When a VB.Net application needs to use a build-in function, you should get familiar with argument data type, returned data type and value. Also you should learn from examples that are provided by the VB.Net online help.

Table 7-1(a) Key Built-in Functions (A-F)

Function	Description	Example
Abs(Number)	Get absolute value of a number	Abs(-10.87)
Asc(String)	Get character code of the first letter in a string	Asc("abcd") = 97
Atn(Number)	Get the arctangent of the number	Atn(1)
CBool (Expression)	To convert an expression to a Boolean Type. See also other functions: CByte(*expression*), CChar(*expression*), CDate(*expression*), CDbl(*expression*), CDec(*expression*), CInt(*expression*), CLng(*expression*), CObj(*expression*), CShort(*expression*), CSng(*expression*), CStr(*expression*)	Check = CBool(A =B)
Chr(CharCode)	Get the string character of a CharCode	Chr(97)
Cos(Number)	Cos(x)	Cos(1) ' Angle in radiant
ChDrive(drive)	Change the current path of a drive	
CurDir(drive)	Get the current path of a drive	CurDir()
CreateObject (class)	Creates and returns a reference to an ActiveX object.	CreateObject (Excel.Application)
Date	Get the current system date	MyDate = Date
Day(date)	Get the day of the month	Day(#March 9, 1963#)
Dir(PathName)	Get a String representing the name of a file, directory, or folder that matches a specified pattern or the volume label of a drive.	Dir("C:/users/")
Environ(String)	Get a String containing an operating system environment variable.	Environ("path")
EOF(fileNumber)	Check if End of File	EOF(1)
Exp(number)	Get e raised to a power of number.	Exp(2)
FileLen(PathName)	Get the length of a file in bytes	FileLen("chapter8.doc")

Table 7-1(b) Key Built-in Functions (F-Z)

Function	Description	Example
Format(expression, [format])	Format the result of the expression	Format(50003.4, "##,##0.00") ' Returns "50,003.40". Format("ce303", ">") ' return "CE303"
GetObject([Pathname] [,class])	Get the reference to an object provided by an ActiveX component	GetObject ("c:\grade.xls")
Hour(time)	Get the hour of the day	Hour(#23:23:21#)
Input(Number, #FileNumber)	Return characters from an opened file	MyFileChar = Input(1, #1)
InputBox(Prompt, Title)	Displays a prompt in a dialog box, waits for the user to input text or click a button, and returns a String containing the contents of the text box.	MyInput = Inputbox("Test","Test")
InStr([start], strring1, string2)	Get a position of the first occurrence of string2 in string1	Instr(3, "It is a test", "is")
Len(string)	Get the number of characters in a string	Len("abcd")
Log(number)	Ln(x)	Log(4)
mid(start, string, length)	Get a subset from a string	mid(1,"this is a test", 4)
Minute(time)	Get the minutes from the time	Minute(#12:34:35#)
Month(date)	Get the month of the date	Month("June 16, 1963")
Msgbox(prompt, title)	Displays a message in a dialog box	Msgbox("Test","Test")
Now	Return the system date and time	Today = now
Rnd(number))	Get a random number	Int((100 * Rnd) + 1)
Second(time)	Get the second of the time	Second(#12:23:34#)
Sin(number)	Sin(x)	Sin(3.0)
Sqrt(number)	Get a square root of a number	Sqrt(4)
Str(number")	Convert a number to a string	Str(1234)
tan(number)	Tan(x)	Tan(3)
Time	Get the current system time	time
Val(string)	Convert a string to a numerical value	Val("1234")
Weekday(date)	Get the day of the week from a specified date	Weekday(#November 22, 1994#
Year(date)	Get the year of the date	Year(#August 26, 1999#)

7.2.2   User-Defined Functions

User-defined functions are similar to built-in functions. A user-defined function is structured with the following template:

```
Private Function FunctionName(ByVal Arg1 as Type1,      _
                ByRef Arg2 as Type2,…) as DataType

            VB Statement 1
            VB Statement 2
            VB statement 3
                  .
                  .
                  .

            VB statement n

      End Function
```

Note that the user-defined function has a sequence of arguments that are declared with either ByVal or ByRef. The body of the function consists of VB.Net statements. One of the statements should be an assignment statement that assigns a retuned value to the function name.

An example user-defined function is as follows:

```
Function RootCheck (        ByVal      A1 as integer,    _
                            ByVal      B1 as integer,    _
                            ByVal      C1 as integer)    _
                            as Boolean
      Dim chk as Long
      Chk = b1^2 - 4*a1*c1
      If chk <  0 then
            RootCheck = FALSE
      Else
            RootCheck = TRUE
      End If

End Sub

Private Sub Calc_Click (ByVal sender As System.Object,   _
      ByVal e As System.EventArgs)                       _
            Handles Calculate.Click

      REM This is a comment statement
      REM Below are Variables a, b, c, rt1, rt2 and
      REM chk declared within this procedure

      Dim a as integer
      Dim b as integer
      Dim c as integer
```

```
Dim rt1 as Double
Dim rt2 as Double
Dim chk as Long
Dim response as integer

' The below three statements are used to check
' if the values of the textboxes are numeric values.
' If they are not, send messages out and terminate
' the execution of the procedure.

If Not IsNumeric(Val_a.text) or Val_a.Text = "" then
    Messagebox.Show ("Please enter a numeric value")
    Exit Sub
End If

If Not IsNumeric(Val_b.text) or Val_b.Text = "" then
    Messagebox.Show ("Please enter a numeric value")
    Exit Sub
End If

If Not IsNumeric(Val_c.text) or Val_c.Text = "" then
    Messagebox.Show ("Please enter a numeric value")
    Exit Sub
End If

' The below three statements get user inputs
' of a, b, and c from the textboxes on the
' form after the check.

A = val(Val_a.text)
B = val(Val_b.text)
C = val(Val_c.text)

'
' Call the user-defined function of QuadraticRootCheck
' calculate the roots if the returned value is true
' from the function.

if RootCheck(a, b, c) then

        '
        ' If there are real roots, calculate the roots
        ' and assign them to two variables called rt1 and
        ' rt2.
        '

        rt1 = (-b+Math.sqrt(chk))/(2*a)
        rt2 = (-b-Math.sqrt(chk))/(2*a)

        ' Output the calculated roots onto the two
        ' textboxes on the form so that users
        ' can see the roots.

        Root1.text = str(rt1)
        Root2.text = str(rt2)
    End if
End Sub
```

In the above example, the user-defined function is called *RootCheck (a,b,c)*. It has three placeholders declared with ByVal. The retuned value of the function is declared to be Boolean.

Within the body of the function, you can find two assignment statements that assign FALSE and TRUE to the function name. The assignment statements provide a mechanism to return result back to the calling procedure. In addition, you can also use pass by reference to return a group of results back to the calling procedure.

The calling procedure uses the function *RootCheck (a,b,c)* in its logical expression. Keep in mind functions cannot be placed at the left side of any assignment statements.

Example 7-2 User-defined functions

Suppose you are asked to develop a VB.Net application that allows a user to insert data into a list. The user adds an item into the data list by entering the item and clicking the *Insert* button. Furthermore, the user can click on the *Calculate* button any time. An event procedure then will calculate the function value based on the following formula:

$$F(x) = \cos(x) + \sin(x) + e^x$$

The results will be listed in the function value list. Figure 7-4 shows the key control names defined for the example.

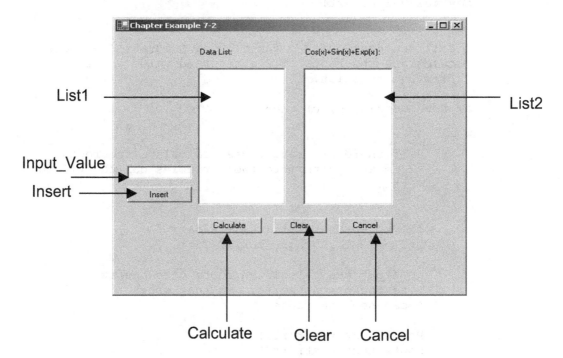

Figure 7-4   Control Names for the Example

There are four event-driven procedures for this example application: *Insert_Click*, *Cancel_Click*, *Clear_Click*, and *Calculate_Click*. The *Insert_Click* procedure adds the data entered in the *Input_Value* textbox to the data list.

The *Calculate_Click* event procedure has a For-Next loop statement to call the user-defined function called cos_sin_exp(x). The cos_sin_exp(x) function has one placeholder declared with byVal. It returns a value with *Double* data type.

```
Private Sub Insert_Click(ByVal sender As System.Object,    _
        ByVal e As System.EventArgs)                       _
        Handles Insert.Click
    If IsNumeric(Input_Value.Text) Then
        List1.Items.Add(Input_Value.Text)
    End If
End Sub


Private Sub Clear_Click(ByVal sender As Object,    _
        ByVal e As System.EventArgs)               _
        Handles Clear.Click
    List1.Items.Clear()
    List2.Items.Clear()
    Input_Value.Text = ""
End Sub


Private Sub Cancel_Click(ByVal sender As Object,    _
        ByVal e As System.EventArgs)                _
        Handles Cancel.Click
    End
End Sub


Private Sub Calculate_Click(ByVal sender As Object,    _
        ByVal e As System.EventArgs)                   _
        Handles Calculate.Click
    Dim count As Integer, ReturnValue As Double
    Dim ValueFromList1 As Double
    For count = 0 To List1.Items.Count - 1
        ValueFromList1 = Val(List1.Items(count))
        ReturnValue = cos_sin_exp(ValueFromList1)
        List2.Items.Add(ReturnValue)
    Next count

End Sub


Private Function cos_sin_exp(ByVal x As Double) As Double
    cos_sin_exp = Math.Cos(x) + Math.Sin(x) + Math.Exp(x)
End Function
```

7.3   VB.Net Modules

We have discussed procedures and functions. As you have already known, the procedures and functions are limited to the form they reside.

A challenging issue we may have is how to make procedures and functions to be used by other forms in a VB.Net application? The solution is modules.

Figure 7-5 shows the relationships between modules, forms, and other components in an application. Note that a VB.Net application consists of code modules and module-level variables, form classes and form-level variables, as well as procedures/functions and procedure/function-level variables.

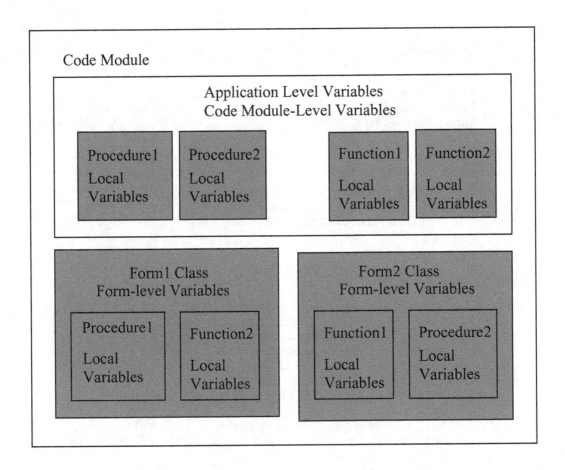

Figure 7-5   Relationships of Code Modules and Forms
in a VB.Net application

A module is a section of code that contains declarations and general procedures and functions. Procedures and functions can be declared with keyword **Private** or **Public**. When declared with **Private**, the procedures and functions can be used only in the module they reside. When declared with **Public**, the procedures and functions can be used any places in the application. All the forms can access and execute these types of procedures and functions.

There are three types of variables that can be declared in a code module: local variables, module-level variables, and application-level variables. Local variables are declared within the procedures and functions in a module. They have their scope in the procedures and functions.

Module-based variables are declared using the Dim statement. They are located outside of the procedures and functions within a module. These variables are scoped within the entire module. Any procedures and functions within the module can access to them.

Application-level variables are declared with the keyword **Public**. They are located outside of all the procedures and functions. These variables can be accessed by all the form classes, modules where the variables do not reside, as well as the functions and procedures within the hosting code module.

Example 7-3 Modules

Suppose we are developing a VB.Net application that summarizes student scores and GPAs. The application has three forms (Form1, Form2, and Form3) and a code module. Users can navigate these three forms easily. The first form, Form1, is the *Scores Input* form. It allows user to enter student scores. The second form, Form2, is the *Score Calculation* form. It allows users to calculate the average score of the students and tally the number of students within each category of A, B, C, D, and F. The third form, Form3, is the GPA Calculation form. It provides an interface to help users to calculate the average GPA of the students.

Form Design

Figure 7-6 shows the layout of Form1 that allows users to 1) enter the exam score of a student into a list from a textbox, 2) clear the list if needed, and 3) click on the *Next Form* button to go for analyses of scores and GPAs in Form2 and Form3, and 4) terminate the application.

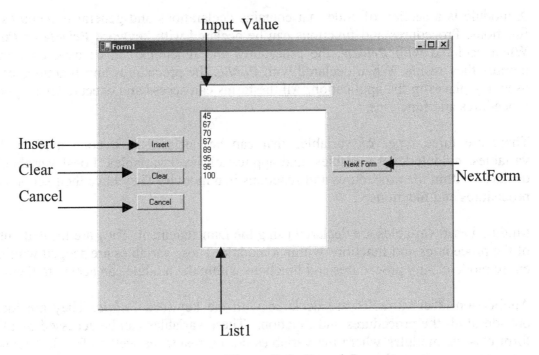

Figure 7-6   Form1 Layout

Figure 7-7 shows the layout of Form2 with key control names. Once the form is initiated and shown to the user, the list is filled with student scores received from Form1. The user click on the *Grade* button, the program will classify the student scores and summarize students with A, B, C, D, and F grade. When the user clicks on the *Average* button, the average scores will be calculated and displayed at the bottom of the list (see *List1_Average* label control). The user can click the *Back* button to go back to the Form1 for enter more student scores. The user can also click the *Forward* button to go for GPA analyses. When the user clicks on the *Cancel* button, the application will be terminated.

Figure 7-8 shows the layout of Form3 with key control names. Once this form is initiated and shown to the user, the student scores from Form2 are transferred and filled in the list on this form. The user click on the *GPA* button, the program will convert the student scores to grades and insert them into the GPA list. When the user clicks on the *Average* button, the average scores and GPA will be calculated and displayed at the bottom of the lists (see *List1_Average* and *List2_Average* label controls). The user can click the *BacktoInsert* button to go back the form1 for enter more student scores. The user can also click the *BacktoGrade* button to go for grade analyses. When the user clicks on the *Cancel*, the application will be terminated.

List1

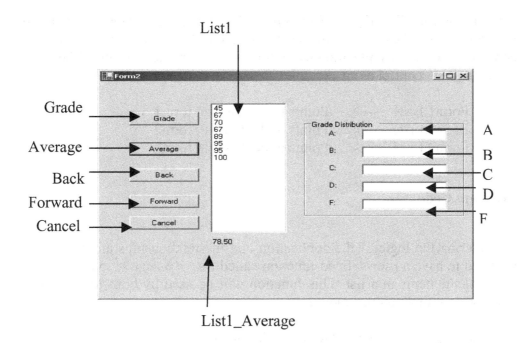

Grade

Average

Back

Forward

Cancel

A

B

C

D

F

List1_Average

Figure 7-7 Form2 Layout

List1   List2

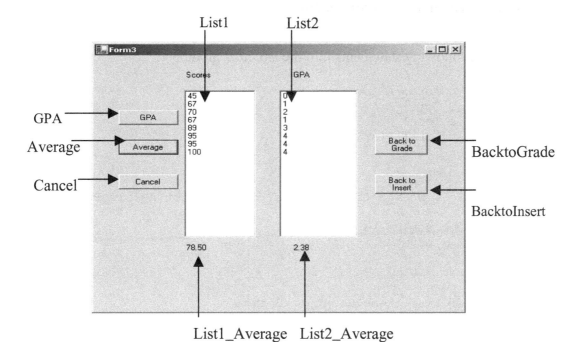

GPA

Average

Cancel

BacktoGrade

BacktoInsert

List1_Average   List2_Average

Figure 7-8 Form3 Layout

Note that Form1, Form2, and Form3 have the same control names such as *Cancel*. This is allowed since the control names are in different forms. We can differentiate the same control names in an application by adding the form name in front of the control names. Take the List1 control as an example:

Form1.List1 ---- >   Points to the List1 in form1
Form2.List1 ---- >   Points to the List1 in form2
Form3.List1 ---- >   Points to the List1 in form3

Program Code

Considering the logic of the application and the relationships among the three forms, we need to have a user-defined function called *List_Average ()* to calculate the average value of the items in a list. This function will be used by both form2 and form3. We will code the function in a module.

To create a module, you need to do the following:

1)   Open the *Project* menu
2)   Choose the *Add Module* option
3)   Double click the *Module* icon in the *Template* Window

Now you are in the *module1* window.

Copy the following statements into the *module1* module.

```
Public Total_A As Integer
Public Total_B As Integer
Public Total_C As Integer
Public Total_D As Integer
Public Total_F As Integer


Public Function List_Average(    ByVal List As ListBox)    _
                                 As String

    Dim sum As Long
    Dim counter As Integer, average As Double

    sum = 0

    If List.Items.Count <> 0 then

        For counter = 0 To List.Items.Count - 1

            sum = sum + Val(List.Items(counter))
        Next counter
        average = sum / List.Items.Count
```

```
            End if
            List_Average = Format(average, "#0.00")

      End Function
```

Note that *Total_A, Total_B, Total_C, Total_D, and Total_F* are the variables that are declared with the keyword *Public*. The keyword *Public* denotes the variables to be available for the entire application. All the form classes can access these variables.

The *List_Average* function is also declared with *Public*. Therefore it can be used in all the form classes. The function returns a string. Note that the function has one argument that is declared as a ListBox. It is allowed in VB.Net to declare a variable to follow a control template. Also note that ByVal is associated with the argument. It indicates that the passage of a List from a calling procedure or function to the *List_Average* function follows the "call by value" rule.

The following procedures are stored in the code window of Form1.

```
Private Sub NextForm_Click(ByVal sender As System.Object,      _
              ByVal e As System.EventArgs)                     _
                    Handles NextForm.Click

      Dim aform2 As New Form2
      aform2.List1.Items.AddRange(List1.Items)

      Me.Hide()
      Total_A = 0
      Total_B = 0
      Total_C = 0
      Total_D = 0
      Total_F = 0
      aform2.A.Text = ""
      aform2.B.Text = ""
      aform2.C.Text = ""
      aform2.D.Text = ""
      aform2.F.Text = ""
      aform2.Show()

End Sub

Private Sub Cancel_Click(    ByVal sender As Object,         _
                             ByVal e As System.EventArgs)    _
                             Handles Cancel.Click
        End
End Sub

Private Sub Clear_Click(    ByVal sender As Object,          _
                            ByVal e As System.EventArgs)     _
                            Handles Clear.Click

      List1.Items.Clear()
```

```
        Input_Value.Text = ""
End Sub


Private Sub Insert_Click(    ByVal sender As Object,        _
                             ByVal e As System.EventArgs)   _
                             Handles Insert.Click
     If Not IsNumeric(Input_Value.Text) Or _
               Input_Value.Text = "" Then
         MsgBox(" Please enter a numeric value ...")
         Exit Sub
     End If

     List1.Items.Add(Val(Input_Value.Text))
     Input_Value.Text = ""

End Sub
```

There are four procedures created for the form: *Insert_Click, Clear_Click, Cancel_Click and NextForm_Click*. The *Insert_Click* procedure adds the scores of a student from the *Input_Value* textbox to the list box. In order for the scores to be inserted into the list, the user will first enter the scores into the *Input_Value* textbox and clicks on the *Insert* button. As you can see, the procedure does have a robust checking mechanism that ensures the validity of the entered scores. When the user enters "abc" into the textbox, the procedure can prompt the user with a message "Please Enter a Numeric Value …".

The *Clear_Click* procedure clears the items inside the list and the *Input_Value* textbox. The *Cancel_Click* procedure terminates the application when it is clicked.

The *NextForm_Click* procedure leads the user to the grade form (Form2) for grade analyses. The procedure first defines a variable to be of Form2 class and creates an instance of the Form2 class. The statement:

```
        aform2.List1.Items.AddRange(List1.Items)
```

transfers all the items in the List1 of the Form1 to the List1 of the Form2. Before the instance of the Form2 class is shown to the user, the Form1 form will be hidden; the variables Total_A, Total_B, Total_C, Total_D, and Total_F will be set to 0; and the A, B, C, D, and F textboxes will be set to be blank.

The following procedures are stored in Form2.

```
Private Sub Cancel_Click(ByVal sender As System.Object,  _
                         ByVal e As System.EventArgs)  _
                         Handles Cancel.Click
     End
```

```
End Sub


Private Sub Back_Click(       ByVal sender As Object,          _
                              ByVal e As System.EventArgs)     _
                              Handles Back.Click
    Dim aForm As New Form1
    aForm.List1.Items.AddRange(List1.Items)

    aForm.Show()
    Me.Hide()
End Sub


Private Sub Forward_Click(ByVal sender As Object,              _
                          ByVal e As System.EventArgs)         _
                          Handles Forward.Click
    Dim aForm As New Form3
    aForm.List1.Items.AddRange(List1.Items)
    aForm.Show()
    Me.Hide()
End Sub



Private Sub Grade_Click(       ByVal sender As Object,         _
                               ByVal e As System.EventArgs)    _
                               Handles Grade.Click
    Dim i As Integer
    Dim aValue As Double

    Total_A = 0
    Total_B = 0
    Total_C = 0
    Total_D = 0
    Total_F = 0

    For i = 0 To List1.Items.Count - 1
        aValue = Val(List1.Items(i))
        Select Case aValue
            Case Is >= 90
                Total_A = Total_A + 1
            Case Is >= 80
                Total_B = Total_B + 1
            Case Is >= 70
                Total_C = Total_C + 1
            Case Is >= 60
                Total_D = Total_D + 1
            Case Is < 60
                Total_F = Total_F + 1
        End Select
    Next i
    A.Text = str(Total_A)
    B.Text = str(Total_B)
    C.Text = str(Total_C)
    D.Text = str(Total_D)
```

```
        F.Text = str(Total_F)

   End Sub

   Private Sub Average_Click(ByVal sender As Object,      _
           ByVal e As System.EventArgs)                   _
           Handles Average.Click
       List1_Average.Text = List_Average(List1)
    End Sub
```

There are five procedures that respond to the events or actions on Form2. The *Grade_Click* procedure classifies the scores in the list by five categories. The select case statement is used inside the For-Next loop. The variable "I" is used as a pointer to go through the list from the first to the last. As the first item has the index of 0, the last item has its index of the total number of the items minus 1. The List1.Items.Count method returns the total number of items in the List1 list.

The *Back_Click* and *Forward_Click* procedures are created to allow the user to navigate to form1 and form3. The *Back_Click* procedure creates an instance of Form1 class. Before it hides its form, it transfers the items in the List1 of Form2 to the List1 on Form1 and displays the instance of the Form2 class. The *Forward_Click* procedure first creates an instance of Form3 class. It then transfers all the items in the List1 of Form2 into the List1 of Form3.

The *Average_Click* procedure calls the List_Average function defined in the module1 and assigns the returned result to the Text property of the list1_average label control on Form2.

The following procedures are stored in Form3.

```
Private Sub BackToGrade_Click(ByVal sender As System.Object,   _
        ByVal e As System.EventArgs)                           _
        Handles BackToGrade.Click
    Dim aForm As New Form2
    aForm.List1.Items.AddRange(List1.Items)
    aForm.Show()
    Me.Hide()
End Sub

Private Sub BacktoInsert_Click(     ByVal sender As Object, _
        ByVal e As System.EventArgs)                        _
        Handles BacktoInsert.Click
    Dim aForm As New Form1
    aForm.List1.Items.AddRange(List1.Items)
    aForm.Show()
    Me.Hide()
End Sub

Private Sub Cancel_Click(     ByVal sender As Object,          _
```

```
                                 ByVal e As System.EventArgs)        _
                                 Handles Cancel.Click
            End
End Sub

Private Sub GPA_Click(  ByVal sender As Object,                     _
                        ByVal e As System.EventArgs)                _
                        Handles GPA.Click
        Dim i As Integer, aScore As Double
        If List1.Items.Count <= 0 Then
            Exit Sub
        End If
        For i = 0 To List1.Items.Count - 1
            aScore = Val(List1.Items(i))
            Select Case aScore
                Case Is >= 90
                    List2.Items.Add(4)
                Case Is >= 80
                    List2.Items.Add(3)
                Case Is >= 70
                    List2.Items.Add(2)
                Case Is >= 60
                    List2.Items.Add(1)
                Case Else
                    List2.Items.Add(0)
            End Select
        Next
End Sub

Private Sub Average_Click(    ByVal sender As Object,                _
                             ByVal e As System.EventArgs)           _
                             Handles Average.Click
            List1_Average.Text = List_Average(List1)
            List2_Average.Text = List_Average(List2)
End Sub
```

The *BacktoGrade_Click* and *BacktoInsert_Click* procedures allow the user to go back to Form1 and Form2. The *BacktoGrade_Click* procedure creates an instance of the Form2 Class and transfers all the items in the List1 of Form3 into the List1 of the Form2. The *BacktoInsert_Click* procedure creates an instance of Form1 and transfers all the items in the List1 of Form3 into the List1 of Form1.

The *Cancel_Click* procedure terminates the application when the user clicks on the *Cancel* button.

The *GPA_Click* procedure translates the scores into GPAs. A For-Next statement is used for the translation. The Select Case statement inside the For-Next loop is used to specify which GPA category the scores should go.

The *Average-Click* procedure uses the function List_Average () to first calculate the average of student scores and GPAs and then put the results at the bottom of the lists.

In summary, the example application has employed the code module to store user-defined functions that can be used by different forms.

7.4   Questions

Q1.   What are the differences between "pass by value" and "pass by reference"?

Q2.   Your project manager gives you a VB.Net application that has the following two procedures:

```
Private Sub aTxBox_KeyPress (ByVal sender As Object,    _
            ByVal e As System.EventArgs)
            Handles aTextBox.KeyPress                      _


        Dim x as double
        Dim y as double
        Dim z as double

        X = val(AtextBox.Text)
        Y = Math.sin(x)

        If Asc(e.KeyChar) = 13 then
            Average(X,Y,Z)
        End IF
        Average1.Text = Z
End Sub


Public Sub Average (    ByVal X as Double,            _
                 ByVal Y as Double,                   _
                 ByRef Z as Double)
        Z = (x+y)/2
End Sub
```

Answer the following questions:

- ❑ What does the aTextBox_Keypress event procedure do?
- ❑ Draw a diagram to show the communications between variables in the calling procedure and the called procedure.
- ❑ If we can change `public sub average` to `private sub average`, is the event procedure still able to call the called function?
- ❑ If 10 is entered into the ATextBox control, what is the value displayed in the Average1 control?

Q3.   VB.Net provides a rich set of functions for manipulating date and time. You are asked to develop an application that can allow users to click a command button and display information about year, month, date, hour, minute, and second of the current system date and time in different textboxes.

Q4.   Explain scope of variables that reside in different declarations sections. Describe code-module-level variables, form-level variables, and local variables.

Q5.   In Example 7-3 of this chapter, every form has a Cancel button. Can the Cancel button be shared by the three forms? If it can be shared, what do you need to do?

Chapter 8
Random Number Generation

Random numbers are useful for computer game, computer simulation and numerical method testing. Random sequences with a variety of statistical properties can be generated in VB.Net using the Rnd () function and the Randomize() statement. We will develop a couple of VB.Net applications that generate random numbers with uniform and Gaussian distributions in this chapter.

8.1   Uniform Distribution and π Estimation

The random sequence that follows uniform distribution is a sequence of numbers in an interval of [a, b] where each number in the interval is equally likely to occur. The probability density function p(x) for a uniformly distributed random numbers is described as follows:

$$p(x) = \begin{cases} \dfrac{1}{b-a} \,, & a \leq x \leq b \\[2ex] 0 \,, & otherwise \end{cases}$$

Figure 8-1 shows the graphical representation of the p(x) for a uniform distribution.

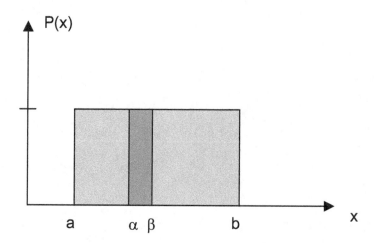

Figure 8-1 Probability Density of a Uniform Distribution

Given a small interval $[\alpha,\beta]$ within the interval [a, b], the probability that a random number will fall in the interval $[\alpha,\beta]$ is

$$p[\alpha \le x \le \beta] = \int_{\alpha}^{\beta} p(x)dx$$

The area bounded by the interval [α,β] is the probability that a random number will fall in the interval [α,β].

The Rnd() function within VB.Net is a random number generator for the interval [0, 1]. It uses a seed value created by the Randomize statement to generate a series of random numbers. When the Randomize statement is executed, it always defines a different seed value based on the universal time of a computer and helps the Rnd () function to create a unique series of random numbers.

Example 8-1 π Estimation

Assume a VB.Net application is needed to estimate π. As you may know, a rough π estimation can be obtained by using random numbers and checking the geometric relationships between a square and its inscribed circle. Suppose there is a square board of 200 * 200 screen units in which an inscribed circle with a radius of 100 units is drawn. When we throw darts on this board randomly, all of the darts are uniformly distributed over the square. In another words, no darts are outside of the board. The probability of darts that fall into the circle is proportional to the ratio of the square and circle areas, as shown below:

$$\text{Prob(darts in circle)} = \frac{p}{n} = \frac{Area\ of\ Circle}{Area\ of\ Square} = \frac{\pi * 100^2}{200^2} = \frac{\pi}{4}$$

Where

Prob (darts in circle)   – Probability of darts that fall in the circle
P   - Number of darts that fall in the circle
N   - Total of darts that are thrown onto the board.

Reformatting the above equation, we will get the approximation of π as follows:

$$\pi = \frac{4 * p}{n}$$

Now we will develop a VB.Net program to simulate the "throwing" process and estimate the π value.

Figure 8-1 shows the form design of the application. As you can see there are a square and its inscribed circle on the form. They will be generated when the form is activated.

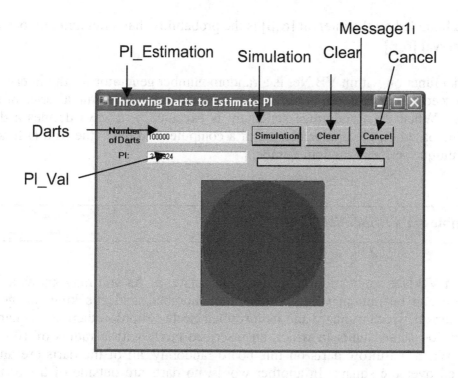

Figure 8-1 Form in the VB.Net Application for π Estimation

Below is the code developed for the VB. Net application:

```
' The below two statements must be placed outside the class.
' They imports the classes within the System.Drawing and
' System.Darwing.Drawing2D into the application

Imports System.Drawing
Imports System.Drawing.Drawing2D


Public Class PI_Estimate

        Inherits System.Windows.Forms.Form

        Windows Form Designer Generated Code
```

```
Private Sub PI_Estimate_Paint(ByVal sender As Object,        _
        ByVal e As System.Windows.Forms.PaintEventArgs)  _
        Handles MyBase.Paint

    Dim myGraphics As Graphics

' E is the object variable. It contains a set of Paint Event
' related arguments inherited from the PI_Estimate form.
' One of the arguments is the Graphics Property of
' the form.
    myGraphics = e.Graphics

' Define a variable to be of Rectangle class.
' The Rectangle class is within the System.Drawing
' library and is imported by the Imports statement.

    Dim myRectangle As Rectangle

    Dim x1 As Integer
    Dim y1 As Integer

' Define a variable to be of Pen class.
' The Pen class is within the System.Drawing
' library and is imported by the Imports statement.
' The Mypen variable is initiated by the pen color
' of Dark Blue.


    Dim myPen As New Pen(Color.DarkBlue)

' Set up the upper left corner of the rectangle or the
' square board (200 * 200 screen units). The term screen
' unit is defined for the window.
' The below two statements get the width and height of
' the active form (or the PI_Estimate form) and offsets
' the corner [-100, -100] from the center point.

    x1 = Val(ActiveForm.Width) / 2 - 100
    y1 = Val(ActiveForm.Height) / 2 - 100

' Make the rectangle to be 200 * 200
    myRectangle = New Rectangle(x1, y1, 200, 200)

' Draw the rectangle in dark blue on the active form

    myGraphics.DrawRectangle(myPen, myRectangle)

' Draw the circle inscribed within the rectangle.

    myGraphics.DrawEllipse(myPen, myRectangle)

End Sub
```

```
Private Sub Simulation_Click(ByVal sender As System.Object, _
              ByVal e As System.EventArgs)                    _
              Handles Simulation.Click


'     The below statements declare three variables of
'     Graphics, Rectangle, and SolidBrush class, respectively.

      Dim myGraphics As Graphics
      Dim myRectangle As Rectangle
      Dim myBrush As SolidBrush

      Dim i As Long
      Dim DeltaX As Integer
      Dim DeltaY As Integer
      Dim centerX As Integer
      Dim centerY As Integer
      Dim radius As Single
      Dim p As Long
      Dim totaldarts As Long


'  The below statement checks if the value in
'  the Darts textbox is a numeric value. If not,
'  Display a message in the Mesage1 label control
'  and exit the procedure.

      If Not IsNumeric(Darts.Text) Then
          Message1.text = "Enter a numeric Value"
          Exit Sub
      End If


'  Get the window handle of the Active form
'  Set a reference of myGraphics to the Graphics
'  property (or object) of the active form.

      myGraphics = Graphics.FromHwnd(ActiveForm().Handle)
'  Get the center point of the Active form

      centerX = Val(ActiveForm.Width) / 2
      centerY = Val(ActiveForm.Height) / 2


'  Set up a seed value for random number generation

      Randomize()



      p = 0
      totaldarts = Val(Darts.Text)

'  Simulate the dart throwing process. The total of
'  throwing times is defined in the Totaldarts variable
'
```

```
        For i = 1 To totaldarts

    ' Determine the position of the dart on the board with
    ' respect to the center point

            DeltaX = Rnd() * 200 - 100
            DeltaY = Rnd() * 200 - 100

    ' Calculate the radius of the dart position in relation
    ' to the center point of the form

            radius = Math.Sqrt(DeltaX ^ 2 + DeltaY ^ 2)

    ' If radius <= 100 then the dart is within the circle
    ' Assign the color of the dart to be green. Otherwise,
    ' Assign the color of the dart to be red.


            If radius > 100 Then
                myBrush = New SolidBrush(Color.Red)
            Else
                myBrush = New SolidBrush(Color.DarkGreen)
                p = p + 1
            End If

    ' Draw a square dot (or the dart) on the board

            myRectangle = New Rectangle(centerX + DeltaX,  _
                          centerY + DeltaY, 3, 3)
            myGraphics.FillEllipse(myBrush, myRectangle)
        Next i

    ' Calculate the approximate of PI value
        PI_Val.Text = Str(p * 4 / totaldarts)


    End Sub


    Private Sub Cancel_Click(ByVal sender As System.Object,  _
            ByVal e As System.EventArgs)                     _
            Handles Cancel.Click

        End
    End Sub


    Private Sub Clear_Click(ByVal sender As System.Object,  _
            ByVal e As System.EventArgs)                    _
            Handles Clear.Click

    ' Clear the Darts and PI_Val textboxes.
    ' Clear the label control

        Darts.Text = ""
```

```
        PI_Val.Text = ""
        Message1.Text = ""
        Dim myGraphics As Graphics
        Dim myRectangle As Rectangle '

        Dim x1 As Integer
        Dim y1 As Integer
        Dim myPen As New Pen(Color.DarkBlue)

        'return the current form as a drawing surface

        myGraphics = Graphics.FromHwnd(ActiveForm().Handle)

'  Clear the graphics aprt of the form by resetting the
'  color to be the original color.

        myGraphics.Clear(Color.LightSteelBlue)


'  Redraw the square and the circle.

        x1 = Val(ActiveForm.Width) / 2 - 100
        y1 = Val(ActiveForm.Height) / 2 - 100

        ' create a rectangle based on
        ' x,y coordinates, width, & height
        myRectangle = New Rectangle(x1, y1, 200, 200)
        myGraphics.DrawRectangle(myPen, myRectangle)
        myGraphics.DrawEllipse(myPen, myRectangle)
    End Sub


  Private Sub Darts_KeyPress(ByVal sender As Object,  _
      ByVal e As System.Windows.Forms.KeyPressEventArgs)  _
      Handles Darts.KeyPress

        Message1.Text = ""
        PI_Val.Text = ""
    End Sub
End Class
```

It is noted that the above code has used a set of new concepts, terms, statements, and functions.

1)   *Imports* Statement.

The *Imports* statement is used to import a *namespace*. Namespaces have been around for quite a while in programming but have only become a requirement for Visual Basic.Net programmers recently. Namespaces are a way to define a set of objects (or classes) into one hierarchical structure.

There are three types of namespaces: Microsoft, System, and the namespace created for a specific application. The Microsoft namespace contains a structured set of objects related to Visual Basic class library (The definition of a class will be described in later chapters.) The System namespace stores a library of classes and objects that are related to the Windows operating system installed on a computer. The namespace for a application contains classes including form classes. You can find all these namespaces by selecting *View -> Object Browser*.

Namespaces that are often used in VB.Net Applications are as follows:

```
System:             includes essential classes and base classes for
                    commonly used data types, events, exceptions,etc.

System.Collections: includes classes and interfaces that define
                    various collections of objects such as list,
                    arrays, etc.

System.Data:        includes classes that handle data from data
                    sources.

System.Drawing:     provides access to drawing methods. We use this
                    namespace in this chapter.

System.IO:          includes classes for data access with files. We
                    use this namespace in this chapter.

System.Net:         provides interface to protocols used on the
                    Internet.

System.Web:         includes classes and interfaces that support
                    browser-server communication.

System.Web.Services: includes classes that help us build and use Web
                    Services

System.Windows.Forms:includes classes for creating Windows based
                    forms. We use this namespace in all the VB.Net
                    Applications that have forms.
```

You can create your name namespaces. For example, if you want to create a namespace called Statistics that contains two classes named *NormDist1* and *NormDist2*, you can use the following statement to define the namespace:

```
Namespace Statistics
     Class NormDist1
          ' Do something here in this class
     End Class
     Class NormDist2
          ' Do something here in this class
     End Class
End Namespace
```

In order to refer to a namespace (no matter whether it is a .Net System namespace or a user-defined namespace), you have to use *Imports* statement and place it outside of any form classes. For example, Math is a namespace provided by VB.Net. To import this namespace, we need to use the following statement:

```
Imports System.Math
```

Using this statement, we do not need to have *Math* in front of each mathematical function. For example, when we use Sqrt(x) and cos(x) in a procedure, we just simply write them as Sqrt(x) and cos(x) instead of Math.Sqrt(x) and Math.Cos(x).

In the π estimation application, the below two Imports statements are used.

```
Imports System.Drawing
Imports System.Drawing.Drawing2D
```

These two statements are placed outside of the form class, *PI_Estimate* to set references to functions, methods, and properties of graphic drawing classes stored in *System.Drawing.Drawing2D* and *System.Drawing*.

2)   Form Paint Event

The application provides a user-defined event procedure to respond to the Paint event of the *PI_Estimate* form. When the *PI_Estimate* form is activated or initiated, the *PI_Estimate_Paint* event procedure will run. This procedure declares five variables. The myGraphics variable has the data type of the *Graphics* class. It refers to the graphics property of the active form (in this case, the *PI_Estimate* form) through the variable *e*. The variable *e* is a VB.Net built-in variable. It passes Paint Event related arguments (including the Graphics property of the active form) down to the procedure it belongs to.

The Form Paint Event procedure draws a square board of 200 * 200 screen units and an inscribed circle with a radius of 100 screen units. It prepares the darting board on which the random darts can be thrown by other procedures.

3)   The Simulation Click Procedure

Once the *Simulation* button is clicked, this procedure first asks users to specify the number of the times the darts should be thrown. If the entered value in the Darts textbox is not a numeric value, a message will be displayed in the label control (*Message1*) below the *Simulation* button. The procedure uses the following statement to set the variable myGraphics to refer to the Graphics property of the *Active Form* (or the *PI_Estimate* form):

```
myGraphics = Graphics.FromHwnd(ActiveForm().Handle)
```

The procedure also uses the Randomize statement to get a seed value for the Rnd() function. A For-Next loop statement is used to generate two sets of random numbers within a range of [-100, 100]. The first set specifies the X position of a dart on the board, while the second set specifies the Y position. If the dart is thrown within the circle, a square dot in green color appears within the circle. The following formula is used to determine if the dart is inside the circle:

$$Radius = \sqrt{\Delta x^2 + \Delta y^2}$$

4)   The Clear Click Procedure

The Clear_Click procedure resets the dart throwing process. It clears the *Darts* and *PI_Val* textboxes. It also clears the drawing board and resets the board with a square and a circle.

8.2   Random Numbers for Gaussian Distributions

With the use of Rnd () function, it is possible to generate random numbers that follow other distributions. For example, we can generate a series of random numbers with Gaussian or normal distribution. The probability density function of a normal distribution is as follows:

$$p(x) = \frac{1}{\sigma\sqrt{2\pi}} \exp\left[\frac{1(x-\mu)^2}{2\sigma^2}\right]$$

Where μ and σ are the mean and the standard deviation of the distribution of random numbers.

This distribution function can be transformed via a pair of uniform distributions using the Box-Muller method. Assume we have two sets of random numbers r_1 and r_2 that are uniformly distributed over [0, 1]. The following formulas can help create random numbers (n_1 and n_2) that follow normal distribution:

$$n_1 = \cos(2\pi r_2)\sqrt{-2\ln(r_1)}$$
$$n_2 = \sin(2\pi r_2)\sqrt{-2\ln(r_1)}$$

The normal distribution here has a mean of $\mu = 0$ and a standard deviation of $\sigma = 1$. We can scale and offset random numbers (n_1 or n_2) to get a more general normal distribution with $\mu = \mu 1$ and $\sigma = \sigma 1$ based on the below formula:

$$Z = \mu + \sigma * x$$

Where   x can be any random number in n_1 or n_2

The normal distribution is noted as $N(\mu, \sigma)$.

Example 8.2	Normal Distribution

Assume a VB.Net application is needed to create a series of normally distributed random numbers. The random numbers will be saved into a text file when a user clicks the **Simulation** button (see Figure 8-2). When the user clicks the **Read Text File** button, you will see the random numbers are loaded into the **RandomNumber** listbox as shown in Figure 8-3.

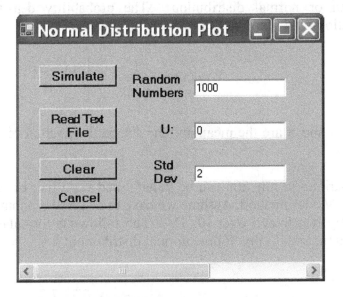

Figure 8-2   Example 8-2 Application

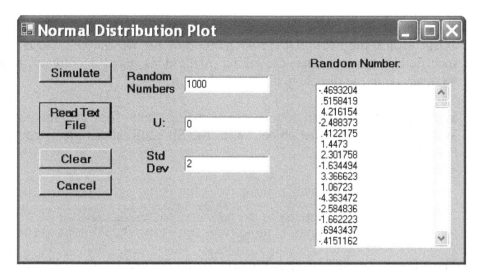

Figure 8-3 List of Random Numbers of Normal Distribution N(0,2)

Before we develop this application, let us prepare ourselves with a few new terms and concepts.

1)   Manage Text files

Microsoft introduced a new, object-oriented method to work with files in VB.Net. The System.IO namespace in the .NET IDE provides several classes to handle text files, binary files, directories, and byte streams. Here we concentrate on the classes for text files.

■   Create and Open a Text File

The System.IO.File class is used to create a new file or open an existing one. This class contains methods for many common file operations, including copying, deleting, file attribute manipulating, and file existence checking. Here, we will use the *CreateText* and *OpenText* methods.

The *CreateText* method creates a new text file and returns a *System.IO.StreamWriter* object. With the StreamWriter object, you can write to a text file. The following code demonstrates how to create a text file:

```
Dim OutputFile As System.IO.File
Dim OutputWrite As System.IO.StreamWriter

If Not OutputFile.Exists("C:\temp1") Then
      Directory.CreateDirectory("c:\temp1")
End If
OutputWrite =
      OutputFile.CreateText("C:\temp1\$$$temp.txt")
```

In the above example, you see an If-Then statement that checks if a specified directory exists. If not, the *CreateDirectory* method of the *Directory* class is used to create the specified directory. The *CreatText* method is used to create a text file called *$$$temp.txt* in the directory or folder *C:\temp1*.

The *OpenText* method opens an existing text file for reading and returns a *System.IO.StreamReader* object. With the StreamReader object, you can read the file. For example,

```
Dim ReadFile As System.IO.File
Dim InputRead As System.IO.StreamReader
InputRead = ReadFile.OpenText("C:\temp1\$$$temp.txt")
```

The above example first open the text file *$$$temp.txt* in the folder *C:\temp1*.

- Writing to a Text File

The methods in the *System.IO.StreamWriter* class for writing to a text file are *Write* and *WriteLine*. The difference between these methods is that the *WriteLine* method appends a newline character at the end of the line while the *Write* method does not. For example,

```
OutputWrite.WriteLine("This is an example")
OutputWrite.Write ("Write a line without new linc character")
outputWrite.Write ()    'Write a blank line to the file
OutputWrite.Close()
```

The statement `OutputWrite.WriteLine("This is an example")` is used to write the string `"This is an example"` into the text file. The second statement writes a string line into the text file without having the new line character at the end of the line. The third statement writes a new line character into the text file. Once all the writing work is done, the statement `OutputWrite.Close()` is used to close the text file for writing.

- Reading from a text file

The System.IO.StreamReader class supports several methods for reading text files and offers a way of determining whether you are at the end of the file. The *Readline* method is often used to read a text line from the opened or newly created text file. For example,

```
While InputRead.Peek <> -1
        aLine = InputRead.ReadLine()
        ListBox1.Items.Add(aLine)
End While
```

Assume a text file is opened through the *InputRead* object. We can use the *ReadLine* method to read the string line and put it into a listbox called *Listbox1*. The while-loop statement is used to determine whether the end of the text file is reached. The Peek method reads the next character in the file without changing the place that we are currently reading. If we have reached the end of the file, Peek returns -1.

With the above terms and concepts clarified, now we can write this VB.Net application. Figure 8-4 shows the form with key control names:

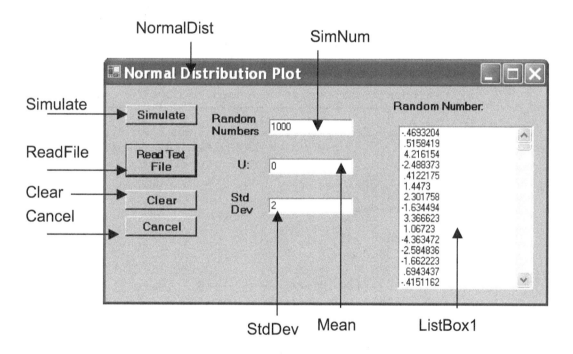

Figure 8-4 Form Design for Example 8-2 Application

Below is the code for the application:

First we have a module to create a function NormDist to generate rand numbers with the normal dirstribution N(u, stddev). The *u* and *stddev* are obtained from the form. Note that the namespace `System.Math` is imported into this module.

```
Imports System.Math
Module Module1
    Public Function NormDist(ByVal u As Single,
                ByVal stddev As Single) As Double

        Const pi As Single = 3.1415026
        Dim r1 As Single
        ' dim r2 as single
        r1 = Cos(2 * pi * Rnd()) * Sqrt(Abs(-2 * Log(Rnd())))

        ' r2 = sin(2 * pi * Rnd()) * Sqrt(Abs(-2 * Log(Rnd())))

        NormDist = u + stddev * r1
    End Function
End Module
```

Second, we need to write a form with the following procedures:

```
Imports System.io
Public Class NormalDist
        Inherits System.Windows.Forms.Form
```

```
┌──────────────────────────────────────────────┐
│     Windows Form Designer Generated Code       │
└──────────────────────────────────────────────┘
```

```
Private Sub Simulate_Click(ByVal sender As System.Object,
                ByVal e As System.EventArgs)
                Handles Simulate.Click

    Dim i As Long
    Dim totalNum As Long
    Dim u As Single
    Dim stddev_val As Single
    Dim randomNumber As Single

    Dim OutputFile As System.IO.File
    Dim OutputWrite As System.IO.StreamWriter


    If Not IsNumeric(SimNum.Text) Then
        MessageBox.Show("Enter a numeric Value")
        Exit Sub
    End If



    If Not IsNumeric(Mean.Text) Then
        MessageBox.Show("Enter a numeric Value")
        Exit Sub
    End If

    If Not IsNumeric(StdDev.Text) Then
        MessageBox.Show("Enter a numeric Value")
        Exit Sub
    End If
```

```
' Place a seed value for random number generation.

  Randomize()
  u = Val(Mean.Text)
  stddev_val = Val(StdDev.Text)

  If Not OutputFile.Exists("C:\temp1") Then
      Directory.CreateDirectory("c:\temp1")
  End If

  OutputWrite = OutputFile.CreateText("C:\temp1\$$$temp.txt")
  For i = 1 To Val(SimNum.Text)

      ' Call the NormDist function created in module1
      ' Generate a series of random numbers with N(u, StdDev)

      randomNumber = NormDist(u, stddev_val)

      ' Write the random numbers within the text file.

      OutputWrite.WriteLine(Str(randomNumber))
  Next i
  OutputWrite.Close()
End Sub




Private Sub NormalDist_Load(ByVal sender As Object,          _
          ByVal e As System.EventArgs)                       _
          Handles MyBase.Load

' Set the form to its original size or the size without the
' listbox1 control is shown.

  Me.Width = 350
  Me.Height = 300
  ListBox1.Visible = False
End Sub




Private Sub ReadFile_Click(ByVal sender As System.Object,   _
          ByVal e As System.EventArgs)                      _
          Handles ReadFile.Click

  Dim aLine As String
  Me.ActiveForm.Width = 550
  Me.ActiveForm.Height = 300
  ListBox1.Visible = True
  RNLabel.Visible = True


  Dim ReadFile As System.IO.File
  Dim InputRead As System.IO.StreamReader
```

```
        InputRead = ReadFile.OpenText("C:\temp1\$$$temp.txt")

        While InputRead.Peek <> -1
            aLine = InputRead.ReadLine()
            ListBox1.Items.Add(aLine)
        End While

        InputRead.Close()

    End Sub


    Private Sub Clear_Click(ByVal sender As System.Object,        _
                ByVal e As System.EventArgs)
                Handles Clear.Click                               _

        SimNum.Text = ""
        Mean.Text = ""
        StdDev.Text = ""
        Me.ActiveForm.Width = 350
        Me.ActiveForm.Height = 300
        ListBox1.Visible = False
        RNLabel.Visible = False
    End Sub

    Private Sub Cancel_Click(ByVal sender As System.Object,       _
                ByVal e As System.EventArgs)
                Handles Cancel.Click                              _
        End
    End Sub
End Class
```

8.3   Questions

Q1.   Which function in VB.Net is used to create a series of random number between [0, 1]?

Q2.   What does the Randomize () statement do?

Q3.   Write a VB.Net function to create a series of random numbers between 0-1000.

Q4.   Assume the board used in Example 8-1 is resized to be 300 * 300 screen units and the inscribed circle has a radius of 300 screen units. What is the formula used for estimating the π value?

Q5.   Write flow charts for all the procedures and functions used in Example 8-1.

Q6.   What is a Namespace? List a set of .Net System namespaces.

Q7.   Show a Namespace statement to define a namespace called *Chapter8*. The namespace has three classes named *Class8_1, Class8_2,* and *Class8_3.*

Q8.   Why do we need to have the following statements before the form class

```
Imports System.Drawing
Imports System.Drawing.Drawing2D


Public Class PI_Estimate

    ...
    ...

    ...
End Class
```

Q9.   What does the keyword "Me" refer to? What does the ActiveForm refer to?

```
Private Sub Clear_Click(ByVal sender As System.Object,    _
        ByVal e As System.EventArgs)                      _
        Handles Clear.Click

    SimNum.Text = ""
     Mean.Text = ""
    StdDev.Text = ""
    Me.ActiveForm.Width = 350
    Me.ActiveForm.Height = 300
    ListBox1.Visible = False
    RNLabel.Visible = False
End Sub
```

Q9.   Write a set of statements in a new *Form_Paint* procedure to draw an intersection as shown below:

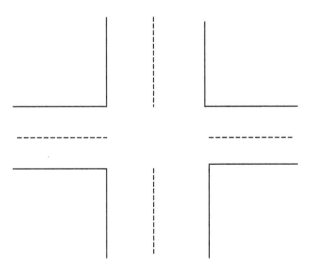

Q10.   Assume you have an existing file called *Chapter8_Data.txt* in *c:\temp* folder. Write a function to read data line by line from this file until the end of file is reached.

Q11.   Write a set of statements to verify a folder called *Chapter8* exists in C:\.

Q12.   Write a function to create a series of random numbers that follow Poisson distribution.

Chapter 9
Development of VB.Net Applications II

This chapter presents a problem with which you can develop a VB.Net application. The problem is to use a computer to estimate an average value of a function over a certain interval. Suppose $f(x)$ is a continuous and monotonic function defined over [a, b]. The average value of $f(x)$ can be expressed in terms of the integral as follows:

$$f_{avg} = \frac{1}{b-a} \int_a^b f(x)dx$$

An approximation to the average value of $f(x)$ can be estimated using a series of random numbers. Given a series of n random numbers, xi, uniformly distributed over [a, b], the function value $f(x_i)$ can then be calculated to estimate the average value f_{avg}. As the set of random numbers increases, the accuracy of the approximation should increase. With the average function value is approximated, the integral of the function over [a, b] can be estimated using the following equation:

$$\int_a^b f(x)dx = (b-a) f_{avg}$$

This approximation technique for the integral of a function is referred to as Monte Carlo integration.

Project I: Monte Carlos Integration

You are asked to develop an error free VB.Net application that can approximate the integral of the following function:

$$\int_a^b f(x)dx = \int_0^1 (x^2 + 2x + 1)dx$$

Figure 9-1 shows an example form for the VB.Net application. The form, when activated, allows a user to enter the interval [a, b] and the times of simulation into three textboxes. As you can see from Figure9-1, the user has entered 0 for a, 1 for b, and 10,000 for the simulation times.

Once the three values are entered, the user can click the *Monte Carlo Simulation* button. The approximate of the integral of the given function over [a, b] will be displayed in the *Approximation* textbox. When the user clicks the *Clear* button, the textboxes will be empty. When the user clicks the *Cancel* button, the program terminates normally.

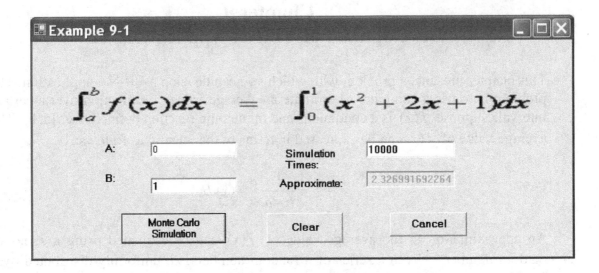

Figure 9-1   An Example Form for the Project I

9.2   Project II: Enhancement of Example 8-2 Application

You are asked to upgrade the Example 8-2 application described in Chapter 8. Figure 9-2 shows an example enhancement of the application. As you can see from Figure 9-2, nine controls are added to the new application: *Min, Max, SampleMean, Sort,* and *SampleStdDev* buttons. The textboxes *MinVal, MaxVal, Mean_List,* and *StdDevVal* are created.

Once a series of random numbers that follow normal distribution is generated and stored in the Listbox, the users can click one of the five buttons and perform statistical analyses on the random numbers.

1)   Min Operation

When the *Min* button is clicked, the program needs to check if the list box is empty. If it is not, the program needs to use a loop statement to get the minimum value within the list box. The minimum value, once found, will be displayed in the textbox next to the *Min* button.

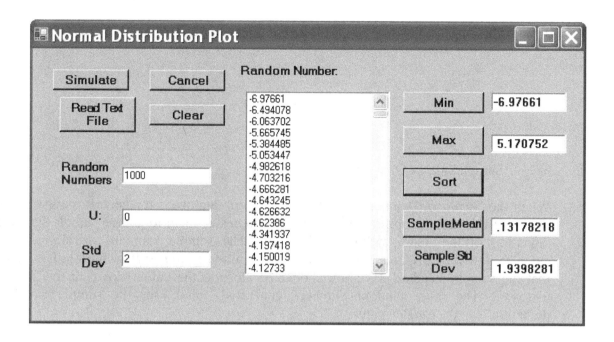

2)   Max Operation

When the *Max* button is clicked, the program needs to check if the list box is empty. If it is not, the program needs to use a loop statement to get the maximum value within the list box. The maximum value, once found, will be displayed in the textbox next to the *Max* button.

3)   Sort Operation

When the *Sort* button is clicked, the program needs to check if the list box is empty. If it is not, the program needs to use a nested loop statement to arrange the values within the list box in ascending order.

4)   SampleMean Operation

When the *SampleMean* button is clicked, the program needs to check if the list box is empty. If it is not, the program needs to use a loop statement to get the average value (or the sample mean value) of the items within the list box. The average value, once calculated, will be displayed in the textbox next to the *SampleMean* button. It is noted that the sample mean value should be close to the value shown in the *Mean* textbox. The more random numbers generated, the closer the sample mean value is to the *Mean* value.

The formula used to calculate the sample mean value is as follows:

$$SampleMeanValue = \frac{\sum\limits_{1}^{n} x_i}{n}$$

5)   SampleStdDev Operation

When the *SampleStdDev* button is clicked, the program needs to check if the list box is empty. If it is not, the program needs to use a loop statement to get the sample standard deviation of the items within the list box. The sample standard deviation, once calculated, will be displayed in the textbox next to the *SampleStdDev* button. It is noted that the sample standard deviation should be close to the value shown in the *StdDev* textbox.   The more random numbers generated, the closer the sample standard deviation is to the *StdDev* value.

The formula used to calculate the sample standard deviation is as follows:

$$SampleStdDev = \sqrt{\frac{\sum\limits_{1}^{n} (x_i - \bar{x})^2}{n-1}}$$

Or

$$SampleStdDev = \sqrt{\frac{n \sum\limits_{1}^{n} x_i^2 - (\sum\limits_{1}^{n} x_i)^2}{n(n-1)}}$$

Chapter 10
A Simple Traffic Animation at an Intersection

Computer animation is a powerful technology that helps people understand the dynamic nature of problems by creating visual movements of features through the use of computers. There are two basic elements within a computer animation application: graphics and their time-based movements. Graphics represents not only the graphical 2D or 3D settings of the environment, but also the moving features in an animation application.

Moving features, once created, can change their positions within an animating environment based on time intervals and an event-trigging mechanism. When a certain time interval is over, an event is activated to update positions and change characteristic of moving graphics.

The *System.Drawing* namespace of the VB.Net IDE provides a great set of classes that can create, edit, update, and dispose graphics. The *Timer* class within the *System.Timers* namespace contains the *Time Interval* property and the *Tick* event-trigging mechanism.

In this chapter we will develop an application that can simulate a car moving through, turning right or left at an intersection. We will first describe how to use the Graphics classes to draw the animation settings. Then we will introduce the *Timer* class and describe how to use this class to create car movements.

10.1   Animation Settings and Moving Objects

In this section, we will show you how to create an intersection and a car in an application. The intersection is considered as the animation setting for the application, while the car is the moving feature. The car will go through the intersection.

As the intersection and the car will be used in various event procedures within the application, we put them into a module called *Module1*.

The procedures to create the *Module1* module are as follows:

1)   In the VB.Net IDE, select *Project -> Add Module ...*
2)   Make sure the name of the module is *Module1*.

You will see the following empty statement for the *Module1*:

```
Imports System.drawing
Module Module1


      ' Add procedure for creating an Intersection
      ' Add procedure to draw a car
      ' Add procedure to clear a car
      ' Add procedure for a car moving forward on X
      ' Add procedure for a car moving backward on X
      ' Add procedure for a car moving upward on Y
      ' add procedure for a car moving downward on Y


End Module
```

The `Imports System.Drawing` is used as the first statement. It refers to the `Drawing` classes within the `System` Namespace.

Create an Intersection

We need to write a user-defined procedure to create an intersection on a form. This procedure requires three arguments. One of them refers to a form on which the intersection is drawn. The other two arguments specify the center position of the intersection on the form.

The code for this procedure is as follows:

```
Public Sub CreateIntersection(ByVal InGraphics As Graphics,    _
              ByVal x As Single, ByVal y As Single)

    ' Define a variable to be of Rectangle class.
    ' The Rectangle class is within the System.Drawing
    ' library and is imported by the Imports statement.

    Dim myRectangle As Rectangle

    Dim x1 As Single
    Dim y1 As Single
    Dim x2 As Single
    Dim y2 As Single

    ' Define a variable to be of Pen class.
    ' The Pen class is within the System.Drawing
    ' library and is imported by the Imports statement.
    ' The Mypen variable is initiated by the pen color
    ' of Dark Blue.


    Dim myPen As New Pen(Color.DarkBlue)

    ' Set up the upper left corner of the rectangle or the
```

```
' square board (200 * 200 screen units). The term screen
' unit is defined for the window.
' The below two statements get the width and height of
' the active form (or the PI_Estimate form) and offsets
' the corner [-100, -100] from the center point.


        x1 = +20
        y1 = y
        x2 = x - 60
        y2 = y

        myPen.DashStyle = Drawing2D.DashStyle.DashDotDot
        InGraphics.DrawLine(myPen, x1, y1, x2, y2)

        myPen.DashStyle = Drawing2D.DashStyle.Solid
        InGraphics.DrawLine(myPen, x1, y1 + 40, x2, y2 + 40)

        InGraphics.DrawLine(myPen, x1, y1 - 40, x2, y2 - 40)

        x1 = x
        y1 = +60
        x2 = x
        y2 = y - 40



        myPen.DashStyle = Drawing2D.DashStyle.DashDotDot
        InGraphics.DrawLine(myPen, x1, y1, x2, y2)
        myPen.DashStyle = Drawing2D.DashStyle.Solid
        InGraphics.DrawLine(myPen, x1 - 60, y1, x2 - 60, y2)

        InGraphics.DrawLine(myPen, x1 + 60, y1, x2 + 60, y2)

        x1 = x + 60
        y1 = y
        x2 = 2 * x - 20
        y2 = y

        InGraphics.DrawLine(myPen, x1, y1 + 40, x2, y2 + 40)
        myPen.DashStyle = Drawing2D.DashStyle.DashDotDot
        InGraphics.DrawLine(myPen, x1, y1, x2, y2)
        myPen.DashStyle = Drawing2D.DashStyle.Solid
        InGraphics.DrawLine(myPen, x1, y1 - 40, x2, y2 - 40)

        x1 = x
        y1 = y + 40
        x2 = x
        y2 = 2 * x - 80
        myPen.DashStyle = Drawing2D.DashStyle.DashDotDot
        InGraphics.DrawLine(myPen, x1, y1, x2, y2)
        myPen.DashStyle = Drawing2D.DashStyle.Solid
        InGraphics.DrawLine(myPen, x1 - 60, y1, x2 - 60, y2)
        InGraphics.DrawLine(myPen, x1 + 60, y1, x2 + 60, y2)
End Sub
```

This procedure uses the *DrawLine* method of the *Graphics* class to construct approaches for the intersection. Also the procedure uses the *Pen* method to specify the color and line style for the lanes within the approaches. Once the intersection is drawn by this procedure, it does not change its position during the animation process.

Draw a Car

We need to write a user-defined procedure to draw a solid, rectangle car on a form. This procedure requires three arguments. One of them refers to a form on which the car is drawn. The other two arguments specify the upper left corner of the car on the form. The size of the car is 10 screen units by 10 screen units. The color of this car is red.

```
Public Sub CarDraw(ByVal inGraphics As Graphics,        _
               ByVal x As Single, ByVal y As Single)

    Dim Myrectangle As Rectangle
    Myrectangle = New Rectangle(x, y, 10, 10)
    Dim myBrush As SolidBrush = New SolidBrush(Color.Red)
    inGraphics.FillRectangle(myBrush, Myrectangle)
End Sub
```

Clear a Car

We need to erase the car from its previous position and draw it in a new position. By doing this, we can see the car moving from one position to another. The below procedure is used to clear a car from the position specified by x and y arguments.

```
Public Sub CarClear(ByVal inGraphics As Graphics,       _
            ByVal x As Single, ByVal y As Single)

    Dim Myrectangle As Rectangle
    Myrectangle = New Rectangle(x, y, 10, 10)
    Dim myBrush As SolidBrush = New SolidBrush(Color.LightGray)
    inGraphics.FillRectangle(myBrush, Myrectangle)
End Sub
```

Move a Car Forward on X direction

The below procedure is used to draw a car one step forward along X direction. It first clears the car from its previous position using the *CarClear* procedure and then draws it in the current position specified by X and Y screen coordinates.

```
Public Sub CarMoveXForward(ByVal inGraphics As Graphics,    _
            ByVal x As Single, ByVal y As Single)

    Dim myBrush As SolidBrush = New SolidBrush(Color.LightGray)
    CarClear(inGraphics, x - 10, y)
```

```
        myBrush.Color = Color.Red
        CarDraw(inGraphics, x, y)
    End Sub
```

Move a Car Backward on X direction

The below procedure is used to draw a car one step backward along X direction

```
    Public Sub CarMoveXBackward(ByVal inGraphics As Graphics,       _
                ByVal x As Single, ByVal y As Single)

        Dim myBrush As SolidBrush = New SolidBrush(Color.LightGray)
        CarClear(inGraphics, x + 10, y)
        myBrush.Color = Color.Red
        CarDraw(inGraphics, x, y)
    End Sub
```

Move a Car Forward on Y direction

The below procedure is used to draw a car one forward (or downward) along Y direction. The car increases its Y screen coordinate step by step.

```
    Public Sub CarMoveYForward(ByVal inGraphics As Graphics,       _
                ByVal x As Single, ByVal y As Single)

        Dim myBrush As SolidBrush = New SolidBrush(Color.LightGray)
        CarClear(inGraphics, x, y - 10)
        myBrush.Color = Color.Red
        CarDraw(inGraphics, x, y)
    End Sub
```

Move a Car Backward on Y direction

The below procedure is used to draw a car one backward (or upward) along Y direction. The car reduces its Y screen coordinate step by step.

```
    Public Sub CarMoveYBackward(ByVal inGraphics As Graphics,       _
                ByVal x As Single, ByVal y As Single)

        Dim myBrush As SolidBrush = New SolidBrush(Color.LightGray)
        CarClear(inGraphics, x, y + 10)
        myBrush.Color = Color.Red
        CarDraw(inGraphics, x, y)
    End Sub
```

Move a Car Left

The below procedure is used to draw a car one step left.

```
Public Sub CarMoveLeft(ByVal inGraphics As Graphics,           _
            ByVal x As Single, ByVal y As Single)

    Dim myBrush As SolidBrush = New SolidBrush(Color.LightGray)
    CarClear(inGraphics, x - 4, y + 4)
    myBrush.Color = Color.Red
    CarDraw(inGraphics, x, y)
End Sub
```

Move a Car Right

The below procedure is used to draw a car one step right.

```
Public Sub CarMoveRight(ByVal inGraphics As Graphics,           _
            ByVal x As Single, ByVal y As Single)

    Dim myBrush As SolidBrush = New SolidBrush(Color.LightGray)
    CarClear(inGraphics, x - 4, y - 4)
    myBrush.Color = Color.Red
    CarDraw(inGraphics, x, y)
End Sub
```

10.2   Timer Class and its Controls

The Timer class allows a computer animation program to set a time interval to execute an event after that interval is elapsed. This class is useful for computer simulation and file archiving. For example, if you want to back up your data processing results into files in every hour, you can use the controls derived from this class to set up the time interval to be one hour. Also you can update the position of a car every second if you set the interval of a *Timer* object 1 second.

Create a Timer Control

To create a *Timer* control, you can drag and drop the *Timer* icon (in the Toolbox window) into the *Form* window and set up its initial time interval in the *Property* window (see Figure 10-1). Note that the *Timer1* control is set with its time interval of 1000 milliseconds or 1 second. You can start and stop the *Timer* control using the following statements:

```
        Timer1.Enabled = True    ` Start the Timer1 control
        Timer1.Enabled = False   ` Stop the Timer1 control
```

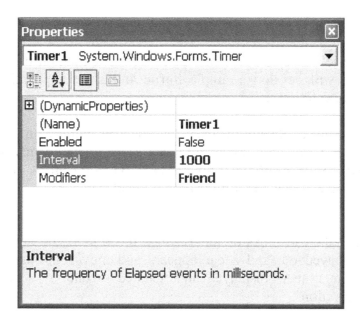

Figure 10-1 Timer Control Property Window

Respond to a *Timer_Tick* Event

The *Timer1* control has an event called *Tick* as mentioned in the previous section. We need to write a group of statements to tell the computer what to do when the time interval of this control is ticked over. Below is an example procedure that responds to the *Timer_Tick* event:

```
Private Sub Timer1_Tick(ByVal sender As Object,          _
               ByVal e As System.EventArgs)             _
               Handles Timer1.Tick
     Label1.Text = "Current Time = " & Now.ToString
     ' Other VB.Net statements.
End Sub
```

This procedure will be executed in every second since the interval of the *Timer1* control is set 1000 milliseconds (or 1 second). Within this event procedure, there is only one statement. The keyword `Now` here returns the current system time of the computer in the format of "`Date Hour:Minute:Second AM`" or "`Date Hour:Minute:Second PM`". For example, the *Lable1* control may display "`Current Time = 8/25/2006 3:02:44 PM`." As the time changes second by second, the *Label1* control shows the changes of time in every second.

10.3   A Simple Traffic Animation Application

With the basic concepts and terms of computer animation described in the previous sections, we will develop a simple traffic animation application. The logic of the application is as follows:

1)   When this application is executed, the user will see an intersection as shown in Figure 10-2. This application has seven menu items: *Through, Left, Right, Reset, Stop, Continue,* and *Cancel.* The *Stop* and Continue menu items are grayed out when the form is initially loaded.

2)   When the use clicks on the *Through* menu item, the *Left* and *Right* menu items are grayed out and a car appears and moves through the intersection. The current time is displayed and updated second by second at the top of the intersection.

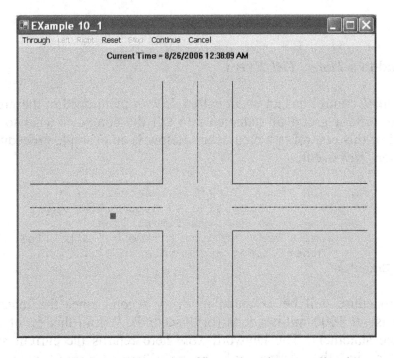

Figure 10-2 A Simple Traffic Animation Application

3)   When the use clicks on the *Left* menu item, the *Through* and *Right* menu items are grayed out and a car appears and makes left turns at the intersection.

4)   When the use clicks on the *Right* menu item, the *Through* and *Left* menu items are grayed out and a car appears and makes right turns at the intersection.

5)   When the car is moving forward and the *Stop* menu item is active, the user can click the menu item. The car will be stopped.

6)   When the car is stopped and the *Continue* menu item is active, the user can click the item to resume the animation. The car will continue going through the intersection. The *Continue* and *Stop* menu items are toggled each other.

7)   The user can click the *Reset* menu item anytime when the car is moving. The *Reset* menu item enforces the animation to reset to its starting states.

Step 1:   Form Design

Figure 10-3 shows the key control names for the application. Note that the control names for the *Left, Right* and *Stop* menu items are *Left1, Right1,* and *Stop1,* respectively.

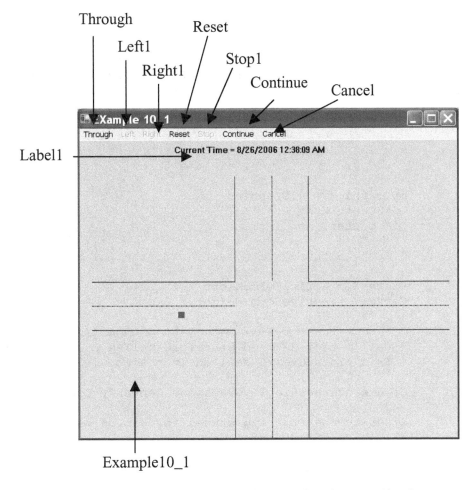

Figure 10-3 Form Design of the Animation Application

Step 2: Application Code

Below is the code for the application:

```
Imports System.Drawing

Public Class Example10_1
        Inherits System.Windows.Forms.Form
```

┌───┐
│   Windows Form Designer generated code   │
└───┘

```
` The below three variables are form-level variables
` They can be used in all the event procedures.



    Dim choice As Integer
    Dim x As Single
    Dim y As Single

` This is the Paint procedure. When the Example10_1 form is loaded,
` this procedure will be executed to draw an intersection on the
` form.

    Private Sub Example10_1_Paint(ByVal sender As Object,      _
                ByVal e As System.Windows.Forms.PaintEventArgs) _
                Handles MyBase.Paint

        Dim myGraphics As Graphics
        ' E is object variable. It contains a set of Paint Event
        ' related arguments inherited from the form.
        ' One of the arguments is the Graphics Property of
        ' the form.
        myGraphics = e.Graphics
        Dim CenterX As Single
        Dim CenterY As Single

        ` Specify the center position of the intersection

        CenterX = ActiveForm.Width / 2
        CenterY = ActiveForm.Height / 2

        `
        ` Call a user defined procedure called CreateIntersection.
        ` This procedure is defined in the Module1 module.

        CreateIntersection(myGraphics, CenterX, CenterY)

        ` Set up the starting states for car animation.

        Timer1.Enabled = False
        stop1.Enabled = False
        Continue.Enabled = False
    End Sub
```

```
' This procedure will be executed when the time interval of the
' Timer1 timer is ticked over. If the interval is set to be 200,
' this procedure will be executed every o.2 second.


    Private Sub Timer1_Tick(ByVal sender As Object,          _
              ByVal e As System.EventArgs) Handles Timer1.Tick

        ' Display the current time in the Label1 control.

        Label1.Text = "Current Time = " & Now.ToString

        Dim myrec As Rectangle
        Dim centerX As Single, CenterY As Single
        Dim limitx As Single = ActiveForm.Width
        Dim Limity As Single

        ' Specify the form where the intersection is drawn.

        Dim myGraphics As Graphics
        myGraphics = Me.CreateGraphics

        ' get the center point of the intersection.

        centerX = ActiveForm.Width / 2
        CenterY = ActiveForm.Height / 2

        ' When the choice is 1, the car goes through the intersection.
        ' When the choice is 2, the car turns left at
        ' the intersection.
        ' When the choice is 3, the car turns right at
        ' the intersection.

        Select Case choice
            Case 1
                x = x + 10
                If x > limitx Then
                    Timer1.Enabled = False
                    Through.Enabled = True
                    Left1.Enabled = True
                    Right1.Enabled = True
                    stop1.Enabled = False
                    Continue.Enabled = False
                    Exit Sub
                End If
                CarMoveXForward(myGraphics, x, y)


            Case 2

            ' When the car is before the stopping line, it moves
            ' forward in X direction.

                If x <= centerX - 30 Then
                    x = x + 10
                    CarMoveXForward(myGraphics, x, y)
                End If
```

```
' When the car is within the intersection area, it
' turns left until it is out of the intersection area.

    If x > centerX - 30 And x <= centerX + 30 Then
        x = x + 4
        y = y - 4
        CarMoveLeft(myGraphics, x, y)
    End If

' When the car moves out of the intersection area,
' it moves backward or upward in Y direction until it
' moves out of the animation limit.

    If x > centerX + 30 Then

        y = y - 10
        CarMoveYBackward(myGraphics, x, y)
    End If
    Limity = 30
    If x > limitx Or y < 30 Then
        Timer1.Enabled = False
        Through.Enabled = True
        Left1.Enabled = True
        Right1.Enabled = True
        stop1.Enabled = False
        Continue.Enabled = False
        Exit Sub
    End If

Case 3


' When the car is within the intersection, it
' turns left until it is out of the intersection area.

    If x <= centerX - 60 Then
        x = x + 10
        y = CenterY + 10
        CarMoveXForward(myGraphics, x, y)
    End If



' When the car is within the intersection area, it
' turns left until it is out of the intersection area.

    If x > centerX - 60 And x <= centerX - 30 Then
        x = x + 4
        y = y + 4
        CarMoveRight(myGraphics, x, y)
    End If

' When the car moves out of the intersection area,
' it moves upward in Y direction until it
' moves out of the animation limit.
```

```
                    If x > centerX - 30 Then

                        y = y + 10
                        CarMoveYForward(myGraphics, x, y)
                    End If

                    Limity = ActiveForm.Height
                    If y > Limity Then
                        Timer1.Enabled = False
                        Through.Enabled = True
                        Left1.Enabled = True
                        Right1.Enabled = True
                        stop1.Enabled = False
                        Continue.Enabled = False
                        Exit Sub
                    End If
            End Select

        End Sub


' When the user clicks the Through menu item, this procedure will be '
executed. This procedure sets the starting position of the car and
' and the choice of 1. Then it starts the animation.


    Private Sub Through_Click(ByVal sender As Object,            _
            ByVal e As System.EventArgs) Handles Through.Click
        Timer1.Enabled = True
        stop1.Enabled = True
        x = 20
        y = ActiveForm.Height / 2 + 10
        choice = 1
        Left1.Enabled = False
        Right1.Enabled = False
    End Sub


' When the user clicks the Left menu item, this procedure will be
' executed. This procedure sets the starting position of the car and
' and the choice of 2. Then it starts the animation.

    Private Sub Left1_Click(ByVal sender As Object,             _
            ByVal e As System.EventArgs) Handles Left1.Click

        Timer1.Enabled = True
        stop1.Enabled = True
        x = 20
        y = ActiveForm.Height / 2 + 10
        choice = 2
        Through.Enabled = False
        Right1.Enabled = False
    End Sub
```

```
' When the user clicks the Right menu item, this procedure will be
' executed. This procedure sets the starting position of the car and
' and the choice of 3. Then it starts the animation.

    Private Sub Right1_Click(ByVal sender As Object,               _
            ByVal e As System.EventArgs) Handles Right1.Click
        Timer1.Enabled = True
        stop1.Enabled = True
        x = 20
        y = ActiveForm.Height / 2 + 10
        choice = 3
        Through.Enabled = False
        Left1.Enabled = False

    End Sub


' When the user clicks the Stop menu item, this procedure will be
' stopped if the car is moving.

    Private Sub stop1_Click(ByVal sender As System.Object,         _
            ByVal e As System.EventArgs) Handles stop1.Click

        If Through.Enabled = True Then
            Timer1.Enabled = False
        End If

        If Left1.Enabled = True Then
            Timer1.Enabled = False
        End If
        If Right1.Enabled = True Then
            Timer1.Enabled = False
        End If
        stop1.Enabled = False
        Continue.Enabled = True

    End Sub


' When the user clicks the Cancel menu item, the application
' terminates normally.

    Private Sub Cancel_Click(ByVal sender As System.Object,        _
            ByVal e As System.EventArgs) Handles Cancel.Click
        End
    End Sub


' When the user clicks the Reset menu item, this procedure will be
' executed. This procedure will reset the animation at its
' starting state.

    Private Sub Reset_Click(ByVal sender As System.Object,         _
            ByVal e As System.EventArgs) Handles Reset.Click

        Through.Enabled = True
        Left1.Enabled = True
```

```
        Right1.Enabled = True
        stop1.Enabled = False
        Continue.Enabled = False
        Label1.Text = ""

        Dim myrec As Rectangle
        Dim myGraphics As Graphics
        Dim myBrush As SolidBrush = New SolidBrush(Color.LightGray)

        myGraphics = Me.CreateGraphics
        CarClear(myGraphics, x, y)
        Timer1.Enabled = False

    End Sub

' When the user clicks the Continue menu item, this procedure will
' resume the animation process.

    Private Sub Continue_Click(ByVal sender As Object,        _
            ByVal e As System.EventArgs) Handles Continue.Click
        If stop1.Enabled = False Then
            Timer1.Enabled = True
            stop1.Enabled = True
            Continue.Enabled = False
        End If
    End Sub
End Class
```

10.4. Improving the Simple Traffic Animation Application

As you can see, the simple traffic animation application can simulate the movements of only one car. We would like to improve this application by generating a series of cars going through, turning left or right. Figure 10-4 shows the new form design of the animation application. Within this application, there are three textboxes added to allow users to enter traffic volumes for three different directions.

The logic of this improved application is as follows:

1)   When the application is executed, the user can enter the volume for through, left turn and right turn traffic.

2)   Once the traffic volumes are in the textboxes, the user can click *Traffic Flow* menu item. The cars generated randomly start approaching to the intersection. The number of cars for the three directions (going through, turning left and turning right) is governed by the ratio of the traffic volumes in the textboxes.

        The Rnd() function is used to create cars in the following rules:

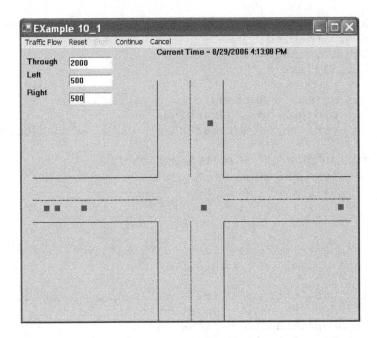

Figure 10-4 Form within the Improved Animation Application

When a time interval of 0.1 second is over, a random number in the range of [0, Rnd() * 36000] is generated. This random number is then compared with the sum of traffic volumes in the three directions. If the random number is greater than the sum, a car is then created and reset to go into the intersection. In other words,

$$\text{Rnd() * 36000} < \text{Vol}_{Th} + \text{Vol}_{LT} + \text{Vol}_{RT}$$

Where

Vol_{Th} - Through Traffic Volume (Vehicles/Hour)
Vol_{LT} - Left Turn Traffic Volume (Vehicles/Hour)
Vol_{RT} - Right Turn Traffic Volume (Vehicles/Hour)

If the above condition is *True*, a car is created. Otherwise, no cars are created within the 0.1 second. For example, the through, left turn and right turn traffic volumes are 2000, 500, 500 veh/hour, respectively. Over the hour, there are 36000 chances to create a car. Using the above logic, about 3000 of the random numbers will be less than 3000. These 3000 random numbers are used to create vehicles for animation. For any given time period, the vehicles will start approaching to the intersection with a Poisson arrival distribution.

When a car is created it is assigned a turn at the beginning of its approach to the intersection. The turns are random based on the ratio of the three traffic volumes for the approach. The logic for splitting turns for each car is as follows:

```
V_total = Vol_Th + Vol_LT + Vol_RT
If      Rnd()  *  V_total  <  Vol_LT   then
               Car makes a left turn
Else
        If Rnd()  *  V_total  <  Vol_LT  + Vol_RT  then
               Car makes a right turn
        Else
               Car goes through the intersection
        End If
End If
```

3)   Other actions are the same as those discussed in the previous animation application.

The procedures to develop the improved animation application are as follows:

Step 1 Form Design

First we need to create a form as shown in Figure 10-5. From this Figure, you can see that the *Stop* Menu item is named *Stop1*.

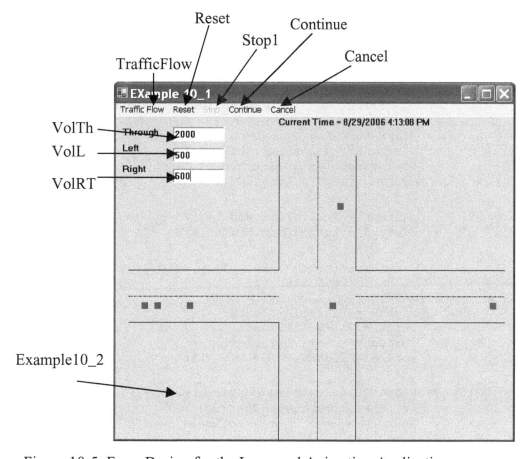

Figure 10-5 Form Design for the Improved Animation Application

Step 2: Code Development

Below is the code for the application:

```
Imports System.Drawing

Public Class Example10_2
    Inherits System.Windows.Forms.Form
```

```
      Windows Form Designer generated code
```

```
    Public x As Single
    Public y As Single

  ' The below three statements are used to define three arrays with
  ' their size undeclared.
  ' Later on you will use REDIM statement to define the size.

    Public choice() As Integer
    Public cars_PosX() As Single
    Public cars_PosY() As Single
    Public volume As Long
    Public carIndex As Long


    Private Sub Timer1_Tick(ByVal sender As Object,
            ByVal e As System.EventArgs) Handles Timer1.Tick
        Label1.Text = "Current Time = " & Now.ToString
        Dim myrec As Rectangle
        Dim centerX As Single, CenterY As Single
        Dim x1 As Single, y1 As Single
        Dim limitx As Single = ActiveForm.Width
        Dim Limity As Single
        Dim i As Integer, randomv As Single
        Dim leftV As Long, rightV As Long, ThroughV As Long
        Dim myGraphics As Graphics
        myGraphics = Me.CreateGraphics

        centerX = ActiveForm.Width / 2
        CenterY = ActiveForm.Height / 2


  ' Receive Through, Left Turn, and Right Turn volumes from
  ' the three textboxes.

        rightV = Val(VolRT.Text)
        leftV = Val(VolLT.Text)
        ThroughV = Val(VolTH.Text)
        volume = rightV + leftV + ThroughV


        ReDim Preserve cars_PosX(volume)
        ReDim Preserve cars_PosY(volume)
        ReDim Preserve choice(volume)


  ' The statement below checks if a car is ready to go into
  ' the intersection. It calls a user-defined function called
```

```
' CarReady(). If the CarReady function returns True, a car
' is ready to go.

  If CarReady(Val(Timer1.Interval), volume) Then
      carIndex = carIndex + 1
      cars_PosX(carIndex) = 20
      cars_PosY(carIndex) = Me.ActiveForm.Height / 2 + 10
      randomv = Rnd() * volume

' Assign a movement for the car: through, left turn, or
' right turn.

      Select Case randomv
          Case Is < leftV
              choice(carIndex) = 2
          Case Is < leftV + rightV
              choice(carIndex) = 1
          Case Else
              choice(carIndex) = 1
      End Select

      If carIndex > volume Then
          carIndex = 0
      End If
  End If


  If carIndex <= 0 Then
      Exit Sub
  End If

  ' Do the animation work here

  For i = 1 To carIndex

      Select Case choice(i)

          Case 1
              cars_PosX(i) = cars_PosX(i) + 10

              If cars_PosX(i) < limitx Then
                  CarMoveXForward(myGraphics, cars_PosX(i), _
                                  cars_PosY(i))
              End If


          Case 2
              If cars_PosX(i) <= centerX - 30 Then
                  cars_PosX(i) = cars_PosX(i) + 10
                  CarMoveXForward(myGraphics, cars_PosX(i), _
                                  cars_PosY(i))
              End If

              ' When the car is within the intersection area, it
              ' turns left until it is out of the intersection
              ' area.

              If cars_PosX(i) > centerX - 30 And            _
```

```
                          cars_PosX(i) <= centerX + 30 Then
                cars_PosX(i) = cars_PosX(i) + 4
                cars_PosY(i) = cars_PosY(i) - 4

                CarMoveLeft(myGraphics, cars_PosX(i),      _
                              cars_PosY(i))
        End If


    ' When the car moves out of the intersection area,
    ' it moves backward or upward in Y direction
    ' until it moves out of the animation limit.

        If cars_PosX(i) > centerX + 30 And              _
                    cars_PosX(i) < limitx Then
            If cars_PosY(i) > 30 Then
                cars_PosY(i) = cars_PosY(i) - 10
                CarMoveYBackward(myGraphics,            _
                        cars_PosX(i), cars_PosY(i))
            End If
        End If


Case 3
    ' When the car is within the intersection, it
    ' turns left until it is out of the intersection
    ' area.

        If cars_PosX(i) <= centerX - 60 Then
            cars_PosX(i) = cars_PosX(i) + 10
            CarMoveXForward(myGraphics, cars_PosX(i),   _
                          cars_PosY(i))
        End If


' When the car is within the intersection area, it
' turns left until it is out of the intersection area.

        If cars_PosX(i) > centerX - 60 And              _
                cars_PosX(i) <= centerX - 30 Then

            cars_PosX(i) = cars_PosX(i) + 4
            cars_PosY(i) = cars_PosY(i) + 4

            CarMoveRight(myGraphics, cars_PosX(i),      _
                          cars_PosY(i))
        End If


' When the car moves out of the intersection area,
' it moves upward in Y direction until it
' moves out of the animation limit.
'
        If cars_PosX(i) < ActiveForm.Height And         _
                cars_PosX(i) > centerX - 30 Then
            cars_PosY(i) = cars_PosY(i) + 10

            CarMoveYForward(myGraphics, cars_PosX(i), _
                          cars_PosY(i))
        End If
```

```
            End Select
      Next i
End Sub




Private Sub Example10_2_Paint(ByVal sender As Object,         _
            ByVal e As System.Windows.Forms.PaintEventArgs) _
                Handles MyBase.Paint

      Dim myGraphics As Graphics
      ' E is object variable. It contains a set of Paint Event
      ' related arguments inherited from the PI_Estimate form.
      ' One of the arguments is the Graphics Property of
      ' the form.
      myGraphics = e.Graphics
      Dim CenterX As Single
      Dim CenterY As Single
      CenterX = ActiveForm.Width / 2
      CenterY = ActiveForm.Height / 2
      CreateIntersection(myGraphics, CenterX, CenterY)
      Timer1.Enabled = False
      stop1.Enabled = False
      Continue.Enabled = False
      carIndex = 0

End Sub




Private Sub TrafficiFlow_Click(ByVal sender As System.Object, _
            ByVal e As System.EventArgs)                      _
            Handles TrafficFlow.Click
      Timer1.Enabled = True
      stop1.Enabled = True
      If Not IsNumeric(VolLT.Text) Or VolLT.Text = 0 Then
          MsgBox("Enter left turn volume")
          Exit Sub
      End If
      If Not IsNumeric(VolRT.Text) Or VolRT.Text = 0 Then
          MsgBox("Enter right turn volume")
          Exit Sub
      End If
      If Not IsNumeric(VolTH.Text) Or VolTH.Text = 0 Then
          MsgBox("Enter through volume")
          Exit Sub
      End If
      carIndex = 0


End Sub
```

```
Private Sub stop1_Click(ByVal sender As System.Object,          _
        ByVal e As System.EventArgs) Handles stop1.Click

    If TrafficFlow.Enabled = True Then
        Timer1.Enabled = False
    End If
    stop1.Enabled = False
    Continue.Enabled = True

End Sub

Private Sub Cancel_Click(ByVal sender As System.Object,         _
        ByVal e As System.EventArgs) Handles Cancel.Click
    End
End Sub



Private Sub Reset_Click(ByVal sender As System.Object,          _
        ByVal e As System.EventArgs) Handles Reset.Click
    Dim i As Long
    TrafficFlow.Enabled = True

    stop1.Enabled = False
    Continue.Enabled = False
    Label1.Text = ""

    Dim myrec As Rectangle
    Dim myGraphics As Graphics
    Dim myBrush As SolidBrush = New SolidBrush(Color.LightGray)

    myGraphics = Me.CreateGraphics
    For i = 1 To carIndex
        CarClear(myGraphics, cars_PosX(i), cars_PosY(i))
    Next i
    Timer1.Enabled = False
    carIndex = 0

End Sub



Private Sub Continue_Click(ByVal sender As Object,              _
        ByVal e As System.EventArgs) Handles Continue.Click
    If stop1.Enabled = False Then
        Timer1.Enabled = True
        stop1.Enabled = True
        Continue.Enabled = False
    End If


End Sub
```

```
    Private Sub Example10_2_Load(ByVal sender As Object,      _
      ByVal e As System.EventArgs) Handles MyBase.Load
        Randomize()
    End Sub
End Class
```

It is noted that the improved application uses the procedures defined in *Module1* as described in the simple traffic animation application. The procedures include *CreateIntersection*, *CreateDraw*, *CarClear*, *CarMoveXForward*, etc.

10.5 Questions

Q1.   There are two basic components required for a computer animation application? What are the two components?

Q2.   The *Timer* class is critical to a VB.Net animation application. What is the property to specify the time interval for a Timer object?

Q3.   List the steps used to create an empty module template.

Q4.   Modify the simple traffic animation application described in Section 10-2 and draw a circle instead of an intersection when the form is initially loaded.

Q5.   Change a car from a solid rectangle to a car image. Modify the code to show the icon moving through the intersection. [Hint: check the *DrawImage* method of the *Graphics* class]

Q6.   Explain the function `Now.toString` in the animation applications?

Q7.   Assume the time interval of a timer control is 2 second. How to do it?

Q8.   Draw flow charts for all the procedures and functions used in the Simple Traffic Animation Application.

Q9.   Draw flow charts for all the procedures and functions used in the Improved Animation Application.

Q10.   In the improved animation application, how to generate cars to reflect the sum of through, left turn, and right turn traffic volumes?

Q11.   After a car is created, this car should be assigned its turn. Explain the logic used
       for the turn assignment.

Q12.   Explain the `CarReady()` function used in the animation applications?

Chapter 11
Object-Oriented Programming

We have already learned a lot of Visual Basic.Net statements in the previous chapters. As a VB.Net project gets more and more statements to implement a solution to a problem, we may feel necessary to use some control templates that cannot be provided in the IDE's toolbox window. Furthermore we may need some functions that are not standard VB.Net functions. What do we do? We need to introduce the concepts of object-oriented programming or component programming.

Object-oriented programming or component programming (later we will use them interchangeably) often involves the use of objects or components in the development of a VB.Net project. We have already explored, in the previous chapters, objects that are provided by VB.Net. For example, forms and various controls created from control templates in the IDE's toolbox window are objects. These types of objects are often called GUI-based objects. Visual Basic.Net also contains many other types of objects that cannot be visually seen. These types of objects are primarily used for programming. We will explore these types of objects in later chapters. Furthermore, Visual Basic.Net also allows third-party objects (or components) to be inserted into the VB.Net IDE for the development of a VB.Net project.

As you can see, the VB.Net IDE is an open-ended development environment. It allows you to work with various types of objects. It employs an object-oriented approach to organize, use and manage objects effectively for a VB.Net project. We will discuss in this chapter the principals of the object-oriented programming and describe how objects are created and used in the VB.Net IDE for projects.

11.1   Classes and Objects

Object-oriented programming involves the use of two important but often confusing terms: classes and objects. Before we describe how to use objects to develop VB.Net projects, we need to have a clear understanding on the differences between classes and objects.

A class is a program structure that defines the behaviors of data. For example, a command button control template is a class that defines the blueprint of the command button controls derived from the template. Objects are instances of a class. When you select the command button control template (or the command button class) from the IDE's toolbox window and place it on a form, you create an instance or an object from the command button class. All the controls that are created from control templates are called objects. Objects created from a class will behave the same ways as those defined in the class.

Behaviors of Classes and Their Derived Objects

Each class and its derived objects have properties, methods, and event procedures to define the behaviors when they are used to communicate with objects of other classes.

Properties define the nature of objects. Let us take the command button class as an example. The command button class has properties such as Width, Height, Text and Name properties. These properties will be available in all the controls or objects derived from the command button class. Suppose you create two command button controls from the command button class. These two controls have the same properties.

Methods are procedures or functions shared by the objects of the class. For example, a textbox control class has two methods called *Focus* and *Refresh*. These two methods are created when a textbox control is created on a form.

Events are actions or operations associated with the objects derived from the class. The textbox has an event called *KeyPress*. In order to respond to the *KeyPress* event, you need to write an event procedure to tell the computer what to do when users key in values into the textbox control.

Explore Classes in the VB.Net IDE

Classes and their objects are the foundation for the development of a VB.Net project. In order to have a powerful program that implements the logic to solve a problem, you should explore the availability of various needed classes in the VB.Net IDE. If you cannot find a class in the IDE, you need to think of creating a new class or purchasing one from a third party.

VB.Net provides you with a powerful tool called Object Browser to explore classes available in the VB.Net IDE. You can do the following to activate the Object Browser:

- ❑ Select *View* on the Menu Bar and Click *Object Browser* on the View drop-down menu, when you are within the VB.Net IDE. The Object Browser Window will appear as shown in Figure 11-1. As you can see, the Object Browser window consists of all the classes available for a project. All these classes are grouped in different libraries. The standard class libraries provided by VB.Net are *System, System.Data, System.DirectoryServices, System.Drawing, System.Windows.Forms, System.XML, Microsoft.VisualBasic, mscorlib, and Example11_1*. The *Example11_1* library stores all the form classes and the controls within the forms, when the *Example11_1* project is created.

- ❑ Besides these libraries, you can add the third-party libraries into the VB.Net IDE. The added class libraries will be listed in the Object Browser view window. Detailed description on how to add a new class library will be provided in later sections.

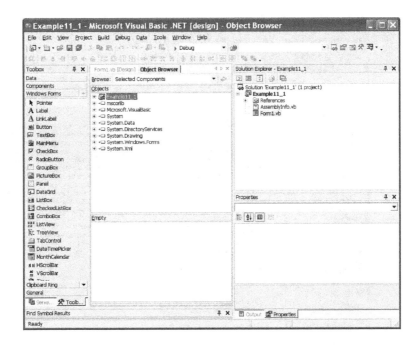

Figure 11-1 Object Browser View Window

❑ You can explore classes in the VB.Net IDE. Suppose you are interested in the *Textbox* class, you can scroll down the *System.Windows.Forms* library and select the *Textbox* class.

❑ By clicking the *Textbox* class, you can see properties, methods, and event procedures listed in the *Members* window for the class. Figure 11-2 shows the list of properties, methods, and even procedures associated with the *Textbox* class.

❑ By moving the curser onto the *Property* icon of the *Text* property, you can see the description of the property. The description indicates that the property is a String data type. It returns or sets a text value to the *Textbox* object through *Textbox.Text*.

The *Textbox* class also inherits a set of properties, methods, and event procedures from its parent and grandparent classes. As you can see in the Object Browser view window, the *TextBoxBase* class is the parent of the *Textbox* class. The *Control* class is the parent class of the *TextBoxBase* class and the grandparent class of the *Textbox* class. *Textbox* controls inherit the *Width* property and the *KeyPress* event from the *Control* class.

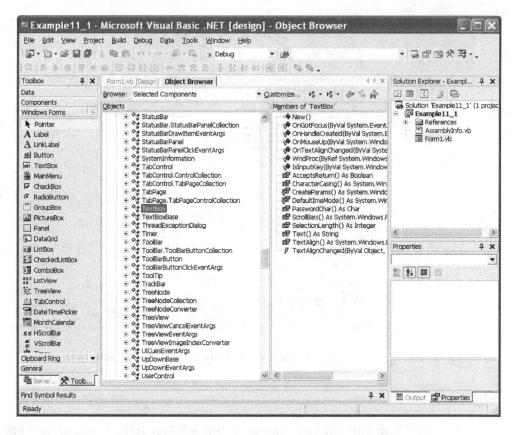

Figure 11-2   Properties, Methods, and Event Procedures of **TextBox** Class

Load Third-Party Classes in the VB.Net IDE

The previous section describes the procedures on how to explore classes that exist in the VB.Net IDE. When you want some classes that are not provided in the VB.Net IDE, what do we do? We need to load these classes in the VB.Net IDE.

Suppose Visual Basic.Net and ArcGIS (a product from the Environmental Systems and Research Institute (ESRI)) are installed in the computer you are working on. Also assume that you are using Visual Basic.Net and ArcGIS to develop a VB.Net application that can perform spatial operations and analyses. The ArcGIS classes are grouped in the *ESRI MapControl* class library.   In order to load the *ESRI MapControl* class library, you have to do the following (see Figure 11-3):

- Start VB.Net and Go to the IDE for a new project
- Select *Tools -> Add/Remove Toolbox Items* …
- Select *COM Components* tab
- Select *ESRI MapControl*
- Click *Ok*

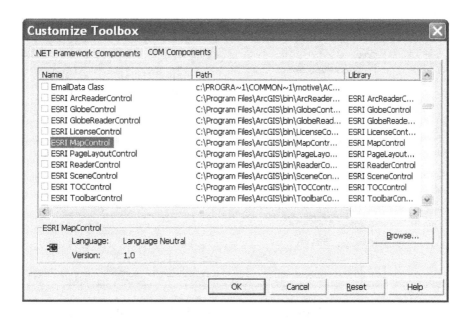

Figure 11-3   Procedures for Loading ESRI's MapControl

Once the *ESRI MapControl* Class Library is loaded in the VB.Net IDE, you can see this library appear on the Toolbox window as a new control template.

It is noted that third-party's class libraries are often protected by a software license. If you want to develop and deliver a commercial product that is based on third-party classes, you have to establish a license agreement with the third-party before you put the product on market.

11.2   Create Your Own Class Libraries and Classes

You can create your own classes for a project in Visual Basic.Net. To add a class to a project, you should do the following steps:

- Select the *Project* Menu in the VB.Net IDE
- Select *Add Class* from the Project drop-down list

The Add Class dialog box will appear as shown in Figure 11-4.

- Select the *Class* Icon in the *Template* window
- Double Click the *Class* icon. A new class is added to the project and appears in the code window. Once you have created a class, you can define a class in the code window. Note that the default class name is *Class1*.

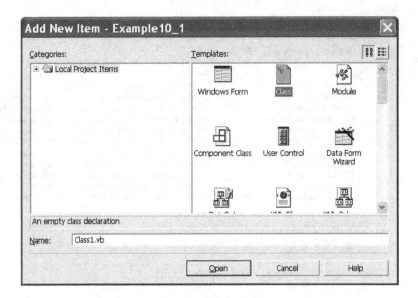

Figure 11-4 The Add Class Dialog Box

❑   Click the *Open* Button. The following class statement template is created:

```
Public Class Class1

End Class
```

With the empty class statement, you need to insert variables, methods, properties and events in the class. There are two types of variables that are defined in a class. These two types of variables are class-level and local variables. Class-level variables are the variables within the class, but they are outside of any procedures, functions, properties, and events. Local variables are the variables located in a procedure, function, property, or event.

Properties are retrieved and set like variables but are implemented using Property Get and Property Set procedures. They provide more control on how values are set or returned. An example used to declare a property for a class is as follows:

```
Public Property a() As Double
      Get
            Return Inside_a
      End Get

      Set(ByVal outside_a As Double)
            Inside_a = Val(outside_a)
      End Set
End Property
```

You can see that in this example, the *Get* and *End Get* are paired and *Set* and *End Set* are paired.

Methods represent the object's built-in procedures or functions. Normally, methods are created by adding Sub routines or functions to the class. A method created with Sub does not return a value, while a Function must return a value as a result. An example used to create a method for a class is as follows:

```
Public Function check() As Boolean
    If Inside_b ^ 2 - 4 * Inside_a * Inside_c >= 0 Then
        check = True
    Else
        check = False
        RaiseEvent NoRealRoot()
        Exit Function
    End If

End Function
```

It is noted that this function has a statement `RaiseEvent NoRealRoot()`, which is used to raise an event called `NoRealRoot`.

Before we raise an event, we need to declare it first using the Event statement. Given the above `NoRealRoot` event, we will have the following statement:

```
Public Event NoRealRoot
```

Example 11-1 Create a New Class Library

Assume we need to create a new class library called *ClassLibrary1* in which there is a class called *QE*. The *QE* class implements the simple logic discussed in Chapter 1, which finds roots for a quadratic equation. It has three properties, three methods, and two events. Let us create this class library and define these properties, methods and event for the *QE* class.

Step 1:   Create the Class Library *ClassLibrary1*

1)   Start *VB.Net*, create a new project
2)   Select the *Class Library* Icon within the *Template* window
3)   Specify the Class Library name to be *ClassLibrary1*

Step 2:   Create the *QE* class

1)   Right Click *Class1.vb* in the Solution Explorer window and select the Delete option. The default class, Class1, is then deleted.

2)   Go to *Project -> Add Class*

Select Class Icon and Change the Class name to be *QE*
Click the *Open* button

An empty class statement is created. Now you can insert the below statements in the class:

```
Imports System.Math
Public Class QE

    Private Inside_a As Double
    Private Inside_b As Double
    Private Inside_c As Double

    Public Property a() As Double
        Get
                Return Inside_a
        End Get

        Set(ByVal outside_a As Double)
                outside_a = Trim(outside_a)
                If Len(outside_a) > 0 Then
                    Inside_a = Val(outside_a)
                Else
                    MsgBox("Parameter a cannot be blank")
                    Exit Property
                End If
        End Set
    End Property


    Public Property b() As Double

    Get
        Return Inside_b
    End Get

        Set(ByVal outside_b As Double)
            outside_b = Trim(outside_b)
            If Len(outside_b) > 0 Then
                    Inside_b = Val(outside_b)
            Else
                    MsgBox("Parameter b cannot be blank")
                    Exit Property
            End If
        End Set
    End Property


    Public Property c() As Double
        Get
                Return Inside_c
        End Get

        Set(ByVal outside_c As Double)
            outside_c = Trim(outside_c)
```

```
            If Len(outside_c) > 0 Then
                    Inside_c = Val(outside_c)
            Else
                    MsgBox("Parameter c cannot be blank")
                    Exit Property
            End If
        End Set
End Property


Public Function check() As Boolean
    If Inside_b ^ 2 - 4 * Inside_a * Inside_c >= 0 Then
        check = True
    Else
        check = False
        RaiseEvent NoRealRoot()
        Exit Function
    End If
End Function


Public Function IsAZero() As Boolean
  If Inside_a = 0 Or Inside_b = 0 Or Inside_c = 0 Then
        RaiseEvent InputZero()
        IsAZero = True
  Else
        IsAZero = False
  End If
End Function




Public Function FindRoots(ByRef root1 As Double,        _
            ByRef root2 As Double) As Boolean

    If Me.check And Not Me.IsAZero Then
        root1 = (-Inside_b + Sqrt(Inside_b ^ 2 - 4 *    _
                Inside_a * Inside_c)) / (2 * Inside_a)
        root2 = (-Inside_b - Sqrt(Inside_b ^ 2 - 4 *    _
                Inside_a * Inside_c)) / (2 * Inside_a)
        FindRoots = True
    Else
        FindRoots = False
    End If

End Function




Public Event InputZero()
Public Event NoRealRoot()

End Class
```

By examining the above code, you can see the statements used for creating properties, methods and events of the QE class. Explanation of these statements is as follows:

Variables: Three variables *Inside_a*, *Inside_b*, and *Inside_c* are declared in the General Declaration section of the class. Since they have the *Private* scope, they can be accessed only within the class itself. No access is permitted from outside of the class.

Properties: Three properties are defined by the Property statements in the class. The *Get* and *Set* procedures are included in each *Property* statement. These procedures are important in protecting invalid access to properties from outside of a class. Take the *Set* statement for property a as an example. The procedure has a checking statement to ensure that the Property a is set by a non-blank value.

Methods: Three methods *IsAZero*, *Check* and *FindRoots* are created for the class. They are declared with the *Public* keyword. They return a value of Boolean data type. The Keyword Me in the *FindRoots* method is used to refer to the method itself.

Events: Two events `InputZero()` and `NoRealRoot ()` are defined in this class. These two events are raised in the `Check` and `IsAZero` methods.

Once you have the above code in the class statement, you can build this class through the following procedures:

1)   Select *Build -> Build ClassLibrary1*

2)   Go to the folder where the *ClassLibrary1* is located.
        Go to the *bin* subfolder and see if the *ClassLibrary1.dll* exists.

Once you see the *ClassLibrary1.dll* file, you can use this class in any VB.Net applications.

11.3   Use of Classes in VB.Net Applications

As discussed in the previous sections, three types of classes (standard control templates, third-party classes, and user-owned classes) can be loaded into the VB.Net IDE for the development of projects. Also we have created our own class called *QE*. A challenging question now is how to use this class and other classes available in the VB.Net IDE environment.

In order to use a class in a project, you have to create an instance of the class by declaring a variable with the class name as its data type. The following example shows how to create an instance of the *QE* class:

```
DIM qe1 as New QE
```

This statement creates a variable named qe1. The *New* keyword enforces the class instance to be created in the memory.

Another way of creating an instance of a class is shown in the below example:

```
DIM qe1 as QE
qe1 = New QE
```

The first DIM statement creates a variable named qe1 but does not create an instance of the *QE* class. The second statement uses the statement with the keyword *New* to create an instance of the class and assigns it to the qe1 variable.

Once an object is created from a class, all the properties, methods, and event procedures can be accessed. Take the qe1 object as an example, you can have the following statements in a project:

```
qe1.a = 1
qe1.b = 2
qe1.c = 3
```

The first statement assigns 1 to the property a of the *qe1* object.

You can also use an assignment statement to retrieve the value of property a. For example,

```
Msgbox    eq1.a
```

This statement first gets the value of the property a, and displays it through the Msgbox window.

Similar to properties of a class, you can also access a method of a class using assignment statements. For example, you can have,

```
Qe1.check
Qe1.FindRoots (root1, root2)
```

Example 11-2 Use of the Class QE in a VB.Net Application

Now that you have an understanding about the concepts of classes and objects, it is the time to explore how to use the *QE* class to develop a VB.Net application.

Figure 11-5 shows the form for the VB.Net application. The logic of the application, as discussed in Chapter 1, is as follows:

When the application is executed, it allows the user to enter values of parameters into three textboxes a, b, and c. When the user clicks the *FindRoot* button, the program will check if roots exist. Then it outputs the roots onto the *root1* and *root2* textboxes when roots exist, otherwise it prompts the user with a warning message saying "No Root Exists". When the user enters 0 in any one of the textboxes a, b, and c, a message also appears to inform the user that a non-zero value is expected for the parameter textboxes.

When the user clicks the *Clear* button, the program will clear the values in the textboxes and make the textboxes empty for the next round of calculation. When the user clicks the *Cancel* button, the program will be terminated.

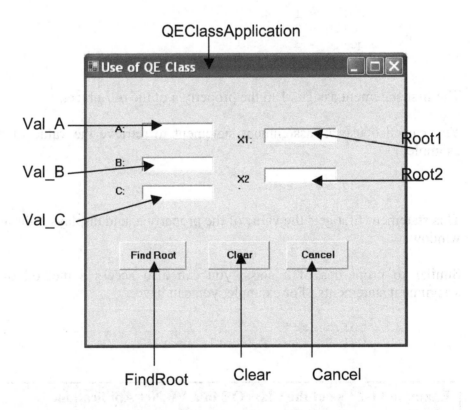

Figure 11-5 Form for the QE Class Application

Once you finish the form design, you need to load the class library *ClassLirary1* into the project. The procedures to load the class library are as follows:

1) Under the VB.Net IDE for the application, you right click *References* within the *Solution Explorer*.
2) Select *Add Reference*. The Add Reference window appears.
3) Select the *Project* Tab and click *Browse* button
4) Browse to the folder where the *ClassLibrary1* class library is located
5) Browse to the *bin* folder and find the *ClassLirary1.dll* file
6) Load the *ClassLirary1.dll* file into the VB.Net IDE.

Below is the code for the project

```
' The imports statement loads the ClassLibrary1 into
' this project

Imports ClassLibrary1

Public Class QEClassApplication

    Inherits System.Windows.Forms.Form

    ┌────────────────────────────────────────┐
    │ Window Form Designer Generated Code    │
    └────────────────────────────────────────┘

    ' The below statement declares the object qe1 with events.

    Public WithEvents qe1 As QE

    Private Sub FindRoot_Click(ByVal sender As System.Object, _
                    ByVal e As System.EventArgs)                _
                    Handles FindRoot.Click

    ' The below statement declares the qe1 to be of QE class
        qe1 = New QE
        Dim rt1 As Double, rt2 As Double
        Dim response As Boolean

        If Not IsNumeric(Val_A.Text) Then
           MsgBox("Enter a numeric value for parameter a")
           Exit Sub
        End If

        If Not IsNumeric(Val_B.Text) Then
           MsgBox("Enter a numeric value for parameter b")
           Exit Sub
        End If

        If Not IsNumeric(Val_C.Text) Then
           MsgBox("Enter a numeric value for parameter c")
           Exit Sub
        End If
```

```
' The below statements assign values from the three
' textboxes to the three properties of the object
' qe1.

    qe1.a = Val(Val_A.Text)
    qe1.b = Val(Val_B.Text)
    qe1.c = Val(Val_C.Text)



' The below statement uses the FindRoots method of the
' qe1 object, find the roots, and assign the roots to
' the two argments. If the roots are found successfully,
' the method returns True, otherwise, it
' returns False.

  response = qe1.FindRoots(rt1, rt2)
    If response Then
         Root1.Text = rt1
         Root2.Text = rt2
    End If

End Sub


Private Sub Clear_Click(ByVal sender As Object,          _
             ByVal e As System.EventArgs)                _
             Handles Clear.Click
    Val_A.Text = ""
    Val_B.Text = ""
    Val_C.Text = ""
    Root1.Text = ""
    Root2.Text = ""
End Sub

Private Sub Cancel_Click(ByVal sender As Object,         _
        ByVal e As System.EventArgs)                     _
             Handles Cancel.Click
    End
End Sub

Private Sub qe1_InputZero() Handles qe1.InputZero
    MsgBox("Paramenter cannot be 0")
    Exit Sub
End Sub

Private Sub qe1_NoRealRoot() Handles qe1.NoRealRoot
    MsgBox("No Root Exists")
    Exit Sub
End Sub
End Class
```

Note that the *FindRoot_Click* event procedure creates an instance of the class *QE* first. The instance is called qe1. The values in the textboxes a, b and c are assigned to the properties a, b, and c in the object qe1, respectively.

With each property of the object assigned with a value, the program calls the *FindRoots* method of the object. Keep in mind that the *FindRoots* method needs two arguments rt1 and rt2. The method first calculates the roots for the object. If the calculation is successful, the method returns *True*, otherwise it returns *False*. The roots calculated by the *FindRoots* method are further displayed in the *root1* and *root2* textboxes.

11.4   Collections of Objects

A collection class is a container that contains a group of objects. It is similar to an array. Each object in a collection instance is called a member. Collections are much more powerful and flexible than arrays. A collection expands when a member is added to it and shrinks when a member is removed from it.

1) Creating a Collection Object

In order to create a collection object, you should use the DIM statement. The following statement declares a collection variable named OC.

```
DIM OC as Collection
Set OC = New Collection
```

2) Adding Objects into a Collection

Once a collection is created, you can add members (or items) in the collection using the add method of the collection object. The syntax of the *Add* method is as follows:

```
Collection.Add <Member>, [Key], [Before], [After]
```

The member is an object to be added into the Collection. Key, Before and After are the three optional arguments that inform how to add a member in the collection.

For example, the following statements show that the *Add* method of the collection object called *OC* is used to add a QE object into the collection. The key value "Tim Jones" that represents a student name is also added into the connection.

```
DIM OC as Collection
Set OC = New Collection

DIM qe1 as QE
Set qe1 = New QE

Qe1.a = "1.0"
Qe1.b = "2.0"
Qe1.c = "3.0"

OC.Add qe1, "Tim Jones"
```

Note that the key value must be unique in the collection. Before you try to add the key value with its member, it is better to check if the key value exists in the collection. The next section shows the way to do the checking.

3) Searching for an Object in a Collection

Collection objects have a method called *Item* for searching for a member in a collection. Its syntax is as follows:

```
<CollectionName>.Item <Expression>
```

The expression can be a numerical value that represents the index of the member in the collection or a string value that represents the key value of the member.

The method can search for a specific member in the collection and return a reference to the member if found. Otherwise, a run-time error will return. The following statements demonstrate how you can trap the run-time error without terminating your program abnormally.

```
Private Sub Add1_Click(ByVal sender As System.Object, _
          ByVal e As System.EventArgs)                  _
          Handles Add1.Click

     DIM OC as Collection
     Set OC = New Collection

     DIM qe1 as QE
     Set qe1 = New QE

     On Error GOTO Errhandler
     Qe1.a = "1"
     Qe1.b = "2"
     Qe1.c = "3"

     OC.Add qe1, "Tim Jones"
     OC.Item ("Tim J")

     Exit sub
ErrHandler:

     Msgbox "No Such Value Key Exists"

End Sub
```

4) Browsing Members in a Collection

You can use For Each Next Loop statement to access individual members of a collection the same way a For Next Loop statement does for an array. Below is an example that goes through all the members in a collection called *ObjCollect* that consists of all the objects from the QE class.

```
Dim ObjCollect as Collection
Dim anObject as QE

For Each anObject in ObjCollect
    Console.Writeline anObject.a, anObject.b, anObject.c
Next
```

5) Removing a Member from a Collection

You can remove a member from a collection by using the Remove method. The *Remove* method has the following syntax:

```
<CollectionName>.Remove <Expression>
```

The expression can be a numerical value that represents the index of the member in the collection or a string value that represents the key value of the member.   An example statement that uses the Remove method is

```
ObjCollect.Remove(2)
ObjCollect.Remove("Tim Jones")
```

6) Deleting a Collection

You can delete a collection object by setting the object to refer to a *Nothing* object. For example,

```
ObjCollect = Nothing
```

Example 11.3	Application with Collections

You are asked to develop a VB.Net application that creates an environment to show how to use the *Add, Search*, and *Remove* methods of a collection.   Figure11-6 shows the form designed for the application. As you can see, the form has three group boxes. The top group box consists of one command button called *Add* and four textboxes: AVal, BVal, CVal, and KeyValue. The group box allows the user to enter a, b, and c parameters and a key value.   Once the values are entered, the user can click the *Add* button and insert a quadratic equation into the collection called ObjCollect. Also the parameters a, b, and c and the key value are listed in the list box on the left of the form.

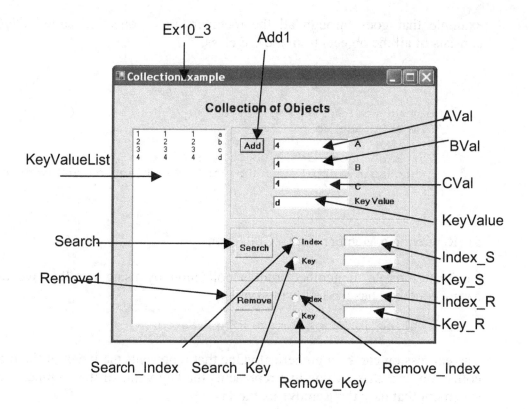

Figure 11-6   Form for the Collection Application

The middle group box has one command button called *Search* and two textboxes. The user can toggle the choice to search for a quadratic equation through the index of the equation object in the collection or through the key value entered in the Key_S textbox.

The bottom group box consists of one command button called *Remove* and two textboxes. The user can toggle the choice to remove a quadratic equation through the index of the equation object in the collection or through the key value entered in the Key_S textbox.

Below is the code for the application:

```
Imports ClassLibrary1

Public Class Example11_3
    Inherits System.Windows.Forms.Form
```

```
Window Form Designer Generated Code
```

```
    Dim ObjCollect As Collection


    Private Sub Ex11_3_Load(ByVal sender As System.Object,     _
                ByVal e As System.EventArgs)                   _
                Handles MyBase.Load
        ObjCollect = New Collection
        ObjCollect = Nothing
    End Sub




    Private Sub Add1_Click(ByVal sender As System.Object,      _
                ByVal e As System.EventArgs)                   _
                Handles Add1.Click

        Dim qe1 As QE, qe2 As QE
        qe1 = New QE
        On Error GoTo errhandler

        Dim astring As String

        If Not IsNumeric(AVal.Text) Then
            MsgBox("Numberical Value for a")
            Exit Sub
        End If
        If Not IsNumeric(BVal.Text) Then
            MsgBox("Numberical Value for b")
            Exit Sub
        End If



        If Not IsNumeric(CVal.Text) Then
            MsgBox("Numberical Value for c")
            Exit Sub
        End If


        qe1.a = Val(AVal.Text)
        qe1.b = Val(BVal.Text)
        qe1.c = Val(CVal.Text)

        ObjCollect.Add(qe1, KeyValue.Text)
        qe2 = ObjCollect.Item(KeyValue.Text)
        astring = Str(qe2.a) + vbTab + Str(qe2.b) +
                vbTab + Str(qe2.c)                             _
        astring = astring + vbTab + KeyValue.Text
        KeyValueList.Items.Add(astring)
        Exit Sub
errhandler:

        MsgBox("The Key Value already Exits")

    End Sub
```

```
Private Sub Search_Click(ByVal sender As System.Object, _
            ByVal e As System.EventArgs) _
            Handles Search.Click

    Dim qe1 As QE
    Dim astring As String


    astring = ""
    On Error GoTo errhandler

    If Index_Search.Checked = True Then
        If  Not IsNumeric(Index_S.Text) Then
            MsgBox("Numberical Value for Index")
            Exit Sub
        End If
        If Val(Index_S.Text) > 0 Then
            qe1 = ObjCollect.Item(Val(Index_S.Text))
        Else
            MsgBox("Index starts from 1")
            Exit Sub
        End If

    End If


    If Key_Search.Checked = True Then
        If Key_S.Text = "" Then
            MsgBox("Numberical Value for Index")
            Exit Sub
        End If

        qe1 = ObjCollect.Item(Key_S.Text)
    End If


    astring = Str(qe1.a) + vbTab + Str(qe1.b) + vbTab   _
            + Str(qe1.c)

    MsgBox(astring)

    Exit Sub
errhandler:

    MsgBox("No Such Value Key Exists")

    End Sub
```

```
Private Sub remove1_Click(ByVal sender As System.Object, _
                ByVal e As System.EventArgs) _
                Handles Remove1.Click

    Dim qe1 As QE
    Dim astring As String
    Dim index As Integer
    Dim akey As Integer
    On Error GoTo errhandler
    If Index_Remove.Checked = True Then
        If Index_R.Text = "" Or _
            Not IsNumeric(Index_R.Text) Then
            MsgBox("Numerical Value for Index")
            Exit Sub
        End If

        Index = Val(Index_R.Text) - 1
        KeyValueList.Items.RemoveAt(Index)
        akey = Val(Index_R.Text)
        ObjCollect.Remove(akey)
    End If

    If Key_Remove.Checked = True Then

        If Key_R.Text = "" Then
            MsgBox("Numerical Value for Index")
            Exit Sub
        End If


        qe1 = ObjCollect.Item(Key_R.Text)
        astring = Str(qe1.a) + vbTab + Str(qe1.b) + _
                vbTab + Str(qe1.c)

        astring = astring + vbTab + Key_R.Text

        KeyValueList.Items.Remove(astring)
        ObjCollect.Remove(Key_R.Text)
    End If
    Exit Sub


errhandler:

    MsgBox("No Such Value Key Exists")

    End Sub
End Class
```

Note that a collection variable *ObjCollect* is created using the following statements:

```
Dim ObjCollect As Collection
```

This collection variable is form-level variable that can be accessed and referenced by all the procedures in the form. The *ObjCollect* collection stores QE objects. The *Form_Load* event procedure sets the ObjCollect variable to refer to a new collection object derived by the Keyword *New*.

The *Add_Click* event procedure first creates an object called *qe1* from the *QE* class and assigns the properties a, b, and c with the values from the textboxes AVal, BVal, and CVal. Before assigning the values from the textboxes to the properties, three IF-THEN statements are used to check if the values in the three textboxes are numerical values. If the value is not a numerical value, exit the procedure.

The *qe1* object is then inserted into the collection *ObjCollect* as a member. Once the object is inserted into the collection, the properties of the object and the key value are retrieved from the collection using the statement:

```
qe2 = ObjCollect.Item(KeyValue.Text)
```

The properties are then concatenated to form a string and inserted into a list called KeyValueList.

The statement On ERROR GOTO ErrHandler is used to monitor the abnormal execution in the procedure. If an execution error is detected, this statement will go to the error-checking statements labeled with ErrHandler. Within the ErrHandler section, the statement *MsgBox* is used to prompt a message to users.

The *Search_Click* procedure first declares a variable to be an instance of QE class. It then uses the statement ON ERROR GOTO ErrHandler to monitor the abnormal execution and handles the errors by the statement labeled with ErrHandler.

There are two options to retrieve a member from a collection: by index or by Key Value. When the Index option is selected, the *Checked* property of the Index_Search control will be true. The procedure will then check if the Index_S textbox is empty or the value in the textbox is anything but a numeric value. If the textbox is empty or the value is not a numeric value, the procedure will inform the user with a message. Otherwise, it retrieves the member from the *ObjCollect* collection using the entered index.

When the Key Value option is selected, the *Checked* property of the Key_Search control will be true. The procedure then will check if the Key_S textbox is empty. If it is not empty, the procedure will search for a member whose key value matches to the entered one.

The object (or the member) found in the collection *ObjCollect* will be assigned to the *qe1* object. The properties of the object will be concatenated and informed to the user through the *MsgBox* statement. If the object cannot be found in the collection, a message will be prompted to indicate that no member exists with the entered index or key value.

The *Remove_Click* event procedure first uses the statement ON ERROR GOTO ErrHandler to monitor the abnormal execution and handles the errors by the statement labeled with ErrHandler.

Similar to Search_Click, there are two options to remove a member from a collection: by index or by Key Value. When the Index option is selected, the *Checked* property of the Index_Remove control will be true. The procedure will then check if the Index_R textbox is empty or the value in the textbox is anything but a numeric value. If the textbox is empty or the value is not a numeric value, the procedure will inform the user with a message. Otherwise, it removes the member from the *ObjCollect* collection using the entered index. Also it removes the items and the key value of the member from the KeyValueList.

When the Key Value option is selected, the *Checked* property of the KeyValue_Remove control will be true. The procedure then will check if the Key_R textbox is empty. If it is not empty, the procedure uses the value in the Key_R textbox to search for the qe1 object. Once a qe1 object is found, the procedure assembles a string and deletes the string from the KeyValueList.

11.5   Questions

Q1.   What is the difference between class and object?

Q2.   How to find all the properties, methods, and events of the label class template?

Q3.   List steps to include third-party classes into the VB.Net IDE for a project?

Q4.   Create a class *Triangle* that has the following characteristics:

```
Property    x1   as Double
Property    y1   as Double
Property    x2   as Double
Property    y2   as Double
Property    x3   as Double
Property    y3   as Double

Method      CalculateArea (x1, y1, x2, y2, x3, y3)
            This method calculates the area of a triangle
            with three given points.

Method      CalcualtePerimeter (x1, y1, x2, y2, x3, y3)
```

This method calculates the perimeter of a triangle with three given points.

Event   IsNotNumeric ()
             When the value for x1, y1, x2, y2, x3, or y3
             is not a numeric value, this event will be
             raised

Q5.   Suppose you want to create an object from the class *Triangle*. List the statements to define this object.

Q6.   What is a Collection of Objects? How to define a collection?

Chapter 12
VB.Net Advanced Topics

We have discussed fundamentals of VB.Net programming in the previous chapters. In this chapter we will introduce you a set of advanced VB.Net topics. As component programming is the trend in computer industry, this chapter will describes the use of **MSChart** control component in a VB.Net application. Through the development of this application, you will have hands-on experiences in component programming.

12.1   MSChart Control Component

The *MSChart* control component is one of the components that come along with the Visual Studio.Net product from Microsoft. This component uses an array to create and display graphs on forms.

The *MSChart* control component, different from the control templates we have discussed in the previous chapters, can not be found in the Visual Basic.Net toolbox. We need to insert it in the VB.Net IDE before we use it.

The procedures used to insert the *MSChart* control component into the toolbox are as follows:

Step 1   Select *Tools -> Add/RemoveToolbox Items ...*
              You will be prompted a window as shown in Figure 12-1.

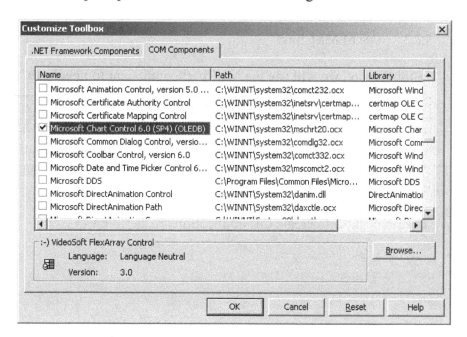

Figure 12-1   Customize Toolbox

Step 2   Select *Com Components* tab
Step 3   Scroll down until the option *Microsoft Chart Control 6.0 (SP4) (OLEDB)* appears

Step 4   Check on the option and click *OK*. Now you will see a template icon inserted into the VB.Net IDE's toolbox. Typically the *MSChart* control will be added at the end of the *Windows Forms* list in the Toolbox.

Step 5   View the Microsoft *MSChart* control component in the toolbox.

Now that we have added the *MSChart* control component to the Toolbox, we can use *MSChart* controls derived from the component in our VB.Net projects.

The *MSChart* control component has a set of properties, methods, and events. You do not need to know all of them. Instead you just need to know some of them to meet your programming needs. As to the VB.Net application to be developed below, you need to know the following properties:

DataType property   This property specifies which type of the chart the *MSCHart* control component should form and display.

DataChart property   This property specifies which set of values that should be used in the chart. If the DataType property specifies a 2D chart, the DataChart property should point to a two-dimensional array in which the first column of the array defines the labels shown on x axes and the second column defines the values for the y axes.

12.2   Use of MSChart

In this section we will use the MSChart component to develop a VB.Net application.

Example 12-1   Use of MSChart

We expand Example 6-1 by adding a chart to show the distribution of random numbers generated by Rnd ( ) function. Figure 12-2 shows the graphical interface of the expanded VB.Net application.

The procedures to create this application are as follows:

Step 1: Form Design

As shown in Figure 12-2, the form for the application has the following key controls:

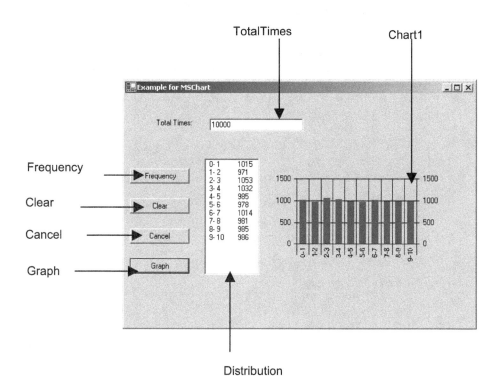

Figure 12-2 Interface of an MSChart Application

Control Name	Type	Property	Setting
MSChartEx	Form	Text	Example for MSChart
TotalTimes	TextBox	Text	
Frequency	Button	Text	Frequency
Clear	Button	Text	Clear
Cancel	Button	Text	Cancel
Graph	Button	Text	Graph
Chart1	MSChart		

It is noted that **_Chart1_** is a control derived from the MSChart data type. Other controls are same as those used in Example 6-1.

Step 2: Application Code

```
Public Class MSChartEx
  Inherits System.Windows.Forms.Form
```

```
┌──────────────────────────────────────────────┐
│ Window Form Designer Generated Code          │
└──────────────────────────────────────────────┘
```

```
' This is the form-level variable. It can be used
' by all the procedures in this form. The scope of this
' variable is the entire form.

Dim A(10) As Long

' This procedure will be executed when the MSChart
' Application is oaded.  This procedure enforces the
' Chart1 control to be invisible.  Also the Application
' form is set with its width of
' 500 screen units and its height of 400 screen units.

Private Sub MSChartEx_Load(ByVal sender As System.Object,
                ByVal e As System.EventArgs)
                    Handles MyBase.Load
     Me.Width = 500
     Me.Height = 400
     Chart1.Visible = False
End Sub

' This procedure, same as the procedure in Chapter 6,
' calculates distribution of random numbers generated by
' the rnd() in 0-1, 1-2, 2-3, 3-4, 4-5, 5-6, 6-7, 7-8,
' 8-9, and 9-10.

Private Sub Frequency_Click(ByVal sender As System.Object, _
                ByVal e As System.EventArgs)
                    Handles Frequency.Click

     Dim i As Long
     Dim RandomNumber As Single
     Dim category As Integer
     Dim TotalNumberofSimulation As Long

     '
     ' Check if the entered value is a numeric value.
     ' If it is not a numeric value, send a message out and
     ' stop the execution of the procedure.
     '
     ' Also Check if the TotalTimes textbox is empty.
     ' If it is, send a message out and stop the execution
     ' of the procedure.

    If Not IsNumeric(TotalTimes.Text) Or
                TotalTimes.Text = "" Then
            MessageBox.Show("Enter a Numeric Value ... ")
            Exit Sub
    End If
```

```
'
'  Reset the value in each element of Array A to be 0
'

   For i = 0 To 9
       A(i) = 0
   Next

   TotalNumberofSimulation = Val(TotalTimes.Text)


'
' Get a random number using RND() function
' Determine which category the random number will
` belong to
' Add 1 to its corresponding category
'

   For i = 1 To TotalNumberofSimulation
       RandomNumber = Rnd()
       category = Int(RandomNumber * 10)
       A(category) = A(category) + 1
   Next i


'
' Clear the Listbox before the distribution is
` inserted in it.
     '

   Distribution.Items.Clear()


'
' Insert the distribution into the listbox
'

   For i = 0 To 9
    Distribution.Items.Add(Str(i) + "-" + Str(i + 1) + _
                         vbTab + Str(A(i)))
   Next i

End Sub

' This procedure, same as the procedure in Chapter 6,
` clears the distribution list and the TotalTimes
` textbox.



Private Sub Clear_Click(ByVal sender As System.Object, _
            ByVal e As System.EventArgs)             _
            Handles Clear.Click



   ' This is the statement to reset the form.
   ` The width of the form is 500 screen units.
   ` The keyword me here refers to the Clear control.
   ` The ActiveForm property of the Clear control refers
   ` to the form where the Clear control is located.
```

```
        Me.ActiveForm.Width = 500
        Dim i As Integer
        TotalTimes.Text = ""
        Distribution.Items.Clear()
        For i = 0 To 9
            A(i) = 0
        Next I
        Chart1.Visible = false
    End Sub



    ' This procedure, same as the procedure in Chapter 6,
    ' terminates the application.


    Private Sub Cancel_Click(ByVal sender As System.Object, _
                ByVal e As System.EventArgs)                  _
                Handles Cancel.Click
        End
    End Sub

    ' This procedure responds to the Click event of the
    ' Graph control and generates a chart that shows
    ' graphically the distribution
    ' of random numbers generated in 0-1, 1-2, 2-3, 3-4,
    ' 4-5, 5-6, 6-7, 7-8, 8-9 and 9-10.

    Private Sub graph_Click(ByVal sender As System.Object, _
                ByVal e As System.EventArgs)                 _
                Handles Graph.Click


    ' First thing to do in the procedure is to make the Chart1
    ' control visible so users can see the distribution of
    ' random numbers.  Also the form window is resized to
    ' include the Chart1 control.

        Chart1.Visible = True
        Me.Width = 750


    ' The below statements create a one-dimensional array
    ' first and extract the number of counts for each
    ' interval (0-1, 1-2, 2-3, etc) from the list.
    ' The number of counts is the number after
    ' Tab on each line of the list.

        Dim AA(10) As String, aItem As String, bitem as string
        Dim i As Integer, pos1 As Integer

        For i = 0 To Distribution.Items.Count - 1
            aItem = str(Distribution.Items(i))
            pos1 = InStr(aItem, vbTab)
            bitem = Mid(aItem, pos1)
            AA(i) = Val(bitem)
        Next
```

```
' The below statement declares a two-dimensional array
' called chdata. The initial value is a group of labels and
' data from the AA array.


    Dim chdata(,) As String = New String(,)  _
    {                                        _
                {"0-1",  AA(0)},             _
                {"1-2",  AA(1)},             _
                {"2-3",  AA(2)},             _
                {"3-4",  AA(3)},             _
                {"4-5",  AA(4)},             _
                {"5-6",  AA(5)},             _
                {"6-7",  AA(6)},             _
                {"7-8",  AA(7)},             _
                {"8-9",  AA(8)},             _
                {"9-10", AA(9)}             _
    }

  Chart1.chartType = MSChart20Lib.VtChChartType.VtChChartType2dBar
  Chart1.ChartData = chdata

End Sub
```

12.3   Questions

Q1.   Assume you have a component called *MapControl* from the Environmental System Research Institute (ESRI). List steps to get this component into the VB.Net IDE for application development.

Q2.   What is the purpose of the `Form_Resize` procedure within the simple browser?

Q3.   Example 12-1 in this chapter shows the uniform distribution of random numbers generated from the Rnd ( ) function. Review the application to allow the normal distribution of random numbers to be shown in the Chart control.

Q4.   You are asked to develop a Visual Basic.Net-based simple browser that allows users to surf on the Internet. A VB.Net template application is provided in this chapter. You should enhance the application by having the following functions as shown in Figure 12-3 [Hint: use Microsoft WebBrowser component].

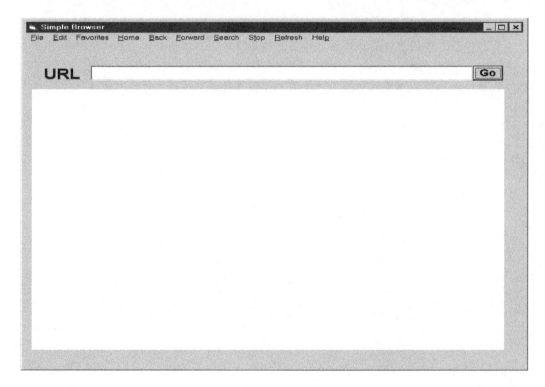

Figure 12-3   A Simple Web Browser

Chapter 13
Introduction to Numeric Methods

Science or engineering problems involve a set of factors whose interactions and relationships are often governed by their principles with certain constraints. In order to understand these interactions and relationships, scientists and engineers commonly formulate various mathematical or computational models to simulate the dynamic characteristics of problems. A common problem-solving process is shown in Figure 13-1.

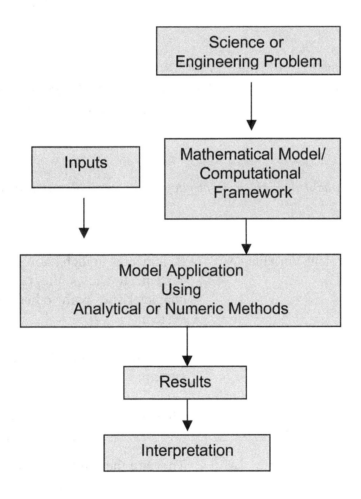

Figure 13-1 Problem-Solving Process

It is noted from Figure 13-1 that a problem is first formulated by a mathematical model or a computational framework. This model or framework is then implemented or applied to solve the problem with different inputs. A set of analytical or numerical methods are used to conduct calculations and find results. The results are further interpreted in the context of the problem.

13.1   Roles of Computers in Numerical Computing

Before computers were invented, mathematical models were often developed in the form of equations, tables, plots, or nomographs. The equations or graphical representations describe the essential features and their relationships of a physical or engineering system (or process). In a mathematical term, equations are shown as follows:

$$Dependent\ Variable1 = f(indepedent\ variables, parameters, constra\operatorname{int} s)$$
$$Dependent\ Variable2 = f(indepedent\ variables, parameters, constra\operatorname{int} s)$$
$$Dependent\ Variable\ i = f(indepedent\ variables, parameters, constra\operatorname{int} s)$$

$$\ldots$$

$$Dependent\ Variablen = f(indepedent\ \operatorname{var} iables, parameters, constra\operatorname{int} s)$$

Where

Dependent Variable i -	It indicates a behavior or characteristic of the system. It shows the relationship between this characteristic with other characteristics of the system.
Independent variables -	They are the characteristics and behaviors of the system.
Parameters -	They are the initial states or values of the system.
Constraints -	They are the limits and constraints that govern the changes of the independent variables.

Graphical representations are the solutions to problems whose characteristics and behaviors can be illustrated graphically.

During the pre-computer time, scientists and engineers spent significant effort on formulation of mathematical models for problems. The mathematical models were normally suitable for solving simple problems. They are of limited practical values since most real systems or problems are complex and difficult, if not impossible, to be formulated in equations or graphical representations.

Computers have provided a powerful tool for solving complicated problems. They have led to the widespread use and development of computer-based numerical methods for handling large systems of equations, nonlinear behaviors of problems, complicated geometries, and uncertainties of systems. A significant change in problem-solving process after the advent of computers is that scientists and engineers can formulate problems not only in mathematical models but also in computational frameworks. Computational frameworks are algorithms, logics or cooking recipes that specify the steps for solving problems. These algorithms are further implemented to yield results for problems.

13.2   Types of Numerical Methods

Many numerical methods are developed for use in computers. These numerical methods can be categorized into the following groups:

- Roots of Equations
- Matrices and Systems of Linear Equations
- Eigenvalues and Eigenvectors
- Optimization
- Curve Fitting
- Numerical Integration
- Ordinary and Partial Differential Equations

The brief descriptions of these numerical methods are as follows:

1)   Roots of Equations

Certain scientific or engineering problems can be formulated by the following single linear equation:

$$f(x) = 0$$

In order to find a root x_0 that meets $f(x_0) = 0$, we can use a set of analytical or numerical methods. When problems are described by a simple, straight forward equation and roots of the equation are expressed in an explicit formula, analytical methods are desirable. When problems are complicated and no explicit formulas are found to calculate roots, numerical methods will be suitable for estimating an approximation of roots. Chapter 14 will provide more information about the analytical and numerical methods used for finding roots of equations.

2)   Matrices and Systems of Linear Equations

Real-life engineering problems have non-linear characteristics. In simplifying these problems and understanding the essential behaviors of factors within the problems, engineers often ignore the effects of nonlinear terms and formulate the problems by a set of linear equations.

Matrices are important in formulating numeric methods for linear systems. They provide a concise way to describe the essential relationships between problem variables. Chapter 15 provides an introduction to matrix theory.

3)   Eigenvalues and Eigenvectors

There are a number of engineering problems that involve vibrations, elasticity, and other oscillating systems. Eigenvalues are specific values that describe the dynamic nature of this type of problems. Due to the limitations of this book, we do not have a comprehensive discussion on Eigenvalues and Eigenvectors. However we do provide methods on how to calculate Eigenvalues in Chapter 16.

4)   Optimization

Engineers are sometimes required to compare a set of feasible alternatives and select a best alternative. This selection process is referred to as optimization. Optimization problems can be formulated mathematically in the following expression:

Minimize or maximize: $f(x)$
Subject to:

$$d_i(x) \le a_i \quad i = 1, 2, 3,...,m$$
$$e_i(x) = b_i \quad i = 1, 2, 3,...,k$$

Where   x   - an n-dimension vector
            $f(x)$ - the objective function
            $d_i(x)$ - inequality constraints
            $e_i(x)$ - equality constraints
            a_i - constant
            b_i - constant

The optimization process is to seek a set of x values or the x vector that satisfies the above constraints and minimizes (or maximizes) the objective function.

Depending on the form of $f(x)$ and constraints, different types of numerical methods are used to seek for the optimal x values. If $f(x)$ and constraints are linear, linear programming methods will be desirable for optimization. If $f(x)$ and constraints are nonlinear, nonlinear programming methods should be used for optimization. Besides linear and nonlinear programming methods, there are other types of numerical methods (such as dynamic programming and integer programming methods) available for finding optimal x values for certain types of problems. The discussion of the numerical methods for optimization is beyond the scope of this book. You can refer to other textbooks if you are interested in this subject.

5)   Curve Fitting

You are sometimes required to fit curves to a set of paired data points. In doing so, you can have a better understanding of the essential relationships among these data points.

One of the curve fitting techniques widely used by engineers is regression. With the regression technique, we can create a single curve to represent the general trend of data points. Detail discussion of the regression method is provided in Chapter 19.

6)   Integration

Certain engineering problems can be formulated by the following expression:

$$I = \int_a^b f(x)dx \cong \int_a^b f_n(x)dx$$

Where

$f_n(x)$ -   A polynomial function

The integral can be approximated using a set of polynomial functions.

Numerical methods used to find approximations of integrals are provided in Chapter 19.

7)   Ordinary and Partial Differential Equations

Ordinary and partial differential equations are important in solving engineering problems. However, we cannot discuss the numerical methods used for these types of equations, due to the limits of the textbook. You can study these types of numerical methods by reading relevant textbooks and references if you are interested in this subject.

13.3   MATLAB and EXCEL

MATLAB is a commercial software product that provides a comprehensive set of numerical methods for engineers and scientists. We will introduce MATLAB in Chapter 17 and describe how to use it for finding roots of equations, performing matrix operations, and fitting curves for data points in Chapters 17 and 18.

Certain numerical methods can be performed in Microsoft EXCEL. Discussion of these methods for performing matrix operations is provided in Chapter 18 and for fitting curves in Chapter19.

13.4   Questions

Q1.   What are the differences of numerical methods before and after computers were invented and widely used for engineering practice?

Q2   List the primary types of numerical methods discussed in this chapter.

Q3.   List two computer programs you can use to apply numerical methods for finding roots of equations.

Q4.   What are the differences between analytical methods and numerical methods?

Chapter 14
Roots of Equations

We will discuss the roots of equations and the numerical methods or algorithms used to find the roots in this chapter. The MATLAB implementation of these algorithms will be provided in Chapter 17.

14.1   Roots of Equations

A root of an equation is defined as a value of x_0 that yields

$$f(x) = f(x_0) = 0$$

Where $f(x)$ can be a polynomial, exponential, logarithmic, or trigonometric function. There are three types of ways used to determine the roots of an equation:

1)   Determinate or closed-form solutions

This method can formulate a closed-form expression for finding roots of an equation. For example, a quadratic equation has a closed-form solution formulated below if $\sqrt{b^2 - 4ac} \geq 0$:

Quadratic: $f(x) = ax^2 + bx + c = 0$

$$x_{1,2} = \frac{-b \pm \sqrt{b^2 - 4ac}}{2a}$$

We can also formulate a cubic equation with a complex closed-form expression for root calculation.   Unfortunately we cannot formulate a closed-form solution for all equations. Mathematicians have already proved that any polynomial equations with order greater than and equal to 4 do not have a closed-form solution. Therefore we cannot rely on the closed-forms to find roots for complicated equations.

2)   Graphical Estimations

Since we cannot get an accurate root of an equation through a closed-form formula, we need to find another way, that is, by plotting the function $f(x)$ and checking its crossing values with the x axis.

There are a number of graphical methods available for root estimation. However these methods are not suitable for computer usage. Recent efforts have been made to improve the methods so that an incremental procedure for searching roots is implemented in computers along the x-axis. In general, graphical approaches do not have an effective searching mechanism. They just simply "march" along the x-axis with a pre-defined interval. They cannot yield precise roots. Estimated roots depend on the intervals chosen for the search. The larger the search interval, the rougher the estimated roots are.

3)   Iterative Approximations

Iterative approximations are the third way of finding roots. They improve graphical approaches by adding an intelligent search mechanism. The search mechanism "march" backward or forward along the x-axis with an interval defined by the characteristics of the function $f(x)$. They repeat a set of search steps to converge to a root x_0.

There are three basic interactive approaches commonly used for root estimation: bisection approach, false-position approach, and Newton-Raphson approach. We will discuss these three approaches in the following sections.

14.2   Bisection Approach

Bisection approach is an iterative approximation method for determining the roots of an equation $f(x) = 0$. It searches for a root by locating an interval within which we know a root exists. It then reduces the interval by half, and checks which divided interval the root is located at. The search continues until an estimated root is close enough to its real root.

This method assumes $f(x)$ is a monotonic function. Given a value x, there is one and only one value for $f(x)$. Since this method requires a guess interval in which a root exists, it is also referred as a bracketing method in other textbooks.

14.2.1   Initial Interval Determination

The determination of the guess interval is critical to the search. Normally the guess interval is determined by a simple plot or by the incremental search method. Suppose an interval $[x_1, x_2]$ is the guess interval within which the function *changes sign*, that is,

$$f(x_1) * f(x_2) < 0$$

If the above inequality satisfies, the interval [x1, x2] has at least one real root and is the guess interval for the search.

14.2.2   Search Rules

Once an guess or initial interval is found, we pick the midpoint x_{mid} to bisect the interval or

$$x_{mid} = \frac{\left(x_2 + x_1\right)}{2}.$$

The value of $f(x_{mid})$ is determined and we check the following product to locate the region in which the root occurs.

$$f(x_1) * f(x_{mid}) \begin{cases} < 0, \text{ then sign change and root in } [x_1, x_{mid}] \\ > 0, \text{ then sign change and root in } [x_{mid}, x_2] \\ = 0, \text{ then } x_3 \text{ is the root, and process stops.} \end{cases}$$

The application of the search rules is shown in Figure 14-1.

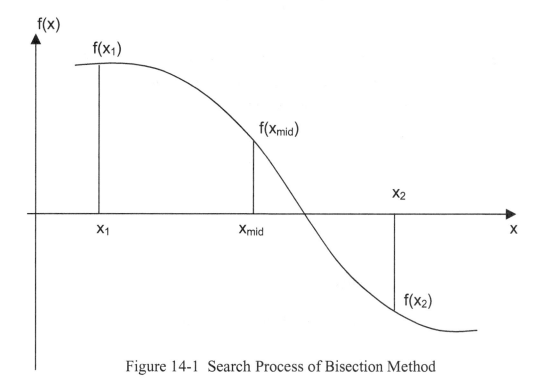

Figure 14-1 Search Process of Bisection Method

14.2.3   Terminating Rules

The search that divides the interval in half continues until the estimated root is within a desired accuracy. Now the question is when to stop. The criteria used for terminating the search are as follows:

Suppose $\hat{x}$ is an approximation of the root and x_0 is the actual root. The search stops when one of the following terminating rules applies:

- When $|\hat{x} - x_0| < \varepsilon$ with ε a small number,
  (As you know x_0 is unknown. We will thus use the comparison of two successive approximated values, $|\hat{x}_n - \hat{x}_{n-1}| < \varepsilon$, to replace the above terminating rule.)

- When $|f(\hat{x})| < \varepsilon$ where ε is a predetermined small number,

- When the ratio of $\dfrac{\hat{x}_n}{\hat{x}_{n-1}}$ is close to unity, say 0.999 and 1.001,

- Stop after n iterations with n pre-defined.

Satisfaction of both $|\hat{x}_n - \hat{x}_{n-1}| < \varepsilon$ and $|f(\hat{x})| < \varepsilon$ would be desirable but almost not possible. In practice, we just care about the terminating rule of $|\overline{x}_n - \overline{x}_{n-1}| < \varepsilon$. Once the search stops, the root can be approximated as

$$\hat{x}_{approximate} = \frac{(\hat{x}_{n-1} + \hat{x}_n)}{2}$$

Or

$$\hat{x}_{approximate} = \hat{x}_n$$

14.2.4   A Bisection Example

Find a root for the following equation with $\varepsilon = 0.01$

$$f(x) = x^2 - 2 = 0$$

Step 1: Determine the guess or initial interval

Suppose the incremental search with an interval of $\frac{1}{2}$, we have

$f(0) = -2$

$f(\frac{1}{2}) = -\frac{7}{4}$

$f(1) = -1$ $\leftarrow$ sign change, $f(1) \times f(\frac{3}{2}) = -1 \times \frac{1}{4} = -\frac{1}{4} < 0$

$f(\frac{3}{2}) = \frac{1}{4}$

Thus a root exists between 1 and 1.5 and we start the bisection method with $x_1 = 1$ and $x_2 = 1.5$.

Step 2: Search for the root (first iteration)

Bisect $x_{mid} = 1.25$; $f(1.25) = -0.4375$; $f(x_1).f(x_{mid}) > 0$

The new bounds are $[x_1, x_{mid}]$ and $[x_{mid}, x_2]$. The root is between $[x_{mid}, x_2]$ that is, $[1.25, 1.5]$.

Step 3: Check if the approximation is close enough. Assume x1 is the first guess of the root.

$|x_{mid} - x_1| = |1.25-1| = 0.25 > 0.01$

Search continues.

Step 4: Search for the root (second iteration)

We assume $[x_1, x_2] = [1.25, 1.5]$

Bisect $x_{mid} = 1.375$; $f(1.375) = -0.1094$; $f(x_1).f(x_{mid}) > 0$
The new bounds are $[x_1, x_{mid}]$ and $[x_{mid}, x_2]$. The root is within $[x_{mid}, x_2]$ or $[1.375, 1.5]$.

Step 5: Check if the approximation is close enough

$|x_{mid} - x_1| = |1.25-1.375| = 0.125 > 0.01$

Search continues.

Step 6: Search for the root (third iteration)

We assume $[x_1, x_2] = [1.375, 1.5]$

Bisect $x_{mid} = 1.438$; $f(1.438) = 0.066$; $f(x_1).f(x_{mid}) < 0$
The new bounds are $[x_1, x_{mid}]$ and $[x_{mid}, x_2]$. The root is within $[x_1, x_{mid}]$ or $[1.375, 1.43]$.

Step 7: Check if the approximation is close enough

$|x_{mid} - x_1| = |1.375 - 1.438| = 0.063 > 0.01$

Search continues.

Step 8: Search for the root (fourth iteration)

We assume $[x_1, x_2] = [1.375, 1.438]$

Bisect $x_{mid} = 1.4063$; $f(1.4063) = -0.0225$; $f(x_1).f(x_{mid}) > 0$
The new bounds are $[x_1, x_{mid}]$ and $[x_{mid}, x_2]$. The root is within $[x_{mid}, x_2]$ or $[1.403, 1.43]$.

Step 9: Check if the approximation is close enough

$|x_{mid} - x_1| = |1.4063 - 1.438| = 0.035 > 0.01$

Search continues.

Step 10: Search for the root (fifth iteration)

We assume $[x_1, x_2] = [1.4063, 1.438]$

Bisect $x_{mid} = 1.422$; $f(1.422) = 0.0217$; $f(x_1).f(x_{mid}) < 0$
The new bounds are $[x_1, x_{mid}]$ and $[x_{mid}, x_2]$. The root is within $[x_1, x_{mid}]$ or $[1.403, 1.417]$.

Step 11: Check if the approximation is close enough

$|x_{mid} - x_1| = |1.422 - 1.4063| = 0.0157 > 0.01$

Search continues.

Step 12: Search for the root (sixth iteration)

We assume $[x_1, x_2] = [1.4063, 1.422]$

Bisect $x_{mid} = 1.4141$; $f(1.4141) = -0.00032$; $f(x_1).f(x_{mid}) > 0$
The new bounds are $[x_1, x_{mid}]$ and $[x_{mid}, x_2]$. The root is within $[x_{mid}, x_2]$ or $[1.4141, 1.417]$.

Step 13: Check if the approximation is close enough

$|x_{mid} - x_1| = |1.417 - 1.4141| = 0.0029 < 0.01$

Search stops.

The root is $\overline{x} = (1.417 + 1.4141)/2 = 1.4155$ within the accuracy of 0.01.

Or the root is 1.4141 if we use $\overline{x}_{approximate} = \overline{x}_{n+1}$.

This approach converges to the actual root with six iterations. We reduce the interval by a factor of $1/2^6$.

Note that this method requires an interval $[x_1, x_2]$ be located within which the sign of the function, $f(x)$, changes. We should be cautious when we select the initial interval for finding roots. If the interval is large, it may contain 1 or any odd number of roots. We might find one root and ignore or miss other roots that may be of interest. If the interval is small, most likely a root does not exist in the interval.

14.3   False-Position Approach

False-position approach determines the roots of an equation by taking advantage of the shape of the function $f(x)$. Using the characteristics of the function, the false-position method converges to an actual root more rapidly than the bisection method.

14.3.1   Initial Interval Determination

Similar to the bisection method, the false-position approach also needs an initial interval within which a root exists. Remember in the previous section, the initial interval is determined by a simple plot or by the incremental search method. Suppose an interval $[x_1, x_2]$ is the interval within which the function is known to *change sign*. This change of sign can be simply determined by checking if:

$$f(x_1) * f(x_2) < 0$$

If the above inequality satisfies, the interval [x1, x2] is the initial interval for the search.

14.3.2   Search Rules

Once an initial interval is found, we then draw the line that goes through two end points $(x_1, f(x_1))$ and $(x_2, f(x_2))$ as shown in Figure 14-2.

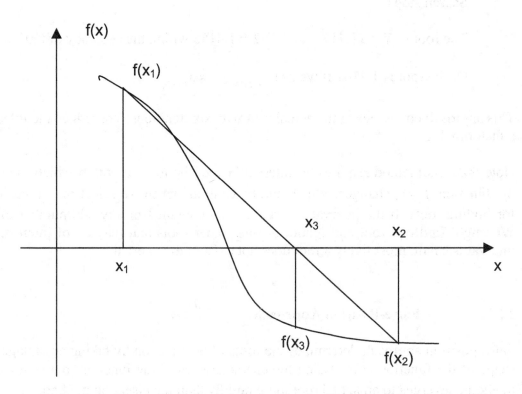

Figure 14-2 Search Rules for the False-Position Approach

$$f(x) = f(x_1) + \frac{f(x_2) - f(x_1)}{x_2 - x_1}(x - x_1)$$

The x intercept of f(x) = 0 becomes a new estimate of the root as $\bar{x} = x_3$ or

$$\bar{x} = x_3 = x_1 - \frac{f(x_1)(x_2 - x_1)}{f(x_x) - f(x_1)}$$

$$\overline{x} = x_3 = \frac{x_1 f(x_2) - x_2 f(x_1)}{f(x_2) - f(x_1)}$$

Note that the intersecting point (x_3) between the line and the x-axis is not the bisecting point of the interval. How to reduce the interval? We go by the following rules:

If $f(x_1)^* f(x_3) < 0$, the search will go to the left side of the intersecting point x_3, that is, the new interval for next iteration will be [x_1, x_3]

If $f(x_1)^* f(x_3) > 0$, the search will go to the right side of the intersecting point x_3, that is, the new interval for next iteration will be [x_3, x_2]

14.3.3   Terminating Rules

We repeat the line-based search until the interval or successive estimates of the root are within tolerance. Similar to the bisection method, the criteria used for terminating the search are as follows:

Suppose $\hat{x}$ is an approximation of the root and x_0 is the actual root. The search stops when one of the following terminating rules applies:

- When $|\hat{x} - x_0| < \varepsilon$ with ε a small number,
  (As you know x_0 is unknown. We will thus use the comparison of two successive approximated values, $|\hat{x}_n - \hat{x}_{n-1}| < \varepsilon$, to replace the above terminating rule.)

- When $|f(\hat{x})| < \varepsilon$ where ε is a predetermined small number,

- When the ratio of $\dfrac{\hat{x}_n}{\hat{x}_{n-1}}$ is close to unity, say 0.999 and 1.001,

- Stop after n iterations with n pre-defined.

Satisfaction of both $|\hat{x}_n - \hat{x}_{n-1}| < \varepsilon$ and $|f(\hat{x})| < \varepsilon$ would be desirable but almost not possible. In practice, we just care about the terminating rule of $|\overline{x}_n - \overline{x}_{n-1}| < \varepsilon$. Once the search stops, the root can be approximated as

$$\hat{x}_{approximate} = \frac{(\hat{x}_{n-1} + \hat{x}_n)}{2}$$

Or

$$\hat{x}_{approximate} = \hat{x}_n$$

14.3.4   Variations of False Position Approach

The false position approach can be modified to improve its search speed. Instead of using the search rules listed in Section 14.3.3, we use the search rule as shown in Figure 14-3:

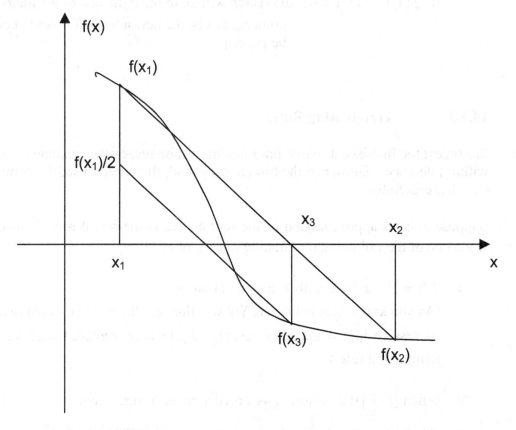

Figure 14-3   Improved Searching Rule for the False Position Approach

Suppose we have found an initial interval $[x_1, x_2]$. The general steps related to the new search rules are as follows:

Step 1:   Calculate $\overline{x} = \dfrac{x_1 f(x_2) - x_2 f(x_1)}{f(x_2) - f(x_1)}$

Step 2:   Compute $f(\bar{x})$

Step 3:   Compute $f(x_1) \times f(\bar{x})$ and check

$$\text{If } f(a) \times f(\bar{x}) \begin{cases} <0 \text{ then} \begin{cases} \bar{x} \text{ becomes new } x_2 \\ f(\bar{x}) \text{ becomes new } f(x_2) \\ f(x_1)/2 \text{ becomes new } f(x_1) \end{cases} \\ \\ =0 \ \bar{x} \text{ is the root, stop} \\ \\ >0 \text{ then} \begin{cases} \bar{x} \text{ becomes new } x_1 \\ f(\bar{x}) \text{ becomes new } f(x_1) \\ f(x_2)/2 \text{ becomes new } f(x_2) \end{cases} \end{cases}$$

Step 4:   Repeat steps 1-3 until convergence is reached.

14.3.5   A False-Position Example

Use the improved false-position method to find a root for the following equation with a small number $\varepsilon_1 = 0.01$

$$x^3 - 3 = 0$$

Two decimal positions are used for simplicity in the following explanation.

Step 1: Initial Interval

   Observe a sign change between $x_1 = 1$ and $x_2 = 2$.

   $$f(0) = (1)^3 - 3 < 0$$
   $$f(1) = (2)^3 - 3 = 5 > 0$$

   We will use the interval [1,2] to be the initial interval. At least a root exists within the interval.

Step 2: Search for the root

   Iteration 0: $x_1 = 1$, $f(1) = -2$ and $x_2 = 2$, $f(2) = 5$

$$\bar{x} = \frac{x_1 * f(x_2) - x_2 * f(x_1)}{f(x_2) - f(x_1)} = \frac{1(5) - 2(-2)}{5 - (-2)} = 1.2857$$

$$f(\bar{x}) = (1.2857)^3 - 3 = -0.8746$$

$$f(x_1) f(\bar{x}) > 0 \quad \therefore \quad x_1 = 1.2857, \ f(x_1) = -0.8746$$

$$x_2 = 2, f(x_2) = \frac{5}{2} = 2.5$$

$|1.2857-1| > 0.01$, search continues.

Iteration 1:

$$\bar{x} = \frac{1.2857(2.5) - 2(-0.8746)}{2.5 + 0.8746} = 1.4708$$

$$f(\bar{x}) = (1.4708)^3 - 3 = 0.1819$$

$$f(x_1) f(\bar{x}) < 0 \quad \therefore \quad x_1 = 1.2857, f(x_1) = \frac{-0.8746}{2} = -0.4373$$

$$x_2 = 1.4708, f(x_2) = 0.1819$$

$|1.4708-1.2857| > 0.01$, search continues.

Iteration 2:

$$\bar{x} = \frac{1.2857(0.1819) - 1.4708(-0.4373)}{0.1819 + 0.4373} = 1.4164$$

$$f(\bar{x}) = (1.4164)^3 - 3 = -0.1583$$

$$f(x_1) f(\bar{x}) > 0 \quad \therefore \quad x_1 = 1.4164, \ f(x_1) = -0.1583$$

$$x_2 = 1.4708, f(x_2) = \frac{0.1819}{2} = 0.0909$$

$|1.4164-1.4708| > 0.01$, search continues.

Iteration 3:

$$\bar{x} = \frac{1.4164(0.0909) - 1.4708(-0.1583)}{0.0909 + 0.1583} = 1.4510$$

$$f(\bar{x}) = 1.4510^3 - 3 = 0.0547$$

$$f(x_1)\, f(\overline{x}) < 0 \quad \therefore \quad x_1 = 1.4164,\ f(x_1) = \frac{-0.1583}{2} = -0.079$$

$$x_2 = 1.4510$$

$$|1.4510\text{-}1.4164| > 0.01,\ \text{search continues}$$

Iteration 4:

$$\overline{x} = \frac{1.4164(0.0547) - 1.4510(-0.079)}{0.0547 + 0.079} = 1.4368$$

$$f(\overline{x}) = 1.4368^3 - 3 = -0.034$$

$$f(x_1)\, f(\overline{x}) > 0 \quad \therefore \quad x_1 = 1.4368$$

$$x_2 = 1.4510,\ f(x_2) = \frac{0.0547}{2} = 0.0273$$

$$|1.4368\text{-}1.4510| > 0.01,\ \text{search continues}$$

Iteration 5:

$$\overline{x} = \frac{1.4368(0.0273) - 1.4510(-0.034)}{0.0273 + 0.034} = 1.4447$$

$$f(\overline{x}) = 1.4447^3 - 3 = 0.015$$

$$f(x_1)\, f(\overline{x}) < 0 \quad \therefore \quad x_1 = 1.4368,\ f(x_1) = \frac{-0.034}{2} = -0.017$$

$$x_2 = 1.447$$

$$|1.4447\text{-}1.4368| < 0.01,\ \text{search stops}$$

Step 3: The root approximation x_0 then is $(1.4447+1.4368)/2 = 1.4407$.

14.4   Newton-Raphson Approach

Both bisection and false position methods require a bounding interval within which a root should exist. The searching rules used in the two approaches ensure the convergent move to the true value of the root. In this section we will introduce the Newton-Raphson method that requires only a single starting point of x for the hunting of the root as shown in Figure 14-4.

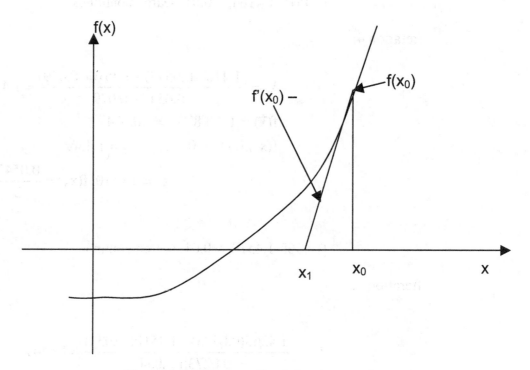

Figure 14-4 Newton-Raphson Approach

14.4.1   Starting Point

The determination of the starting value is critical to the search. A wrong starting value could diverge or move away from the actual root when the iterations continue. As shown in Figures 14-5, convergence may not be reached to the root due to the shape of the curve and the wrong location of the starting point. A suggestion to choose a starting point is to observe the shape of the curve before the starting point is located along the x-axis.

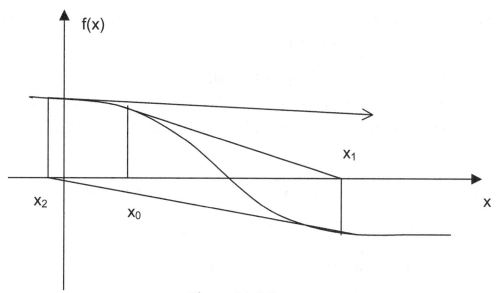

Figure 14-5 Convergence Issue

14.4.2   Searching Rules

The Newton-Raphson method substitutes the local tangent to the function f(x) as a straight line and calculate the x intercept as an approximation to the root.

The tangent to the function at x_k is

$$f(x) = y(x) = f(\overline{x}_k) + f'(\overline{x}_k)(x - \overline{x}_k) = 0$$

Solving for $x = \overline{x}_{k+1}$ yields:

$$\overline{x}_{k+1} = \overline{x}_k - \frac{f(\overline{x}_k)}{f'(\overline{x}_k)}$$

When this method works, it converges quite rapidly. To avoid from the problems as shown in Figure 14-5, we need to investigate the local characteristics of the function $f(x)$.

14.4.3   Terminating Rules

We repeat the search until the interval or successive estimates of the root are within tolerance. Similar to the bisection and the false position methods, the criteria used for terminating the search are as follows:

Suppose $\hat{x}$ is an approximation of the root and x_0 is the actual root. The search stops when one of the following terminating rules applies:

❏ When $|\hat{x} - x_0| < \varepsilon$ with ε a small number,
(As you know x_0 is unknown. We will thus use the comparison of two successive approximated values, $|\hat{x}_n - \hat{x}_{n-1}| < \varepsilon$, to replace the above terminating rule.)

❏ When $|f(\hat{x})| < \varepsilon$ where ε is a predetermined small number,

❏ When the ratio of $\dfrac{\hat{x}_n}{\hat{x}_{n-1}}$ is close to unity, say 0.999 and 1.001,

❏ Stop after n iterations with n pre-defined.

Satisfaction of both $|\hat{x}_n - \hat{x}_{n-1}| < \varepsilon$ and $|f(\hat{x})| < \varepsilon$ would be desirable but almost not possible. In practice, we just care about the terminating rule of $|\overline{x}_n - \overline{x}_{n-1}| < \varepsilon$. Once the search stops, the root can be approximated as

$$\hat{x}_{approximate} = \frac{(\hat{x}_{n-1} + \hat{x}_n)}{2}$$

Or

$$\hat{x}_{approximate} = \hat{x}_n$$

14.4.4   A Newton-Raphson Example

Find the root of the given polynomial that occurs around $x_0 = -1$, $\varepsilon = 0.02$

$$f(x) = x^4 - 2x^3 - 2x^2 + 3x - 2 = 0$$

Determine $f'(x)$: $f'(x) = 4x^3 - 6x^2 - 4x + 3$

$x_0 = -1$

$$f(-1) = (-1)^4 - 2(-1)^3 - 2(-1)^2 + 3(-1) - 2 = -4$$
$$f'(-1) = 4(-1)^3 - 6(-1)^2 - 4(-1) + 3 = -3$$

$$x_1 = -1 - \frac{-4}{-3} = -2.3333$$

$$f(-2.3333) = 35.1581$$
$$f'(-2.3333) = -71.1452$$

$$x_2 = -2.3333 - \frac{35.1581}{-71.1452} = -1.83913$$

$$f(-1.83913) = 9.5997$$
$$f'(-1.83913) = -34.8206$$

$$x_3 = -1.83913 - \frac{9.5997}{-34.8206} = -1.56344$$

$$f(-1.56344) = 2.0389$$
$$f'(-1.56344) = -20.6987$$

$$x_4 = -1.56344 - \frac{2.0389}{-20.6987} = -1.4649$$

$$f(-1.4649) = 0.2056$$
$$f'(-1.4649) = -16.5903$$

$$x_5 = -1.4649 - \frac{0.2056}{-16.5903} = -1.4525$$

Terminate because $|x_5 - x_4| = |-1.4525 - (1.4649)| < 0.02$

The approximation of the root is -1.4525.

14.5   Questions

Q1.   Which method, Bisection, False Position or Newton-Raphson, is the quickest to converge the root of an equation? Explain why?

Q2.   Use the Bisection method to manually determine a root for the following function:

$$F(x) = x^2 - 5 = 0$$

Q3.   Use the Bisection-based VB application provided in this chapter to determine the function:

$$F(x) = e^x - 3 = 0$$

Q4.   Use the False Position method to manually determine a root for the following function:

$$F(x) = x^2 - 3 = 0$$

Q5.   Use the False Position-based VB application provided in this chapter to determine the function:

$$F(x) = \log(x) = 0, \text{ where } x > 0$$

Chapter 15
Matrices

As discussed in Chapter 13, many engineering problems are formulated in a system of linear equations. Solving these linear equations requires a good understanding of matrix algebra or theory since matrices are used extensively in simplifying the representation of the linear equations. In this chapter we will introduce matrix algebra. The topics to be covered include matrix determinant and operations. In Chapters 17 and 18, we will discuss the implementation of matrix operations in EXCEL and MATLAB.

15.1   Matrix

A matrix is defined as a rectangular arrangement of elements in rows and columns. The elements can be numbers, variables, functions, etc.

$$[A] = [a_{ij}] = \begin{bmatrix} a_{11} & a_{12} & \cdots & a_{1j} & \cdots & a_{1m} \\ a_{21} & a_{22} & & & & \vdots \\ \vdots & & \ddots & & & \vdots \\ a_{i1} & & & a_{ij} & & a_{im} \\ \vdots & & & & \ddots & \vdots \\ a_{n1} & \cdots & \cdots & a_{nj} & \cdots & a_{nm} \end{bmatrix}$$

The above matrix A has an order of n by m. The first subscript for an element a_{ij} specifies its row position and the second subscript specifies its column position.

There are different ways of arranging elements. When elements are arranged in a single row, we call the row the row matrix. For example, a 1 x 10 row matrix can be written as:

$$[A] = [a_1, a_2, ..., a_{10}]$$

When elements are arranged in a single column, we call the column the column matrix. For example, a 5 x 1 column matrix can be written as:

$$A = \begin{bmatrix} a_1 \\ a_2 \\ a_3 \\ a_4 \\ a_5 \end{bmatrix}$$

When elements are arranged in n rows and n columns, we call the matrix a square matrix. An example of a square matrix may look like:

$$A = \begin{bmatrix} a_{11} & a_{12} & \cdots & a_{1n} \\ a_{21} & a_{22} & \cdots & a_{2n} \\ & & \ddots & \\ a_{n1} & a_{n1} & \cdots & a_{nn} \end{bmatrix}$$

When all the elements of a square matrix are zero except those along the principal diagonal positions that runs down from top left to down right, we call the matrix a diagonal matrix. For example,

$$[D] = \begin{bmatrix} d_{11} & 0 & \cdots & 0 \\ 0 & d_{22} & & \vdots \\ \vdots & & \ddots & \vdots \\ 0 & \cdots\cdots & & d_{nn} \end{bmatrix}$$

A scalar matrix is a special diagonal matrix in which all of the principal diagonal elements are equal.

$$[a] = \begin{bmatrix} a & 0 & \cdots & 0 \\ 0 & a & & \vdots \\ \vdots & & \ddots & \vdots \\ 0 & \cdots\cdots & & a \end{bmatrix}$$

A scalar matrix with diagonal elements equal to unity is a unit or identity matrix.

$$[I] = \begin{bmatrix} 1 & 0 & \cdots & 0 \\ 0 & 1 & & \vdots \\ \vdots & & \ddots & \vdots \\ 0 & \cdots\cdots & & 1 \end{bmatrix}$$

A symmetric matrix is a square matrix that satisfies $d_{ij} = d_{ji}$

$$[D] = \begin{bmatrix} 2 & 1 & 5 \\ 1 & 3 & -6 \\ 5 & -6 & 4 \end{bmatrix}$$

A skew-symmetric matrix is a square matrix such that $a_{ij} = -a_{ji}$ and the diagonal elements are zero.

$$[A] = \begin{bmatrix} 0 & 1 & 5 \\ -1 & 0 & -6 \\ -5 & 6 & 0 \end{bmatrix}$$

A matrix with all elements equal to zero is a zero or null matrix.

An upper triangular (**U**) matrix is a square matrix in which all elements below the principal diagonal elements are zero.

$$[U] = \begin{bmatrix} u_{11} & u_{12} & \cdots & u_{1n} \\ 0 & u_{22} & \cdots & u_{2n} \\ \vdots & & \ddots & \vdots \\ 0 & 0 & \cdots & u_{nn} \end{bmatrix}$$

An example of an upper triangular matrix is

$$[U] = \begin{bmatrix} 1 & 2 & 1 \\ 0 & 2 & 4 \\ 0 & 0 & -1 \end{bmatrix}$$

A unit upper triangular matrix is one in which the principal diagonal elements are equal to unity and below these diagonal elements are 0s.

$$[U] = \begin{bmatrix} 1 & u_{12} & \cdots & u_{1n} \\ 0 & 1 & \cdots & u_{2n} \\ \vdots & & \ddots & \vdots \\ 0 & 0 & \cdots & 1 \end{bmatrix}$$

A lower triangular matrix (**L**) is similar to the upper triangular except that the zero elements are those above the principal diagonal elements.

$$[L] = \begin{bmatrix} l_{11} & 0 & \cdots & 0 \\ l_{21} & l_{22} & & \vdots \\ \vdots & & \ddots & 0 \\ l_{n1} & l_{n2} & \cdots & l_{nn} \end{bmatrix}$$

An example of a lower triangular matrix is

$$[L] = \begin{bmatrix} 1 & 0 & 0 \\ 3 & 5 & 0 \\ -1 & 2 & 4 \end{bmatrix}$$

15.2   Determinants

A determinant is a scalar numerical value that represents a unique characteristic of a square matrix.

$$D = |A| = |a_{ij}| = \begin{vmatrix} a_{11} & a_{12} & \cdots & a_{1j} & \cdots & a_{1n} \\ a_{21} & a_{22} & & & & \vdots \\ \vdots & & \ddots & & & \vdots \\ a_{i1} & & & a_{ij} & & a_{in} \\ \vdots & & & & \ddots & \vdots \\ a_{n1} & \cdots & \cdots & a_{nj} & \cdots & a_{nn} \end{vmatrix}$$

Elements of a_{11}, a_{22}, ..., a_{ii}, ..., a_{nn} are the diagonal elements of the determinant.

Before we look at the value of the determinant we will introduce a few needed definitions.

Minor (Mij)

Minor (M_{ij}) is associated with element a_{ij} of a square matrix. It is defined as the determinant of the matrix whose order is n–1. For example, if we have a 4 * 4 determinant below

$$D = \begin{vmatrix} a_{11} & a_{12} & a_{13} & a_{14} \\ a_{21} & a_{22} & a_{23} & a_{24} \\ a_{31} & a_{32} & a_{33} & a_{34} \\ a_{41} & a_{42} & a_{43} & a_{44} \end{vmatrix} = \begin{vmatrix} 3 & 4 & 0 & 1 \\ 4 & 2 & 1 & 5 \\ 2 & 7 & 6 & 8 \\ 2 & 1 & 0 & 5 \end{vmatrix}$$

The minor M_{32} for element a_{32} (or 7) is formulated as:

$$M_{32} = \begin{vmatrix} a_{11} & a_{13} & a_{14} \\ a_{21} & a_{23} & a_{24} \\ a_{41} & a_{43} & a_{44} \end{vmatrix} = \begin{vmatrix} 3 & 0 & 1 \\ 4 & 1 & 5 \\ 2 & 0 & 5 \end{vmatrix}$$

Note that M_{32} is formed by eliminating the ith row and the jth column of the 4 * 4 determinant. There are a total of 16 minors within the 4 by 4 matrix. Generally speaking, an n * n matrix has a total of n^2 minors.

Cofactor (Coij)

Cofactor (Co_{ij}) is associated with element a_{ij} of a square matrix. It is defined as the minor M_{ij} of element a_{ij} with a plus or minus sign associated with the position.

$$Co_{ij} = (-1)^{i+j} M_{ij}$$

Given the below determinant,

$$D = \begin{vmatrix} a_{11} & a_{12} & a_{13} & a_{14} \\ a_{21} & a_{22} & a_{23} & a_{24} \\ a_{31} & a_{32} & a_{33} & a_{34} \\ a_{41} & a_{42} & a_{43} & a_{44} \end{vmatrix} = \begin{vmatrix} 3 & 4 & 0 & 1 \\ 4 & 2 & 1 & 5 \\ 2 & 7 & 6 & 8 \\ 2 & 1 & 0 & 5 \end{vmatrix}$$

$$Co_{32} = (-1)^{(3+2)} M_{32} = - \begin{vmatrix} a_{11} & a_{13} & a_{14} \\ a_{21} & a_{23} & a_{24} \\ a_{41} & a_{43} & a_{44} \end{vmatrix} = - \begin{vmatrix} 3 & 0 & 1 \\ 4 & 1 & 5 \\ 2 & 0 & 5 \end{vmatrix}$$

Laplace's Determinant

A determinant is the symbolic representation of an expression that yields the scalar value. It can be calculated based on the Laplace expansion by row or by column. Given the below determinant,

$$D = \begin{vmatrix} a_{11} & a_{12} & a_{13} & a_{14} \\ a_{21} & a_{22} & a_{23} & a_{24} \\ a_{31} & a_{32} & a_{33} & a_{34} \\ a_{41} & a_{42} & a_{43} & a_{44} \end{vmatrix}$$

$$D = \sum_{i=1}^{n} a_{ij} Co_{ij} \qquad \text{Expand by column j}$$

or

$$D = \sum_{j=1}^{n} a_{ij} Co_{ij} \qquad \text{Expand by row i}$$

Consider $D = \begin{vmatrix} a_{11} & a_{12} & a_{13} \\ a_{21} & a_{22} & a_{23} \\ a_{31} & a_{32} & a_{33} \end{vmatrix}$ in the expansion by the **second** row.

$$D = a_{21} Co_{21} + a_{22} Co_{22} + a_{23} Co_{23}$$

$$D = - a_{21} \begin{vmatrix} a_{12} & a_{13} \\ a_{32} & a_{33} \end{vmatrix} + a_{22} \begin{vmatrix} a_{11} & a_{13} \\ a_{31} & a_{33} \end{vmatrix} - a_{23} \begin{vmatrix} a_{11} & a_{12} \\ a_{31} & a_{32} \end{vmatrix}$$

$$D = - a_{21}(a_{12}a_{33} - a_{13}a_{32}) + a_{22}(a_{11}a_{33} - a_{31}a_{13}) - a_{23}(a_{11}a_{32} - a_{12}a_{31})$$

For example, we expand by the first column, we have

$$D = \begin{vmatrix} 3 & 2 & 1 \\ 2 & 3 & 1 \\ 1 & -4 & 1 \end{vmatrix} = 3\begin{vmatrix} 3 & 1 \\ -4 & 1 \end{vmatrix} - 2\begin{vmatrix} 2 & 1 \\ -4 & 1 \end{vmatrix} + 1\begin{vmatrix} 2 & 1 \\ 3 & 1 \end{vmatrix}$$

$$= 3(3x1 + 4x1) - 2(2x1 + 4x1) + 1(2x1 - 3x1)$$

$$= 3(7) - 2(6) - 1(1)$$

$$D = \mathbf{8}$$

Notice that the Laplace method requires the calculation of **n(n–1)(n–1)** determinants in order to evaluate an **n by n** determinant. The number of operations may become enormous for moderate or large size determinants. Considering the time-consuming nature of the Laplace method, we do not use the method in practice. Instead we calculate determinants based on their properties.

Properties of Determinants

There are totally six properties that are related to the determinant of a square matrix. Let us see these six properties one by one below:

Property 1   The value of a determinant (D) is unchanged if rows and columns are interchanged. For example,

$$D = \begin{vmatrix} 3 & 2 & 6 \\ 1 & 2 & 5 \\ 4 & 3 & 2 \end{vmatrix} = \begin{vmatrix} 3 & 1 & 4 \\ 2 & 2 & 3 \\ 6 & 5 & 2 \end{vmatrix} = -27$$

Property 2   If any two rows (or columns) of D are interchanged, only the sign of the determinant changes. For example,

$$D = \begin{vmatrix} 3 & 2 & 6 \\ 1 & 2 & 5 \\ 4 & 3 & 2 \end{vmatrix} = -27 \quad D = \begin{vmatrix} 3 & 2 & 6 \\ 4 & 3 & 2 \\ 1 & 2 & 5 \end{vmatrix} = 27 \quad D = \begin{vmatrix} 3 & 6 & 2 \\ 1 & 5 & 2 \\ 4 & 2 & 3 \end{vmatrix} = 27$$

Property 3   If the elements of any two rows (or columns) of D are equal, then D is zero. For example,

$$D = \begin{vmatrix} 3 & 2 & 6 \\ 3 & 2 & 6 \\ 4 & 3 & 2 \end{vmatrix} = 0$$

Property 4   Multiplying all elements of a row (or a column) by a constant is the same as multiplying the value of D by that constant. For example,

$$D = \begin{vmatrix} 2*3 & 2 & 6 \\ 2*1 & 2 & 5 \\ 2*4 & 3 & 2 \end{vmatrix} = 2* \begin{vmatrix} 3 & 2 & 6 \\ 1 & 2 & 5 \\ 4 & 3 & 2 \end{vmatrix} = 2*(-27) = -54$$

Property 5   If the elements of a row (or a column) are proportional to the corresponding elements of another row (or column), the value of D is zero.

For example,

$$D = \begin{vmatrix} 6 & 3 & 2 \\ 2 & 1 & 2 \\ 8 & 4 & 3 \end{vmatrix} = \begin{vmatrix} 2*3 & 3 & 2 \\ 2*1 & 1 & 2 \\ 2*4 & 4 & 3 \end{vmatrix} = 2* \begin{vmatrix} 3 & 3 & 2 \\ 1 & 1 & 2 \\ 4 & 4 & 3 \end{vmatrix} = 0$$

Property 6   The value of a determinant remains unchanged if the elements of a row (or a column) are increased by values that are equal to or proportional to the corresponding elements of another row (or column).

For example, we reduce element values of row 1 (R1) from the corresponding element values from row 2 (R2), we will have,

$$D = \begin{vmatrix} 6 & 3 & 2 \\ 2 & 0 & 2 \\ 8 & 5 & 3 \end{vmatrix} \overset{R2-R1}{=} \begin{vmatrix} 6 & 3 & 2 \\ -4 & -3 & 0 \\ 8 & 5 & 3 \end{vmatrix}$$

Property 6 allows us to manipulate rows and/or columns to reduce the array to a convenient form that will save operations in Laplace's expansion.

For example, determine the value of the determinant given below.

$$D = \begin{vmatrix} 1 & 3 & 3 & 4 \\ -1 & 1 & 1 & 1 \\ -2 & 2 & 3 & 0 \\ -1 & 1 & 1 & 3 \end{vmatrix}$$

Here, notice that if we change column 2 by adding the elements of column 1 to it (that is, C2 +C1), we will have,

$$D = \begin{vmatrix} 1 & 3 & 3 & 4 \\ -1 & 1 & 1 & 1 \\ -2 & 2 & 3 & 0 \\ -1 & 1 & 1 & 3 \end{vmatrix} \overset{C2+C1}{=} \begin{vmatrix} 1 & 4 & 3 & 4 \\ -1 & 0 & 1 & 1 \\ -2 & 0 & 3 & 0 \\ -1 & 0 & 1 & 3 \end{vmatrix} = -4 \begin{vmatrix} -1 & 1 & 1 \\ -2 & 3 & 0 \\ -1 & 1 & 3 \end{vmatrix}$$

Note that C2 is placed first. In a general term, the row or column to be operated is always placed first in an operator for equal transformation. Otherwise, the determinant is changed.

Now, if we add column 1 to column 2 and expand the determinant by the second column, we get,

$$D = -4 \begin{vmatrix} -1 & 1 & 1 \\ -2 & 3 & 0 \\ -1 & 1 & 3 \end{vmatrix} \overset{C2+C1}{=} -4 \begin{vmatrix} -1 & 0 & 1 \\ -2 & 1 & 0 \\ -1 & 0 & 3 \end{vmatrix}$$

$$= -4 \left(1 \begin{vmatrix} -1 & 1 \\ -1 & 3 \end{vmatrix} \right) = (-4) * [(-1(3) - (-1)1)]$$

$$= 8$$

We can generalize this procedure to convert the determinant array to an **upper triangular form** (sometimes called **Gauss Method**) as

$$|A| \overset{Transofrmation}{=} k|U| = k \begin{vmatrix} u_{11} & u_{12} & \cdots & u_{1n} \\ 0 & u_{22} & \cdots & u_{2n} \\ \vdots & \vdots & \ddots & \vdots \\ 0 & 0 & \cdots & u_{nn} \end{vmatrix} = k(u_{11})(u_{22})\cdots(u_{nn})$$

The value **k** is generated when we apply Property 6 and do row operations to transform |A| to |U|.

For example, given the below determinant

$$|A| = \begin{vmatrix} 1 & 4 & 2 & -1 \\ 3 & 0 & 6 & 1 \\ 1 & 0 & 4 & 5 \\ 1 & 1 & 0 & 7 \end{vmatrix}$$

Find |A| using the upper triangular method.

Solution:

First,   Use multiple of row 1 (R1 or R_1) to eliminate elements below in column 1.

(1)   If $a_{11} = 0$, interchange first row with another row and only the sign of the determinant changes.

(2)   If $a_{11} \neq 1$, factor out a_{11} and proceed.

$$|A| = \begin{vmatrix} 1 & 4 & 2 & -1 \\ 3 & 0 & 6 & 1 \\ 1 & 0 & 4 & 5 \\ 1 & 1 & 0 & 7 \end{vmatrix} \begin{matrix} \\ R_2 - 3R_1 \\ R_3 - R_1 \\ R_4 - R_1 \end{matrix} = \begin{vmatrix} 1 & 4 & 2 & -1 \\ 0 & -12 & 0 & 4 \\ 0 & -4 & 2 & 6 \\ 0 & -3 & -2 & 8 \end{vmatrix}$$

Note that the operator $R_2 - 3R_1$ reduces the element values of Row 2 by 3 times the corresponding element values of Row 1. R_2 is placed first.

Use multiples of R_2 to eliminate elements below in column 3.

$$|A| = \begin{vmatrix} 1 & 4 & 2 & -1 \\ 0 & -12 & 0 & 4 \\ 0 & -4 & 2 & 6 \\ 0 & -3 & -2 & 8 \end{vmatrix} = 4\begin{vmatrix} 1 & 4 & 2 & -1 \\ 0 & -3 & 0 & 1 \\ 0 & -4 & 2 & 6 \\ 0 & -3 & -2 & 8 \end{vmatrix} \begin{matrix} \\ \\ R3 - 4/3R2 \\ R4 - R2 \end{matrix} = 4\begin{vmatrix} 1 & 4 & 1 & -1 \\ 0 & -3 & 0 & 1 \\ 0 & 0 & 2 & 6-\dfrac{4}{3} \\ 0 & 0 & -2 & 7 \end{vmatrix}$$

Continue with similar operations working from left top diagonal until reach lower right diagonal.

$$|A| = 4\begin{vmatrix} 1 & 4 & 1 & -1 \\ 0 & -3 & 0 & 1 \\ 0 & 0 & 2 & 6-\dfrac{4}{3} \\ 0 & 0 & -2 & 7 \end{vmatrix} \begin{matrix} \\ \\ \\ R_4 + R3 \end{matrix} = 4\begin{vmatrix} 1 & 4 & 1 & -1 \\ 0 & -3 & 0 & 1 \\ 0 & 0 & 2 & 6-\dfrac{4}{3} \\ 0 & 0 & 0 & 13-\dfrac{4}{3} \end{vmatrix}$$

Expand to obtain

$$|A| = 4(1)(-3)(2)(13-\frac{4}{3}) = -280$$

Pivotal Condensation

Pivotal condensation is another method we can use to calculate a determinant. It uses Property 6 to calculate the determinant of an n x n matrix by a series of 2 x 2 determinants only, regardless of the size of the array.

Consider the below determinant of a 3 x 3 matrix. First factor out b_{ii} as shown:

$$|B| = \begin{vmatrix} b_{11} & b_{12} & b_{13} \\ b_{21} & b_{22} & b_{23} \\ b_{31} & b_{32} & b_{33} \end{vmatrix} = b_{11}\begin{vmatrix} 1 & \dfrac{b_{12}}{b_{11}} & \dfrac{b_{13}}{b_{11}} \\ b_{21} & b_{22} & b_{23} \\ b_{31} & b_{32} & b_{33} \end{vmatrix}$$

Now we use row 1 to reduce b_{21} and b_{31} to zero, and expand by column 1.

$$|B| = b_{11} \begin{vmatrix} 1 & \dfrac{b_{12}}{b_{11}} & \dfrac{b_{13}}{b_{11}} \\ 0 & b_{22} - (\dfrac{b_{12}}{b_{11}})b_{21} & b_{23} - (\dfrac{b_{13}}{b_{11}})b_{21} \\ 0 & b_{32} - (\dfrac{b_{12}}{b_{11}})b_{31} & b_{33} - (\dfrac{b_{12}}{b_{11}})b_{31} \end{vmatrix} = b_{11} \begin{vmatrix} b_{22} - (\dfrac{b_{12}}{b_{11}})b_{21} & b_{23} - (\dfrac{b_{13}}{b_{11}})b_{21} \\ b_{32} - (\dfrac{b_{12}}{b_{11}})b_{31} & b_{33} - (\dfrac{b_{12}}{b_{11}})b_{31} \end{vmatrix}$$

Now get out $\dfrac{1}{b_{11}}$ from both rows,

$$|B| = \frac{b_{11}}{b_{11}b_{11}} \begin{vmatrix} b_{11}b_{22} - b_{12}b_{21} & b_{11}b_{23} - b_{13}b_{21} \\ b_{11}b_{32} - b_{12}b_{31} & b_{11}b_{33} - b_{13}b_{31} \end{vmatrix} = \frac{1}{b_{11}} \begin{vmatrix} \begin{vmatrix} b_{11} & b_{12} \\ b_{21} & b_{22} \end{vmatrix} & \begin{vmatrix} b_{11} & b_{13} \\ b_{21} & b_{23} \end{vmatrix} \\ \begin{vmatrix} b_{11} & b_{12} \\ b_{31} & b_{32} \end{vmatrix} & \begin{vmatrix} b_{11} & b_{13} \\ b_{31} & b_{33} \end{vmatrix} \end{vmatrix}$$

In general for an n x n determinant (n > 2),

$$|B| = (b_{11})^{2-n} \begin{vmatrix} \begin{vmatrix} b_{11} & b_{12} \\ b_{21} & b_{22} \end{vmatrix} & \begin{vmatrix} b_{11} & b_{13} \\ b_{21} & b_{23} \end{vmatrix} & \cdots & \begin{vmatrix} b_{11} & b_{1n} \\ b_{21} & b_{2n} \end{vmatrix} \\ \begin{vmatrix} b_{11} & b_{12} \\ b_{31} & b_{32} \end{vmatrix} & \begin{vmatrix} b_{11} & b_{13} \\ b_{31} & b_{33} \end{vmatrix} & \cdots & \begin{vmatrix} b_{11} & b_{1n} \\ b_{31} & b_{3n} \end{vmatrix} \\ \vdots & \vdots & \ddots & \vdots \\ \begin{vmatrix} b_{11} & b_{12} \\ b_{n1} & b_{n2} \end{vmatrix} & \begin{vmatrix} b_{11} & b_{13} \\ b_{n1} & b_{n3} \end{vmatrix} & \cdots & \begin{vmatrix} b_{11} & b_{1n} \\ b_{n1} & b_{nn} \end{vmatrix} \end{vmatrix}$$

For example, find the following 4 x 4 determinant.

$$|A| = \begin{vmatrix} 1 & 4 & 2 & -1 \\ 3 & 0 & 6 & 1 \\ 1 & 0 & 4 & 5 \\ 1 & 1 & 0 & 7 \end{vmatrix} = (1)^{2-4} \begin{vmatrix} \begin{vmatrix} 1 & 4 \\ 3 & 0 \end{vmatrix} & \begin{vmatrix} 1 & 2 \\ 3 & 6 \end{vmatrix} & \begin{vmatrix} 1 & -1 \\ 3 & 1 \end{vmatrix} \\ \begin{vmatrix} 1 & 4 \\ 1 & 0 \end{vmatrix} & \begin{vmatrix} 1 & 2 \\ 1 & 4 \end{vmatrix} & \begin{vmatrix} 1 & -1 \\ 1 & 5 \end{vmatrix} \\ \begin{vmatrix} 1 & 4 \\ 1 & 1 \end{vmatrix} & \begin{vmatrix} 1 & 2 \\ 1 & 0 \end{vmatrix} & \begin{vmatrix} 1 & -1 \\ 1 & 7 \end{vmatrix} \end{vmatrix} = (1)^{-2} \begin{vmatrix} -12 & 0 & 4 \\ -4 & 2 & 6 \\ -3 & -2 & 8 \end{vmatrix}$$

$$= (1)^{-2}(12)^{-1} \begin{Vmatrix} \begin{vmatrix} -12 & 0 \\ -4 & 2 \\ -12 & 0 \\ -3 & -2 \end{vmatrix} & \begin{vmatrix} -12 & 4 \\ -4 & 6 \\ -12 & 4 \\ -3 & 8 \end{vmatrix} \end{Vmatrix} = (1)^{-2}(12)^{-1} \begin{vmatrix} -24 & -56 \\ 24 & -84 \end{vmatrix} = -280$$

15.3   Matrix Operations

Before we discuss the matrix operations, we need to define equality of matrices. Two matrices are said to be equal if and only if they are of the same order and corresponding elements in the matrices are equal.

$$[A]_{mn} = [B]_{mn} \quad \text{if} \quad a_{ij} = b_{ij} \quad \text{for all } i \text{ and } j$$

For example,

$$A = \begin{bmatrix} 1 & 2 & 3 \\ 4 & 0 & 5 \end{bmatrix} \qquad B = \begin{bmatrix} 1 & 2 & 3 \\ 4 & 0 & 5 \end{bmatrix}$$

We can say that A = B because elements in A are the same as those in B.

There are basically five matrix operations: 1) adding two matrices together, 2) subtracting one matrix from another, 3) multiplying two matrices, 4) determining the inverse of a matrix, and 5) transposing a matrix. Let us look at these operations one by one.

Add Two Matrices

Two matrices can be added if and only if two matrices are of the same order. The result is a matrix [C] that satisfies $c_{ij} = a_{ij} + b_{ij}$.

Given

$$[A] = \begin{bmatrix} 1 & 2 & 3 \\ 4 & 5 & 6 \end{bmatrix}, \quad [B] = \begin{bmatrix} 2 & 3 & 4 \\ 5 & 6 & 7 \end{bmatrix},$$

we will yield

$$[C] = \begin{bmatrix} 1 & 2 & 3 \\ 4 & 5 & 6 \end{bmatrix} + \begin{bmatrix} 2 & 3 & 4 \\ 5 & 6 & 7 \end{bmatrix} = \begin{bmatrix} 3 & 5 & 7 \\ 9 & 11 & 13 \end{bmatrix}$$

Adding matrices together follows the commutative and associative rules, that is

$$[A] + [B] = [B] + [A]$$
$$[A] + ([B] + [C]) = ([A] + [B]) + [C]$$

Subtract One Matrix from Another

We can subtract one matrix from another if and only if two matrices are of the same order. The result is a matrix [C] that satisfies $c_{ij} = a_{ij} - b_{ij}$. Given,

$$[A] = \begin{bmatrix} 1 & 2 & 3 \\ 4 & 5 & 6 \end{bmatrix}, \quad [B] = \begin{bmatrix} 2 & 3 & 4 \\ 5 & 6 & 7 \end{bmatrix},$$

we will yield

$$[C] = \begin{bmatrix} 1 & 2 & 3 \\ 4 & 5 & 6 \end{bmatrix} - \begin{bmatrix} 2 & 3 & 4 \\ 5 & 6 & 7 \end{bmatrix} = \begin{bmatrix} 1-2 & 2-3 & 3-4 \\ 4-5 & 5-6 & 6-7 \end{bmatrix} = \begin{bmatrix} -1 & -1 & -1 \\ -1 & -1 & -1 \end{bmatrix}$$

Multiply Two Matrices

There are two types of multiplication included in matrix operations: scale matrix multiplication and matrix product. Scale matrix multiplication is defined to multiply each element of a matrix by a scalar quantity. In general,

$$k[A] = [k\, a_{ij}]$$

For example, $3\begin{bmatrix} 1 & 2 & 3 \\ 3 & 0 & 5 \\ 5 & 6 & 7 \end{bmatrix} = \begin{bmatrix} 3 & 6 & 9 \\ 9 & 0 & 15 \\ 15 & 18 & 21 \end{bmatrix}$

It is noted that when you move 3 into $\begin{bmatrix} 1 & 2 & 3 \\ 3 & 0 & 5 \\ 5 & 6 & 7 \end{bmatrix}$, you multiply 3 to each element in the matrix.

There are two types of matrix product: dot product and cross product. Dot product requires two matrices to be of same dimension. The result of a dot product is a matrix that satisfies $c_{ij} = a_{ij} * b_{ij}$. Give the two below matrices,

$$A = \begin{bmatrix} 1 & 2 & 3 & 0 \\ 2 & 3 & 1 & 4 \\ 3 & 5 & 2 & 6 \end{bmatrix} \qquad B = \begin{bmatrix} 2 & 4 & 6 & 1 \\ 0 & 4 & 1 & 3 \\ 1 & 1 & 2 & 1 \end{bmatrix}$$

The dot product of the two matrices is

$$C = A \text{ dot } B \quad = \begin{bmatrix} 1*2 & 2*4 & 3*6 & 0*1 \\ 2*0 & 3*4 & 1*1 & 4*3 \\ 3*1 & 5*1 & 2*2 & 6*1 \end{bmatrix}$$

$$= \begin{bmatrix} 2 & 8 & 18 & 0 \\ 0 & 12 & 1 & 12 \\ 3 & 5 & 4 & 6 \end{bmatrix}$$

A cross product requires two matrices to be conformable, that is, the number of columns in the first matrix should be the same as the number of rows in the second matrix. If [C] is the cross product of two matrices [A] and [B], thus

$$\underset{mxp}{[C]} = \underset{mxn}{[A]} \underset{nxp}{[B]}$$

It is noted that $\underset{nxp}{[B]}\underset{mxn}{[A]}$ is not possible since the number of columns in [B] and the number of rows in [A] are not the same (p ≠ m).

The product $\underset{mxp}{[C]} = \underset{mxn}{[A]}\underset{nxp}{[B]}$ is defined, where $c_{ij} = \sum_{k=1}^{n} a_{ik} b_{kj}$.

For example,

Given $[A] = \begin{bmatrix} a_{11} & a_{12} & a_{13} \\ a_{21} & a_{22} & a_{23} \end{bmatrix}$ and $[B] = \begin{bmatrix} b_{11} & b_{12} \\ b_{21} & b_{22} \\ b_{31} & b_{32} \end{bmatrix}$, we form the product [C] = [A][B]

Solution: $[C]=[A][B]=\begin{bmatrix} (a_{11}b_{11}+a_{12}b_{21}+a_{13}b_{31}) & (a_{11}b_{12}+a_{12}b_{22}+a_{13}b_{32}) \\ (a_{21}b_{11}+a_{22}b_{21}+a_{23}b_{31}) & (a_{21}b_{12}+a_{22}b_{22}+a_{23}b_{32}) \end{bmatrix}$

It is convenient and instructive to place the matrices as shown below for hand calculations.

$$\begin{bmatrix} b_{11} & b_{12} \\ b_{21} & b_{22} \\ b_{31} & b_{32} \end{bmatrix}$$

$$\begin{bmatrix} a_{11} & a_{12} & a_{13} \\ a_{21} & a_{22} & a_{23} \end{bmatrix} \begin{bmatrix} c_{11} & c_{12} \\ c_{21} & c_{22} \end{bmatrix}$$

For example,

$$\begin{Bmatrix} 0 \\ 4\downarrow \\ 1 \end{Bmatrix} \qquad \text{and} \qquad \begin{bmatrix} 1 & 0 & 3 \\ 1 & 1 & 2 \end{bmatrix}$$

$$\begin{bmatrix} 1 & 1 & 3 \end{bmatrix} 7 \qquad \qquad \begin{bmatrix} 1 & 0 \\ 0 & 2 \end{bmatrix}\begin{bmatrix} 1 & 0 & 3 \\ 2 & 2 & 4 \end{bmatrix}$$

In general, $[A][B] \neq [B][A]$,   non-commutative property.

In fact, even when the two cross products are conformable this inequality is also true. For example,

$$[C][D]=\begin{bmatrix} 1 & 1 \\ 1 & 1 \end{bmatrix}\begin{bmatrix} 1 & -1 \\ 1 & -1 \end{bmatrix} = \begin{bmatrix} 2 & -2 \\ 2 & -2 \end{bmatrix}, \text{ but } [D][C]=\begin{bmatrix} 1 & -1 \\ 1 & -1 \end{bmatrix}\begin{bmatrix} 1 & 1 \\ 1 & 1 \end{bmatrix} = \begin{bmatrix} 0 & 0 \\ 0 & 0 \end{bmatrix}$$

Matrix multiplication follows the associative and distributive rules. For example,

$$([A][B])[C] = [A]([B][C])$$
$$[A]([B] + [C]) = [A][B] + [A][C]$$

In general: $[I][A] = [A] = [A][I]$
$$[0][A] = [0] = [A][0]$$

When [A][B] = [0], it does not imply that either of [A] and/or [B] are [0].

Transpose a Matrix

The transpose of a matrix [A] is formed by interchanging the rows for the columns of [A] and is denoted as $[A]^T$ or $[A]'$. For example, if we have a matrix below,

$$[A] = \begin{bmatrix} 2 & 0 & 2 \\ 3 & 5 & 8 \end{bmatrix}$$

The transpose of the matrix is

$$[A]^T = \begin{bmatrix} 2 & 3 \\ 0 & 5 \\ 2 & 8 \end{bmatrix}$$

A transposed matrix has the following properties:

- $([A] + [B])^T = [A]^T + [B]^T$
- $(k [A])^T = k [A]^T$
- $([A][B])^T = [B]^T [A]^T$

For example, if we have $[A] = \begin{bmatrix} 3 & 1 \\ 1 & 0 \end{bmatrix}$ and $[B] = \begin{bmatrix} 2 & 1 \\ 1 & 1 \end{bmatrix}$

$$([A][B])^T = (\begin{bmatrix} 3 & 1 \\ 1 & 0 \end{bmatrix} * \begin{bmatrix} 2 & 1 \\ 1 & 1 \end{bmatrix})^T = \begin{bmatrix} 7 & 4 \\ 2 & 1 \end{bmatrix}^T = \begin{bmatrix} 7 & 2 \\ 4 & 1 \end{bmatrix}$$

$$([A][B])^T = [B]^T [A]^T = \begin{bmatrix} 2 & 1 \\ 1 & 1 \end{bmatrix}\begin{bmatrix} 3 & 1 \\ 1 & 0 \end{bmatrix} = \begin{bmatrix} 7 & 2 \\ 4 & 2 \end{bmatrix}$$

Get the Inverse of a Matrix

Matrix division is not defined, but the operation similar to the division of two numerical values is called *inversion* or *inverse of a matrix*.

Consider a scalar equation $a\,x = b$

x can be obtained by multiplying $\dfrac{1}{a}$, that yields,

$$\frac{1}{a}.ax = \frac{1}{a}.b$$

or $x = \dfrac{1}{a}.b = a^{-1}.b$

Similarly, the matrix inverse ($[A]^{-1}$) is defined by,

$$[A]^{-1}[A] = [I] = [A][A]^{-1}$$

Assume we have $[A][x] = [B]$, we can multiply $[A]^{-1}$ on both side, then we can get

$$[A]^{-1}[A]\,[x] = [x] = [A]^{-1}[B]$$

The *Classical Inverse* of a matrix is defined as:

$$[A]^{-1} = \frac{(Co[A])^T}{|A|}$$

Where $(Co[A])^T$ - Transpose of the cofactor matrix of [A]. This is a
                                    matrix of same size as [A] whose elements are the
                                    element cofactors.

                $|A|$ - Determinant of matrix [A]

Example:

Given $[S] = \begin{bmatrix} 2 & 1 & 0 \\ 0 & 1 & 2 \\ 1 & 0 & 1 \end{bmatrix}$, find the inverse of [S] and show that it is indeed the inverse of

[S].

Solution: $|S| = 4$

$$Co[S] = \begin{bmatrix} \begin{vmatrix} 1 & 2 \\ 0 & 1 \end{vmatrix} & -\begin{vmatrix} 0 & 2 \\ 1 & 1 \end{vmatrix} & \begin{vmatrix} 0 & 1 \\ 1 & 0 \end{vmatrix} \\ -\begin{vmatrix} 1 & 0 \\ 0 & 1 \end{vmatrix} & \begin{vmatrix} 2 & 0 \\ 1 & 1 \end{vmatrix} & -\begin{vmatrix} 2 & 1 \\ 1 & 0 \end{vmatrix} \\ \begin{vmatrix} 1 & 0 \\ 1 & 2 \end{vmatrix} & -\begin{vmatrix} 2 & 0 \\ 0 & 2 \end{vmatrix} & \begin{vmatrix} 2 & 1 \\ 0 & 1 \end{vmatrix} \end{bmatrix} = \begin{bmatrix} 1 & 2 & -1 \\ -1 & 2 & 1 \\ 2 & -4 & 2 \end{bmatrix}$$

$$(Co[S])^{T} = \begin{bmatrix} 1 & -1 & 2 \\ 2 & 2 & -4 \\ -1 & 1 & 2 \end{bmatrix}$$

thus, $\qquad [S]^{-1} = \dfrac{1}{4}\begin{bmatrix} 1 & -1 & 2 \\ 2 & 2 & -4 \\ -1 & 1 & 2 \end{bmatrix}$

Now, if this is the inverse then $[S]^{-1}[S]$ must equal $[I]$

$$\frac{1}{4}\begin{bmatrix} 1 & -1 & 2 \\ 2 & 2 & -4 \\ -1 & 1 & 2 \end{bmatrix}\begin{bmatrix} 2 & 1 & 0 \\ 0 & 1 & 2 \\ 1 & 0 & 1 \end{bmatrix} = \begin{bmatrix} 1 & 0 & 0 \\ 0 & 1 & 0 \\ 0 & 0 & 1 \end{bmatrix} = [I] \quad \textit{Check!}$$

15.4   Questions

Q1.   Given the following matrices:

$$A = \begin{bmatrix} 1 & 1 & 3 \\ 5 & 2 & 1 \\ 2 & 3 & 1 \end{bmatrix} \quad B = \begin{bmatrix} 2 & 3 & 5 \\ 3 & 1 & -1 \\ 1 & 3 & 4 \end{bmatrix} \quad C = \begin{bmatrix} 2 & 1 \\ 3 & 4 \\ 2 & 5 \end{bmatrix} \quad D = \begin{bmatrix} 1 & 1 & 1 \\ 1 & 3 & 2 \\ 1 & 2 & 5 \end{bmatrix}$$

Determine: A+ B, B+ A, B+ C, B-A, A – C, AC and BC, CA
Calculate AB and BA and Demonstrate AB ≠ BA
Show that $(AB)^T = B^T A^T$

Determine $[D]^{-1}$ and show that it is the inverse by demonstrating $[D]^{-1}[D] = [I]$

Q2.   How many determinant properties do we discussed in this chapter?

Q3.   True-False Questions (Hint: Answer questions using properties of determinant)

a) $\begin{vmatrix} 2 & 3 & 4 \\ 4 & 1 & 2 \\ 6 & 5 & 3 \end{vmatrix} = \begin{vmatrix} 2 & 4 & 6 \\ 3 & 1 & 5 \\ 4 & 2 & 3 \end{vmatrix}$ (*True   or   False*)

b) $\begin{vmatrix} 2 & 3 & 4 \\ 4 & 1 & 2 \\ 6 & 5 & 3 \end{vmatrix} = \begin{vmatrix} 4 & 1 & 2 \\ 2 & 3 & 4 \\ 6 & 5 & 3 \end{vmatrix}$ (*True   or   False*)

c) $\begin{vmatrix} 2 & 3 & 4 \\ 6 & 9 & 12 \\ 65 & 1 & 2 \end{vmatrix} = 0$ (*True   or   False*)

d) $\begin{vmatrix} 4 & 6 & 8 \\ 2 & 3 & 4 \\ 65 & 1 & 2 \end{vmatrix} = 2 * \begin{vmatrix} 2 & 3 & 4 \\ 2 & 3 & 4 \\ 65 & 1 & 2 \end{vmatrix}$ (*True   or   False*)

e) $\begin{vmatrix} 4 & 1 & 2 \\ 2 & 3 & 4 \\ 65 & 1 & 2 \end{vmatrix} = \begin{vmatrix} 2 & -2 & -2 \\ 2 & 3 & 4 \\ 65 & 1 & 2 \end{vmatrix}$ (*True   or   False*)

Q4.   Determine and verify the inverse of the following matrix

$$A = \begin{bmatrix} 1 & 1 & 1 \\ 1 & 3 & 2 \\ 1 & 2 & 5 \end{bmatrix}$$

Q5.   Evaluate the following determinant

$$\det[A] = \begin{vmatrix} 3 & 0 & 1 & 2 \\ 1 & 1 & 0 & 2 \\ 2 & -1 & 2 & 1 \\ 3 & -1 & 4 & 1 \end{vmatrix}$$

Chapter 16
Systems of Linear Equations

With a good understanding of matrix algebra, we will describe systems of linear equations in this chapter. We will cover the concepts and principals of the numerical methods used for solving linear equations simultaneously. In Chapters 17 and 18, we will discuss the implementation of these numerical methods in EXCEL and MATLAB.

16.1   Linear Equations

Simultaneous linear algebraic equations can be formulated as follows:

$$
\begin{aligned}
a_{11}x_1 + a_{12}x_2 + a_{13}x_3 + \ldots + a_{1n}x_n &= b_1 \\
a_{21}x_1 + a_{22}x_2 + a_{23}x_3 + \ldots + a_{2n}x_n &= b_2 \\
&\vdots \\
a_{n1}x_1 + a_{n2}x_2 + a_{n3}x_3 + \ldots + a_{nn}x_n &= b_n
\end{aligned}
$$

Where a_{ij} is the constant coefficient and b_i is the constant.

The above linear equations can also be written in the following matrix form:

$$
\begin{bmatrix}
a_{11} & a_{12} & \cdots & a_{1j} & \cdots & a_{1n} \\
a_{21} & a_{22} & & & & \vdots \\
\vdots & & \ddots & & & \vdots \\
a_{i1} & & & a_{ij} & & a_{in} \\
\vdots & & & & \ddots & \vdots \\
a_{n1} & \cdots & \cdots & a_{nj} & \cdots & a_{nn}
\end{bmatrix}
\begin{bmatrix}
x_1 \\ x_1 \\ \vdots \\ \vdots \\ \vdots \\ x_n
\end{bmatrix}
=
\begin{bmatrix}
b_1 \\ b_2 \\ \vdots \\ \vdots \\ \vdots \\ b_n
\end{bmatrix}
$$

Or $[A][X] = [B]$

How to solve these linear equations? A naïve thinking of solving them is to divide both $[A][X]$ and $[B]$ by $[A]$ and get the values for $[x]$. However, such division is not possible in matrix algebra. We should consider the nature of matrices when we solve the problem.

There are two basic categories of methods used to solve the linear equations:

1)   "Exact" methods

The "Exact" solution methods use a definite number of operations to produce exact solutions. With the advent of powerful, computers, these methods are the most commonly used one.

2)   Iteration methods

This group of methods approaches the exact solution through an iterative process of approximation. The number of steps for approximation is dependent on accuracy required. These methods are more likely to be used when limited computing capacity is available.

16.2   "Exact" Methods

Methods that fall in this category include 1) direct inverse method, 2) Cramer method, 3) various elimination Methods. The most efficient elimination methods consist of Gaussian Elimination Method, Jordan's Modification to Gaussian elimination (Gauss-Jordan), Crout's Method, and Choleski's Method (or Square Root Method).

16.2.1   Direct Inverse Method

Direct inverse method is commonly used for small systems since the inverse calculation is efficient. Given the below system of linear equations

$$[A][X] = [B]$$

The solution to the system is

$$[X] = [A]^{-1}[B]$$

For example, solve the following problem of form [A][X] =[B]

$$
\begin{bmatrix} 1 & -3 & 1 \\ 1 & 2 & -6 \\ 2 & -1 & 3 \end{bmatrix}
\begin{Bmatrix} x_1 \\ x_2 \\ x_3 \end{Bmatrix}
=
\begin{Bmatrix} 2 \\ 3 \\ 1 \end{Bmatrix}
$$

We will have

$$
\begin{bmatrix} x_1 \\ x_2 \\ x_3 \end{bmatrix}
=
\begin{bmatrix} 1 & -3 & 1 \\ 1 & 2 & -6 \\ 2 & -1 & 3 \end{bmatrix}^{-1}
\begin{bmatrix} 2 \\ 3 \\ 1 \end{bmatrix}
=
\begin{bmatrix} 1 \\ -0.5 \\ -0.5 \end{bmatrix}
$$

16.2.2 Cramer Method

The Cramer method is a simple method that uses determinants to find the solution. This method is applicable for small systems due to its inefficiencies in evaluating determinants.

Given a system of linear equations below

$$[A][X] = [B]$$

Where

$$
[A] = [a_{ij}] =
\begin{bmatrix}
a_{11} & a_{12} & \cdots & a_{1j} & \cdots & a_{1n} \\
a_{21} & a_{22} & & & & \vdots \\
\vdots & & \ddots & & & \vdots \\
a_{i1} & & & a_{ij} & & a_{in} \\
\vdots & & & & \ddots & \vdots \\
a_{n1} & \cdots & \cdots & a_{nj} & \cdots & a_{nn}
\end{bmatrix}
$$

[A] is the square matrix of coefficients. These coefficients represent the physical parameters that control a system.

$$[B] = \begin{Bmatrix} b_1 \\ b_2 \\ \vdots \\ b_n \end{Bmatrix}$$ It is the right hand side (RHS) vector of constants. These values represent the "driving forces" that will generate a solution [x].

$$[X] = \begin{Bmatrix} x_1 \\ x_2 \\ \vdots \\ x_n \end{Bmatrix}$$ It is the vector of unknowns that represent a solution to the system.

Note that the notation $[A_{bn}]$ is a matrix where the nth column of [A] is replaced by the RHS vector [B].

$$[A_{b1}] = \begin{bmatrix} b_1 & a_{12} & \cdots & a_{1n} \\ b_2 & a_{22} & & a_{2n} \\ \vdots & \vdots & \ddots & \vdots \\ b_2 & a_{2n} & \cdots & a_{nn} \end{bmatrix}, \quad [A_{b2}] = \begin{bmatrix} a_{11} & b_1 & \cdots & a_{1n} \\ a_{21} & b_2 & & a_{2n} \\ \vdots & \vdots & \ddots & \vdots \\ a_{n1} & b_n & \cdots & a_{nn} \end{bmatrix}, \cdots, \text{etc.}$$

Cramer's Rule defines the solution values of x_i as:

$$x_1 = \frac{|A_{b1}|}{|A|}, \quad x_2 = \frac{|A_{b2}|}{|A|}, \quad \cdots, \quad x_i = \frac{|A_{bi}|}{|A|}$$

Note that there is no solution when $|A| = 0$.

For example, solve the following problem of form [A][x] =[b]

$$\begin{bmatrix} 1 & -3 & 1 \\ 1 & 2 & -6 \\ 2 & -1 & 3 \end{bmatrix} \begin{Bmatrix} x_1 \\ x_2 \\ x_3 \end{Bmatrix} = \begin{Bmatrix} 2 \\ 3 \\ 1 \end{Bmatrix}$$

$$\det[A] = \begin{vmatrix} 1 & -3 & 1 \\ 1 & 2 & -6 \\ 2 & -1 & 3 \end{vmatrix} = 40$$

$$\det[A_{b1}] = \begin{vmatrix} 2 & -3 & 1 \\ 3 & 2 & -6 \\ 1 & -1 & 3 \end{vmatrix} = 40$$

$$\det[A_{b2}] = \begin{vmatrix} 1 & 2 & 1 \\ 1 & 3 & -6 \\ 2 & 1 & 3 \end{vmatrix} = -20$$

$$\det[A_{b3}] = \begin{vmatrix} 1 & -3 & 2 \\ 1 & 2 & 3 \\ 2 & -1 & 1 \end{vmatrix} = -20$$

thus,

$$x_1 = \frac{40}{40} = 1, \ x_2 = \frac{-20}{40} = -0.5, \ x_3 = \frac{-20}{40} = -0.5$$

$$\begin{Bmatrix} x_1 \\ x_2 \\ x_3 \end{Bmatrix} = \begin{Bmatrix} 1 \\ -0.5 \\ -0.5 \end{Bmatrix}, \text{ as a check } \begin{bmatrix} 1 & -3 & 1 \\ 1 & 2 & -6 \\ 2 & -1 & 3 \end{bmatrix} \begin{Bmatrix} 1 \\ -0.5 \\ -0.5 \end{Bmatrix} = \begin{Bmatrix} 2 \\ 3 \\ 1 \end{Bmatrix}$$

16.2.3 Elimination Methods

Elimination methods reduce the system of linear equations to an equivalent but simpler system that leads to the solution easily.

Gaussian Elimination

This method transforms the system into an upper triangular matrix form from which a solution can readily be obtained by a "back substitution". Symbolically this method can be represented as:

$$[A][X] = [B] \qquad \text{transform to} \qquad [U][X] = [B']$$

Where [U] is an upper triangular or a unit upper triangular matrix

We will consider a 4 x 4 system to show the general process.

$$a_{11}x_1 + a_{12}x_2 + a_{13}x_3 + a_{14}x_4 = b_1 \quad \text{eq (1)}$$
$$a_{21}x_1 + a_{22}x_2 + a_{23}x_3 + a_{24}x_4 = b_2 \quad \text{eq (2)}$$
$$a_{31}x_1 + a_{32}x_2 + a_{33}x_3 + a_{34}x_4 = b_3 \quad \text{eq (3)}$$
$$a_{41}x_1 + a_{42}x_2 + a_{43}x_3 + a_{44}x_4 = b_4 \quad \text{eq (4)}$$

If $a_{11} \neq 0$, divide the first equation by a_{11}. If $a_{11} = 0$, we look at the first column coefficients of other equations, select an equation whose first column coefficient is not zero, and swap the equation with the first equation. This process is called *partial pivoting*.

Now we get,

$$x_1 + a_{12}^1 x_2 + a_{13}^1 x_3 + a_{14}^1 = b_1^1$$

We now multiply this equation by a_{21} and subtract from eq (2). Similarly we multiply it by a_{31} and a_{41} and subtract the result from eq (3) and eq (4), respectively. The resulting equations are:

$$x_1 + a_{12}^1 x_2 + a_{13}^1 x_3 + a_{14}^1 x_4 = b_1^1 \quad \text{eq (1)}$$
$$a_{22}^1 x_2 + a_{23}^1 x_3 + a_{24}^1 x_4 = b_2^1 \quad \text{eq (2)}$$
$$a_{32}^1 x_2 + a_{33}^1 x_3 + a_{34}^1 x_4 = b_3^1 \quad \text{eq (3)}$$
$$a_{42}^1 x_2 + a_{43}^1 x_3 + a_{44}^1 x_4 = b_4^1 \quad \text{eq (4)}$$

Now check that a_{22}^1 is not zero (again use pivoting if it is) and divide eq (2) by a_{22}^1. Multiply the result by a_{32}^1 and a_{42}^1, and subtract the result from equation (3) and (4), respectively. We will get:

$$x_1 + a_{12}^1 x_2 + a_{13}^1 x_3 + a_{14}^1 x_4 = b_1^1 \quad \text{eq (1)}$$
$$x_2 + a_{23}^2 x_3 + a_{24}^2 x_4 = b_2^2 \quad \text{eq (2)}$$
$$a_{33}^2 x_3 + a_{34}^2 x_4 = b_3^2 \quad \text{eq (3)}$$
$$a_{43}^2 x_3 + a_{44}^2 x_4 = b_4^2 \quad \text{eq (4)}$$

Following the same approach and divide eq (4) by a^4_{33} to obtain the value of x_4, we get the following final triangular form:

$$x_1 + a^1_{12}x_2 + a^1_{13}x_3 + a^1_{14}x_4 = b^1_1 \quad \text{eq (1)}$$
$$x_2 + a^2_{23}x_3 + a^2_{24}x_4 = b^2_2 \quad \text{eq (2)}$$
$$x_3 + a^3_{34}x_4 = b^3_3 \quad \text{eq (3)}$$
$$x_4 = b^4_4 \quad \text{eq (4)}$$

The "back-substitution" process involves:

1)   substitute x_4 into eq (3) and solve for x_3
2)   substitute x_4 and x_3 into eq (2) and solve for x_2
3)   substitute x_4, x_3, x_2 into eq(1) and solve for x_1

We get,

$$x_3 = b^3_3 - a^3_{34}x_4$$
$$x_2 = b^2_2 - a^2_{23}x_3 - a^2_{24}x_4$$
$$x_1 = b^1_1 - a^1_{12}x_2 - a^1_{13}x_3 - a^1_{14}x_4$$

In matrix form we have performed the transformation:

$$\begin{bmatrix} a_{11} & a_{12} & a_{13} & a_{14} \\ a_{21} & a_{22} & a_{23} & a_{24} \\ a_{31} & a_{32} & a_{33} & a_{34} \\ a_{41} & a_{42} & a_{43} & a_{44} \end{bmatrix} \begin{bmatrix} x_1 \\ x_2 \\ x_3 \\ x_4 \end{bmatrix} = \begin{bmatrix} b_1 \\ b_2 \\ b_3 \\ b_4 \end{bmatrix} \xrightarrow{\text{transform}} \begin{bmatrix} 1 & a^1_{12} & a^1_{13} & a^1_{14} \\ 0 & 1 & a^2_{23} & a^2_{24} \\ 0 & 0 & 1 & a^3_{34} \\ 0 & 0 & 0 & 1 \end{bmatrix} \begin{bmatrix} x_1 \\ x_2 \\ x_3 \\ x_4 \end{bmatrix} = \begin{bmatrix} b^1_1 \\ b^2_2 \\ b^3_3 \\ b^4_4 \end{bmatrix}$$

For example, consider the following system and solve by Gauss Elimination and back substitution:

$$2x_1 - 3x_2 + 2x_3 - x_4 = 4 \quad R_1$$
$$x_1 + 2x_2 - 3x_3 + 2x_4 = 3 \quad R_2$$
$$x_1 - x_2 + 3x_3 - x_4 = 1 \quad R_3$$
$$x_1 - x_2 + x_3 - x_4 = 1 \quad R_4$$

Solution: First step elimination

$$x_1 - 1.5x_2 + x_3 - 0.5x_4 = 2 \qquad R_1/2$$
$$3.5x_2 - 4x_3 + 2.5x_4 = 1 \qquad R_2 - 1*R_1$$
$$0.5x_2 + 2x_3 - 0.5x_4 = -1 \quad R_3 - 1*R_1$$
$$0.5x_2 + 0x_3 - 0.5x_4 = -1 \quad R_4 - 1*R_1$$

Second step elimination

$$x_1 - 1.5x_2 + x_3 - 0.5x_4 = 2$$
$$x_2 - 1.143x_3 + 0.714x_4 = 0.286 \qquad R_2/3.5$$
$$2.571x_3 - 0.857x_4 = -1.143 \qquad R_3 - 0.5*R_2$$
$$0.571x_3 - 0.857x_4 = -1.143 \qquad R_4 - 0.5*R_2$$

Third step elimination

$$x_1 - 1.5x_2 + x_3 - 0.5x_4 = 2$$
$$x_2 - 1.143x_3 + 0.714x_4 = 0.286$$
$$x_3 - 0.333x_4 = -0.444 \qquad R_3/2.571$$
$$-0.667x_4 = -0.889 \qquad R_4 - 0.571*R_3$$

Back substitution yields

$$x_4 = -0.889/-0.667 = 1.333$$
$$x_3 = -0.444 + 0.333*1.333 = 0$$
$$x_2 = 0.286 + 1.143*0.000 - 0.714*1.333 = -0.665$$
$$x_1 = 2 + 1.5*(-0.665) - 0.000 + 0.5*1.333 = 1.668$$

The matrix transformation in this case was

$$\begin{bmatrix} 2 & -3 & 2 & -1 \\ 1 & 2 & -3 & 2 \\ 1 & -1 & 3 & -1 \\ 1 & -1 & 1 & -1 \end{bmatrix} \begin{bmatrix} x_1 \\ x_2 \\ x_3 \\ x_4 \end{bmatrix} = \begin{bmatrix} 4 \\ 3 \\ 1 \\ 1 \end{bmatrix} \xrightarrow{\text{transform}} \begin{bmatrix} 1 & -1.5 & 1 & -0.5 \\ 0 & 1 & -1.143 & 0.714 \\ 0 & 0 & 1 & -0.333 \\ 0 & 0 & 0 & 1 \end{bmatrix} \begin{bmatrix} x_1 \\ x_2 \\ x_3 \\ x_4 \end{bmatrix} = \begin{bmatrix} 2 \\ 0.286 \\ -0.444 \\ 1.333 \end{bmatrix}$$

$$\begin{bmatrix} x_1 \\ x_2 \\ x_3 \\ x_4 \end{bmatrix} = \begin{bmatrix} 1.668 \\ -0.665 \\ 0 \\ 1.333 \end{bmatrix}$$

As you can see, the process is not easy to follow. In practice, we use a more compact, computer-oriented format to form the augmented matrix and find the solution.

For the above example, the compact format is as follows:

$$[A \vdots B] = \begin{bmatrix} 2 & -3 & 2 & -1 & \bigm| & 4 \\ 1 & 2 & -3 & 2 & \bigm| & 3 \\ 1 & -1 & 3 & -1 & \bigm| & 1 \\ 1 & -1 & 1 & -1 & \bigm| & 1 \end{bmatrix}$$

$$\begin{bmatrix} 1 & -1.5 & 1 & -0.5 & \bigm| & 2 \\ 0 & 3.5 & -4 & 2.5 & \bigm| & 1 \\ 0 & 0.5 & 2 & -0.5 & \bigm| & -1 \\ 0 & 0.5 & 0 & -0.5 & \bigm| & -1 \end{bmatrix} \begin{matrix} \\ R_2 - R_1 \\ R_3 - R_1 \\ R_4 - R_1 \end{matrix}$$

$$\begin{bmatrix} 1 & -1.5 & 1 & -0.5 & \bigm| & 2 \\ 0 & 1 & -1.143 & 0.714 & \bigm| & 0.286 \\ 0 & 0 & 2.571 & -0.857 & \bigm| & -1.143 \\ 0 & 0 & 0.571 & -0.857 & \bigm| & -1.143 \end{bmatrix} \begin{matrix} \\ R_2 / 3.5 \\ R_3 - R_2 * 0.5 \\ R_4 - R_2 * 0.5 \end{matrix}$$

$$\begin{bmatrix} 1 & -1.5 & 1 & -0.5 & \bigm| & 2 \\ 0 & 1 & -1.143 & 0.714 & \bigm| & 0.286 \\ 0 & 0 & 1 & -0.333 & \bigm| & -0.444 \\ 0 & 0 & 0 & 1 & \bigm| & 1.333 \end{bmatrix} \begin{matrix} \\ \\ R_3 / 2.571 \\ R_4 - R_2 * 0.571; R_4 /(-0.667) \end{matrix}$$

Back-substituting for each RHS column yields

$$\begin{bmatrix} x_1 \\ x_2 \\ x_3 \\ x_4 \end{bmatrix} = \begin{bmatrix} 1.668 \\ -0.665 \\ 0 \\ 1.333 \end{bmatrix}$$

Gauss-Jordan Elimination

This method is the same as Gauss but involves eliminations both above and below the principal diagonal elements. This process can be conveniently performed on an "augmented" matrix formed from the original [A] matrix with the RHS added as an $(n+1)^{st}$ column.

$$\begin{bmatrix} a_{11} & a_{12} & \cdots & a_{1n} & b_1 \\ a_{21} & a_{22} & \cdots & a_{2n} & b_2 \\ \cdots & & \ddots & \vdots & \vdots \\ a_{n1} & a_{n2} & \cdots & a_{nn} & b_n \end{bmatrix} \xrightarrow{\text{transform}} \begin{bmatrix} 1 & 0 & \cdots & 0 & x_1 \\ 0 & 1 & & 0 & x_2 \\ \vdots & & \ddots & \vdots & \vdots \\ 0 & 0 & \cdots & 1 & x_n \end{bmatrix}$$

For example,

$$\begin{bmatrix} 1 & -3 & 1 \\ 1 & 2 & -6 \\ 2 & -1 & 3 \end{bmatrix} \begin{Bmatrix} x_1 \\ x_2 \\ x_3 \end{Bmatrix} = \begin{Bmatrix} 2 \\ 3 \\ 1 \end{Bmatrix}$$

Form an augmented matrix - add 4th column of RHS

$$\begin{bmatrix} 1 & -3 & 1 & 2 \\ 1 & 2 & -6 & 3 \\ 2 & -1 & 3 & 1 \end{bmatrix} \Rightarrow \begin{bmatrix} 1 & -3 & 1 & 2 \\ 0 & 5 & -7 & 1 \\ 0 & 5 & 1 & -3 \end{bmatrix} \begin{matrix} R_1 * 1 \\ R_2 - 1 * R_1 \\ R_3 - 2 * R_1 \end{matrix}$$

$$\Rightarrow \begin{bmatrix} 1 & -3 & 1 & 2 \\ 0 & 5 & -7 & 1 \\ 0 & 0 & 8 & -4 \end{bmatrix} \begin{matrix} \\ R_2 \\ R_3 - R_2 \end{matrix} \Rightarrow \begin{bmatrix} 1 & 0 & 0 & 1 \\ 0 & 1 & 0 & -0.5 \\ 0 & 0 & 1 & -0.5 \end{bmatrix} \begin{matrix} R_1 + 3*R_2 - R_3 \\ (R_2 + 7*R_3)/5 \\ R_3 / 8 \end{matrix}$$

$$\text{or} \begin{bmatrix} 1 & 0 & 0 \\ 0 & 1 & 0 \\ 0 & 0 & 1 \end{bmatrix} \begin{Bmatrix} x_1 \\ x_2 \\ x_3 \end{Bmatrix} = \begin{Bmatrix} 1 \\ -0.50 \\ -0.50 \end{Bmatrix} = \begin{Bmatrix} x_1 \\ x_2 \\ x_3 \end{Bmatrix} \quad \text{Answer}$$

Notice that in this process, the solution is obtained directly from the last column without back substitution.

When we transform the original matrix [A] into an identity [I] and operate on an identity matrix [I] at the same time (in augmented matrix form), the transformed identity matrix will be the inverse of the original matrix, or

$$\left[A \vdots I \right] \xrightarrow{\ transform\ } \left[I \vdots A^{-1} \right]$$

For example,

$$\left[A \vdots I \right] = \begin{bmatrix} 1 & -3 & 1 & 1 & 0 & 0 \\ 1 & 2 & -6 & 0 & 1 & 0 \\ 2 & -1 & 3 & 0 & 0 & 1 \end{bmatrix} \xrightarrow{\ transform\ } \begin{bmatrix} 1 & 0 & 0 & 0 & 0.2 & 0.4 \\ 0 & 1 & 0 & -0.375 & 0.025 & 0.175 \\ 0 & 0 & 1 & -0.125 & -0.125 & 0.125 \end{bmatrix}$$

We have,

$$A^{-1} = \begin{bmatrix} 0 & 0.2 & 0.4 \\ -0.375 & 0.025 & 0.175 \\ -0.125 & -0.125 & 0.125 \end{bmatrix}$$

Note that with the inverse matrix, we can form the solution to the system [A][X]=[B] as

$$[X] = [A]^{-1}[B]$$

$$\text{Given } [B] = \begin{bmatrix} 2 \\ 3 \\ 1 \end{bmatrix} \text{ then } \begin{bmatrix} x_1 \\ x_2 \\ x_3 \end{bmatrix} = \begin{bmatrix} 0 & 0.2 & 0.4 \\ -0.375 & 0.025 & 0.175 \\ -0.125 & -0.125 & 0.125 \end{bmatrix} \begin{Bmatrix} 2 \\ 3 \\ 1 \end{Bmatrix} = \begin{Bmatrix} 1 \\ -0.5 \\ -0.5 \end{Bmatrix}$$

Crout Method

This method results in the same upper triangular form as Gauss Method, but in the process we save the transformation information as a lower triangular matrix.

Given $[A][X] = [B]$

Operations on the system can yield $[U][X] = [C]$

Where [U] is a <u>unit</u> upper triangular matrix (users determine a choice of either a unit upper matrix vs. an upper matrix)

$$[U] = \begin{bmatrix} 1 & u_{12} & u_{13} & \cdots & u_{1n} \\ 0 & 1 & u_{23} & \cdots & u_{2n} \\ 0 & 0 & 1 & \cdots & \vdots \\ \vdots & & & \ddots & \vdots \\ 0 & 0 & \cdots & \cdots & 1 \end{bmatrix}$$

Consider that we can find a lower triangular matrix

$$[L] = \begin{bmatrix} l_{11} & 0 & 0 & \cdots & 0 \\ l_{21} & l_{22} & 0 & \cdots & 0 \\ l_{31} & l_{32} & l_{33} & & \vdots \\ \vdots & & & & \vdots \\ l_{n1} & l_{n2} & \cdots & \cdots & l_{nn} \end{bmatrix}$$

such that

$$[L]([U][X] - [C]) = [A][X] - [B]$$

$$\therefore \qquad [L][U] = [A] \xrightarrow{\ yields\ } \qquad [L] \text{ and } [U]$$

$$\text{then} \qquad [L][C] = [B] \xrightarrow{\ yields\ } \qquad \text{form } [C] \text{ for } \underline{any} \ [B]$$

$$\text{and} \qquad [U][X] = [C] \xrightarrow{\ yields\ } \qquad [X] \text{ solution by back-substitution}$$

For convenience we will augment [U] with an extra column consisting of [C] and [A] with an extra column consisting of [B], such that

$$
\begin{bmatrix}
l_{11} & 0 & 0 & \cdots & 0 \\
l_{21} & l_{22} & 0 & \cdots & 0 \\
l_{31} & l_{32} & l_{33} & \cdots & 0 \\
\vdots & & & \ddots & \vdots \\
l_{n1} & l_{n2} & l_{n3} & \cdots & l_{nn}
\end{bmatrix}
\begin{bmatrix}
1 & u_{12} & u_{13} & \cdots & u_{1n} & c_1 \\
0 & 1 & u_{23} & & u_{2n} & c_2 \\
0 & 0 & 1 & & u_{3n} & c_3 \\
\vdots & & & \ddots & \vdots & \vdots \\
0 & 0 & 0 & \cdots & 1 & c_n
\end{bmatrix}
=
\begin{bmatrix}
a_{11} & a_{12} & a_{13} & \cdots & a_{13} & b_1 \\
a_{21} & a_{22} & a_{23} & & a_{2n} & b_2 \\
a_{31} & a_{32} & a_{33} & & a_{3n} & b_3 \\
\vdots & & & \ddots & \vdots & \vdots \\
a_{n1} & a_{n2} & a_{n3} & \cdots & a_{nn} & b_n
\end{bmatrix}
$$

We can systematically determine the values of l_{ij} and u_{ij} when we equate the product matrices on the LHS to the required result on the RHS. For example, the product that equals a_{11} is

$$l_{11} * 1 = a_{11}$$

Similarly for the first column, we have,

$$l_{i1} = a_{i1} \qquad (i = 1, 2, 3, \ldots, n)$$

With the first column, we can determine the elements of the first row of [U]. By forming the products on the left and equating to terms on the right, we get

$$l_{11} u_{ij} = a_{ij}$$

$$\text{Given} \quad u_{1j} = \frac{a_{1j}}{l_{11}} \qquad (j = 2, 3, \ldots, n+1)$$

The n+1 element is c_1

We continue in this pattern to form a column of [L] and a row of [U]. Using the general terms, we get

$$l_{ij} = a_{ij} - \sum_{k=1}^{j-1} l_{ik} u_{kj} \quad \text{for} \quad j = 2, 3, \cdots, n \text{ and } i = j, \cdots, n \text{ for each } j$$

$$u_{ij} = \frac{a_{ij} - \sum_{k=1}^{i-1} l_{ik} u_{kj}}{l_{ii}} \quad \text{for} \quad i = 2, 3, \cdots, n \text{ and } j = i+1, \cdots, n+1 \text{ for each } i$$

Consider a 4 x 4 system listed below. We solve this system by using the LU decomposition or the Crout method.

$$\begin{bmatrix} 1 & 0 & 2 & -1 \\ 2 & 1 & 4 & -2 \\ 1 & -2 & 1 & 2 \\ 0 & 1 & -1 & -3 \end{bmatrix} \begin{Bmatrix} x_1 \\ x_2 \\ x_3 \\ x_4 \end{Bmatrix} = \begin{Bmatrix} 0 \\ 0 \\ 2 \\ -2 \end{Bmatrix}$$

Solution:

$$\begin{bmatrix} l_{11} & 0 & 0 & 0 \\ l_{21} & l_{22} & 0 & 0 \\ l_{31} & l_{32} & l_{33} & 0 \\ l_{41} & l_{42} & l_{43} & l_{44} \end{bmatrix} \begin{bmatrix} 1 & u_{12} & u_{13} & u_{14} & | & c_1 \\ 0 & 1 & u_{23} & u_{24} & | & c_2 \\ 0 & 0 & 1 & u_{34} & | & c_3 \\ 0 & 0 & 0 & 1 & | & c_4 \end{bmatrix} = \begin{bmatrix} 1 & 0 & 2 & -1 & | & 0 \\ 2 & 1 & 4 & -2 & | & 0 \\ 1 & -2 & 1 & 2 & | & 2 \\ 0 & 1 & -1 & -3 & | & -2 \end{bmatrix}$$

1st col of [L]:

$$l_{11} * 1 + 0 * 0 + 0 * 0 + 0 * 0 = 1 \quad => l_{11} = 1$$
$$l_{21} * 1 + 0 * 0 + 0 * 0 + 0 * 0 = 2 \quad => l_{21} = 2$$
$$l_{31} * 1 + 0 * 0 + 0 * 0 + 0 * 0 = 1 \quad => l_{31} = 1$$
$$l_{41} * 1 + 0 * 0 + 0 * 0 + 0 * 0 = 0 \quad => l_{41} = 0$$

1st row of [U]

$$l_{11} * u_{12} + 0 * \quad 1 + 0 * \quad 0 + 0 * 0 = 0 \quad => 1 * u_{12} = 0 \quad => u_{12} = 0$$
$$l_{11} * u_{13} + 0 * u_{23} + 0 * \quad 1 + 0 * 0 = 2 \quad => 1 * u_{13} = 2 \quad => u_{13} = 2$$
$$l_{11} * u_{14} + 0 * u_{24} + 0 * u_{34} + 0 * 1 = -1 \quad => 1 * u_{14} = -1 => u_{14} = -1$$
$$l_{11} * \quad c_1 + 0 * c_2 + 0 * c_3 + 0 * c_4 = 0 \quad => 1 * \quad c_1 = 0 => \quad c_1 = 0$$

2nd col of [L]

$$l_{21} * u_{12} + l_{22} * 1 + \quad 0 * 0 + \quad 0 * 0 = 2(0) + l_{22}(1) = 1 \quad => l_{22} = 1$$
$$l_{31} * u_{12} + l_{32} * 1 + \quad l_{33} * 0 + \quad 0 * 0 = 1(0) + l_{32}(1) = -2 \quad => l_{32} = -2$$
$$l_{41} * u_{12} + l_{42} * 1 + \quad l_{43} * 0 + l_{44} * 0 = 1(0) + l_{42}(1) = 1 \quad => l_{42} = 1$$

2nd row of [U]

$$l_{21}*u_{13}+l_{22}*u_{23}+ 0*1 + 0*0 = 4 \Rightarrow 2(2) + 1\, u_{23}=4 \qquad \Rightarrow u_{23}=0$$
$$l_{21}*u_{14}+l_{22}*u_{24}+ 0*u_{34} + 0*1 = -2 \Rightarrow 2(-1)+1\, u_{24}=-2 \qquad \Rightarrow u_{24}=0$$
$$l_{21}*c_1 +l_{22}* c_2+0*c_3+0*c_4 = 0 \Rightarrow 2(0) + 1\, c_2 = 0 \qquad \Rightarrow c_2 = 0$$

3rd col of [L]

$$l_{31}*u_{13}+l_{32}*u_{23}+l_{33}*1 + 0*0 = 1 \Rightarrow (1)(2)\ -2*0+l_{33}=1 \qquad \Rightarrow l_{33}=-1$$
$$l_{41}*u_{13}+l_{42}*u_{23}+l_{43}*1 + l_{44}*0 = -1 \Rightarrow 0(2)\ +1*0+l_{43}=-1 \qquad \Rightarrow l_{43}=-1$$

3rd row of [U]

$$l_{31}*u_{14}+l_{32}*u_{24}+l_{33}*u_{34} + 0*1 = 2 \Rightarrow (1)(-1) + (-2)(0)+(-1)*u_{34}=2$$
$$u_{34} = -3$$

$$l_{31}*c_1 +l_{32}* c_2+l_{33}* c_3 + 0*c_4 = 2 \Rightarrow (1)(0) + (-2)*0 + (-1)* c_3 = 2$$
$$c_3 = -2$$

4th col of [L]
$$l_{41}*u_{14}+l_{42}*u_{24}+l_{43}*u_{34}+l_{44}*1 = -2$$
$$0(-1) + (1)(0) + (-1)(-3)+ l_{44}(1) = -2 \Rightarrow l_{44}=-6$$

4th row of [U]

$$l_{41}*c_1+l_{42}*c_2+l_{43}*c_3+l_{44}*c_4 = -2$$
$$0(0) + (1)(0) + (-1)(-2) + (-6)c_4 = -2 \qquad \Rightarrow c_4 = 2/3$$

$$\begin{bmatrix} 1 & 0 & 0 & 0 \\ 2 & 1 & 0 & 0 \\ 1 & -2 & -1 & 0 \\ 0 & 1 & -1 & -6 \end{bmatrix} \begin{bmatrix} 1 & 0 & 2 & -1 & | & 0 \\ 0 & 1 & 0 & 0 & | & 0 \\ 0 & 0 & 1 & -3 & | & -2 \\ 0 & 0 & 0 & 1 & | & 2/3 \end{bmatrix} = \begin{bmatrix} 1 & 0 & 2 & -1 & | & 0 \\ 2 & 1 & 4 & -2 & | & 0 \\ 1 & -2 & 1 & 2 & | & 2 \\ 0 & 1 & -1 & -3 & | & -2 \end{bmatrix}$$

$$\begin{bmatrix} 1 & 0 & 2 & -1 \\ 0 & 1 & 0 & 0 \\ 0 & 0 & 1 & -3 \\ 0 & 0 & 0 & 1 \end{bmatrix} \begin{Bmatrix} x_1 \\ x_2 \\ x_3 \\ x_4 \end{Bmatrix} = \begin{Bmatrix} 0 \\ 0 \\ -2 \\ 2/3 \end{Bmatrix}$$

Back substitution, we get

$$\begin{bmatrix} x_1 \\ x_2 \\ x_3 \\ x_4 \end{bmatrix} = \begin{bmatrix} 0.6667 \\ 0 \\ 0 \\ 0.6667 \end{bmatrix}$$

Choleski Method

This method is particularly appropriate for systems of linear equations where the [A] matrix is symmetric and banded. We decompose the system such that

$$[A \mid B] = [U]^T[U \mid C] = [L][L^T \mid C]$$

[U] is not a unit upper matrix. By carrying out the product on the RHS and equating it to the LHS terms, we obtain the general terms

$$u_{11} = \sqrt{a_{11}} \quad \text{and} \quad u_{1j} = \frac{a_{1j}}{u_{11}}$$

$$u_{ii} = \sqrt{a_{ii} - \sum_{k=1}^{i-1} u_{ki}^2} \quad \text{for } i > 1$$

$$u_{ij} = \frac{1}{u_{ii}}\left(a_{ij} - \sum_{k=1}^{i-1} u_{ki} u_{kj}\right) \quad \text{for } j > 1, i > 1, i < j$$

and

$$u_{ij} = 0 \quad \text{for } i > j$$

For example, we solve the following system by $U^T U$ decomposition or the Choleski method:

$$\begin{bmatrix} 4 & 1 & 0 & 0 \\ 1 & 16 & 5 & 0 \\ 0 & 5 & 4 & 2 \\ 0 & 0 & 2 & 4 \end{bmatrix} \begin{Bmatrix} x_1 \\ x_2 \\ x_3 \\ x_4 \end{Bmatrix} = \begin{Bmatrix} 10 \\ 6 \\ -2 \\ 1 \end{Bmatrix}$$

Solution:

$$\begin{bmatrix} l_{11} & 0 & 0 & 0 \\ l_{21} & l_{22} & 0 & 0 \\ l_{31} & l_{32} & l_{33} & 0 \\ l_{41} & l_{42} & l_{43} & l_{44} \end{bmatrix} \begin{bmatrix} u_{11} & u_{12} & u_{13} & u_{14} & | & c_1 \\ 0 & u_{22} & u_{23} & u_{24} & | & c_2 \\ 0 & 0 & u_{33} & u_{34} & | & c_3 \\ 0 & 0 & 0 & u_{44} & | & c_4 \end{bmatrix} = \begin{bmatrix} 4 & 1 & 0 & 0 & | & 10 \\ 1 & 16 & 5 & 0 & | & 6 \\ 0 & 5 & 4 & 2 & | & -2 \\ 0 & 0 & 2 & 4 & | & 1 \end{bmatrix}$$

1st row

$$u_{11}^2 = 4 \qquad \rightarrow \qquad u_{11} = 2$$
$$2u_{12} = 1 \qquad \rightarrow \qquad u_{12} = 0.5$$
$$2u_{13} = 0 \qquad \rightarrow \qquad u_{13} = 0$$
$$2u_{14} = 0 \qquad \rightarrow \qquad u_{14} = 0$$
$$2c_1 = 10 \qquad \rightarrow \qquad c_1 = 5$$

2nd row

$$u_{12}^2 + u_{22}^2 = (0.5)^2 + u_{22}^2 = 16 \qquad \rightarrow \quad u_{22} = 3.9686$$
$$u_{12}*u_{13} + u_{22}*u_{23} = 0.5*0 + 3.9686*u_{23} = 5 \qquad \rightarrow \quad u_{23} = 1.2599$$
$$u_{12}*u_{14} + u_{22}*u_{24} = 0.5*0 + 3.9686*u_{24} = 0 \qquad \rightarrow \quad u_{24} = 0$$
$$u_{12}*c_1 + u_{22}*c_2 = 0.5*5 + 3.9686*c_2 = 6 \qquad \rightarrow \quad c_2 = 0.8819$$

3rd row

$$u_{13}^2 + u_{23}^2 + u_{33}^2 = (0)^2 + (1.2599)^2 + u_{33}^2 = 4 \qquad \rightarrow \quad u_{33} = 1.5532$$
$$u_{13}*u_{14} + u_{23}*u_{24} + u_{33}*u_{34} =$$
$$0*0 + 1.2599*0 + 1.5532\, u_{34} = 2 \qquad \rightarrow \quad u_{34} = 1.2877$$
$$u_{13}*c_1 + u_{23}*c_2 + u_{33}*c_3 =$$
$$0*(5) + 1.2599(0.8819) + 1.5532\, c_3 = -2 \qquad \rightarrow \quad c_3 = -2.003$$

4th row

$$u_{14}^2 + u_{24}^2 + u_{34}^2 + u_{44}^2 =$$
$$(0)^2 + (0)^2 + 1.2877^2 + u_{44}^2 = 4 \qquad \rightarrow \quad u_{44} = 1.5303$$
$$u_{14}*c_1 + u_{24}*c_2 + u_{34}*c_3 + u_{44}*c_4 =$$
$$0(5) + 0(0.8819) + 1.2877(-2.003) + 1.5303c_4 = 1 \qquad \rightarrow \quad c_4 = 2.3389$$

Thus

$$\begin{bmatrix} 2 & 0.5 & 0 & 0 \\ 0 & 3.9686 & 1.2599 & 0 \\ 0 & 0 & 1.5532 & 1.2877 \\ 0 & 0 & 0 & 1.5303 \end{bmatrix} \begin{Bmatrix} x_1 \\ x_2 \\ x_3 \\ x_4 \end{Bmatrix} = \begin{Bmatrix} 5 \\ 0.8682 \\ -2.003 \\ 2.3389 \end{Bmatrix}$$

Back substitution yields $\quad \{x\} = \begin{Bmatrix} 2.2424 \\ 1.0304 \\ -2.5567 \\ 1.5284 \end{Bmatrix}$

16.3   Iterative Methods

"Exact" methods are sensitive to round-off and computational errors. Another group of methods is the iterative techniques. Iterative methods require an "educated" guess and converge to an answer through a repetitive procedure. Methods falling into this category are:

- ❑   Jacobi's Method
- ❑   Gauss-Seidel Method

Jacobi Method

Consider the following equations:

$$a_{11}x_1 + a_{12}x_2 + a_{13}x_3 = b_1 \quad \text{eq (1)}$$
$$a_{21}x_1 + a_{22}x_2 + a_{23}x_3 = b_2 \quad \text{eq (2)}$$
$$a_{31}x_1 + a_{32}x_2 + a_{33}x_3 = b_3 \quad \text{eq (3)}$$

Solve the first equation for x_1, the second for x_2 and the third for x_3, to obtain

$$x_1 = c_1 - \frac{a_{12}}{a_{11}}x_2 - \frac{a_{13}}{a_{11}}x_3$$

$$x_2 = c_2 - \frac{a_{21}}{a_{22}}x_1 - \frac{a_{23}}{a_{22}}x_3$$

$$x_3 = c_3 - \frac{a_{31}}{a_{33}}x_1 - \frac{a_{32}}{a_{33}}x_2$$

or

$$\begin{Bmatrix} x_1 \\ x_2 \\ x_3 \end{Bmatrix}_{k+1} = \begin{Bmatrix} c_1 \\ c_2 \\ c_3 \end{Bmatrix} - \begin{bmatrix} 0 & b_{12} & b_{13} \\ b_{21} & 0 & b_{23} \\ b_{31} & b_{32} & 0 \end{bmatrix} \begin{Bmatrix} x_1 \\ x_2 \\ x_3 \end{Bmatrix}_k$$

Where $\quad c_i = \dfrac{b_i}{a_{ii}} \quad for \quad i = 1,\ 2,\ 3$

$$b_{ij} = \dfrac{a_{ij}}{a_{ii}}$$

k - the kth iteration.

We can iterate to the solution $\{x\}$ by starting at $k = 0$ with

$$\begin{Bmatrix} x_1 \\ x_2 \\ x_3 \end{Bmatrix}_0 = \begin{Bmatrix} 0 \\ 0 \\ 0 \end{Bmatrix}$$

For example, given the following system, solve the equation using the Jacobi method:

$$\begin{bmatrix} 20 & 2 & 2 \\ 1 & 10 & 2 \\ 0 & 2 & 4 \end{bmatrix} \begin{Bmatrix} x_1 \\ x_2 \\ x_3 \end{Bmatrix} = \begin{Bmatrix} 1 \\ 2 \\ 1 \end{Bmatrix}$$

Solution: The iterative scheme is formed as

$$\begin{Bmatrix} x_1 \\ x_2 \\ x_3 \end{Bmatrix}_{k+1} = \begin{Bmatrix} 0.05 \\ 0.2 \\ 0.25 \end{Bmatrix} - \begin{bmatrix} 0 & 0.1 & 0.1 \\ 0.1 & 0 & 0.2 \\ 0 & 0.5 & 0 \end{bmatrix} \begin{Bmatrix} x_1 \\ x_2 \\ x_3 \end{Bmatrix}_k$$

Starting with $\begin{Bmatrix} x_1 \\ x_2 \\ x_3 \end{Bmatrix}_0 = \begin{Bmatrix} 0 \\ 0 \\ 0 \end{Bmatrix}$

$k = 1$

$$\begin{Bmatrix} x_1 \\ x_2 \\ x_3 \end{Bmatrix}_1 = \begin{Bmatrix} 0.05 \\ 0.2 \\ 0.25 \end{Bmatrix} - \begin{bmatrix} 0 & 0.1 & 0.1 \\ 0.1 & 0 & 0.2 \\ 0 & 0.5 & 0 \end{bmatrix} \begin{Bmatrix} 0 \\ 0 \\ 0 \end{Bmatrix} = \begin{Bmatrix} 0.05 \\ 0.2 \\ 0.25 \end{Bmatrix}$$

$k = 2$

$$\begin{Bmatrix} x_1 \\ x_2 \\ x_3 \end{Bmatrix}_1 = \begin{Bmatrix} 0.05 \\ 0.2 \\ 0.25 \end{Bmatrix} - \begin{bmatrix} 0 & 0.1 & 0.1 \\ 0.1 & 0 & 0.2 \\ 0 & 0.5 & 0 \end{bmatrix} \begin{Bmatrix} 0.05 \\ 0.2 \\ 0.25 \end{Bmatrix} = \begin{Bmatrix} 0.005 \\ 0.145 \\ 0.15 \end{Bmatrix}$$

$k = 3$

$$\begin{Bmatrix} x_1 \\ x_2 \\ x_3 \end{Bmatrix}_1 = \begin{Bmatrix} 0.05 \\ 0.2 \\ 0.25 \end{Bmatrix} - \begin{bmatrix} 0 & 0.1 & 0.1 \\ 0.1 & 0 & 0.2 \\ 0 & 0.5 & 0 \end{bmatrix} \begin{Bmatrix} 0.005 \\ 0.145 \\ 0.15 \end{Bmatrix} = \begin{Bmatrix} 0.0205 \\ 0.1695 \\ 0.1775 \end{Bmatrix}$$

$k = 4$, ... , $k = 9$, $k = 10$

$$\begin{Bmatrix} x_1 \\ x_2 \\ x_3 \end{Bmatrix}_4 = \begin{Bmatrix} 0.015 \\ 0.1624 \\ 0.1652 \end{Bmatrix}, \quad \cdots\cdots , \quad \begin{Bmatrix} x_1 \\ x_2 \\ x_3 \end{Bmatrix}_9 = \begin{Bmatrix} 0.0167 \\ 0.1648 \\ 0.1676 \end{Bmatrix}, \quad \begin{Bmatrix} x_1 \\ x_2 \\ x_3 \end{Bmatrix}_{10} = \begin{Bmatrix} 0.0167 \\ 0.1648 \\ 0.1676 \end{Bmatrix}$$

The process continues until the vector is within the preset tolerance.

The real solution is

$$\begin{Bmatrix} x_1 \\ x_2 \\ x_3 \end{Bmatrix}_{real} = \begin{Bmatrix} 0.0168 \\ 0.1648 \\ 0.1676 \end{Bmatrix}$$

Note that this iterative method may not converge to a real solution. A rule of thumb in judging if the Jacobi method is applicable to a system of linear equation is to check the principal diagonal elements. If the magnitude of the diagonal element is greater than the sum of the magnitude of the element in each row, the Jacobi method can lead to the convergence to the real solution.

Gauss-Seidel Method

The Gauss-Seidel method differs from the Jacobi method in that it uses each x_i to calculate next x value immediately after x_i is calculated. Take the same example used for the Jacobi method to describe the difference,

$k = 1$, calculate x_1 with $x_2 = x_3 = 0$

$$x_1 = 0.05 - 0.1(0) - 0.1(0) = 0.05$$
$$x_2 = 0.2 - 0.1(0.05) - 0.2(0) = 0.15 \qquad (note - use\ x_1\ immediately)$$
$$x_3 = 0.25 - 0(0.05) - 0.5(0.15) = 0.1775 \qquad (note - use\ x_1\ and\ x_2\ immediately)$$

$k = 2$

$$x_1 = 0.05 - 0.1(0.15) - 0.1(0.1775) = 0.01725$$
$$x_2 = 0.2 - 0.1(0.01725) - 0.2(0.1775) = 0.1628$$
$$x_3 = 0.25 - 0(0.01725) - 0.5(0.1628) = 0.1686$$

etc

$$\cdots\cdots, \begin{Bmatrix} x_1 \\ x_2 \\ x_3 \end{Bmatrix}_8 = \begin{Bmatrix} 0.0167 \\ 0.1648 \\ 0.1676 \end{Bmatrix}, \begin{Bmatrix} x_1 \\ x_2 \\ x_3 \end{Bmatrix}_9 = \begin{Bmatrix} 0.0167 \\ 0.1648 \\ 0.1676 \end{Bmatrix}$$

16.4   Eigenvalue Problem

In previous sections we discuss systems of linear equations and solutions to these systems using different types of numerical methods. As you already know, these types of system are formulated as follows:

$$[A][X] = [B], \text{ where } [B] \neq 0$$

When [B] = 0, we call the system to be an Eigenvalue system. We use the following vector of equations to represent Eigenvalue problems:

$$[P][X] = [0]$$

One obvious solution is [X] = [0]. In practice, we are not interested in this solution. Instead, we are looking for other solutions that represent characteristics of linear systems. Using the Cramer method, we get,

$$x_j = \frac{\det\left[P_j \right]}{\det\left[P \right]}$$

Where $[P_j]$ is [P] with j^{th} column replaced by [0], $\det[P_j] = 0$.

To enforce x_j to be non-zero, a necessary and sufficient condition must be:

$$\det[P] = 0$$

Let us assume that [P] is actually the difference between two matrices [A] and [D], where $[D] = \lambda[I]$. The parameter λ is a scalar called the *characteristic value* or *eigenvalue*, and

$$[P] = [A] - \lambda[I]$$

$[P][X] = [0]$ is then represented by the following form:

$$[[A] - \lambda[I]]|X| = |0|$$

or

$$(a_{11} - \lambda) \, x_1 + (a_{12} - \lambda) \, x_2 + \cdots + (a_{1n} - \lambda) \, x_n = 0$$
$$(a_{21} - \lambda) \, x_1 + (a_{22} - \lambda) \, x_2 + \cdots + (a_{2n} - \lambda) \, x_n = 0$$
$$\vdots$$
$$(a_{n1} - \lambda) \, x_1 + (a_{n2} - \lambda) \, x_2 + \cdots + (a_{nn} - \lambda) \, x_n = 0$$

Then a necessary and sufficient condition for a non-zero solution to the system is

$$\det[[A] - \lambda[I]] = 0$$

or

$$\begin{vmatrix} (a_{11} - \lambda) & (a_{12} - \lambda) & \cdots & (a_{12} - \lambda) \\ (a_{21} - \lambda) & (a_{22} - \lambda) & & (a_{2n} - \lambda) \\ \vdots & & \ddots & \vdots \\ (a_{n1} - \lambda) & (a_{n2} - \lambda) & \cdots & (a_{nn} - \lambda) \end{vmatrix} = 0$$

Expanding this determinant, we will get the below polynomial of nth order:

$$\lambda^n + q_1 \lambda^{n-1} + q_2 \lambda^{n-2} + \cdots + q_{n-1} \lambda^1 + q_n = 0$$

This polynomial equation has n roots. We call these roots the *eigen* or *characteristic values* of the system. Corresponding to each eigenvalue λ_i is an eigenvector $[X]_i$. Let us take the below 2 x 2 linear system as an example to see how to solve it:

$$1x_1 + 4 \, x_2 = \lambda \, x_1$$
$$2 \, x_1 + x_2 = \lambda \, x_2$$

or, in matrix form

$$\begin{bmatrix} 1 & 4 \\ 2 & 1 \end{bmatrix} \begin{Bmatrix} x_1 \\ x_2 \end{Bmatrix} = \lambda \begin{Bmatrix} x_1 \\ x_2 \end{Bmatrix}$$

$$\begin{bmatrix} (1-\lambda) & 4 \\ 2 & (1-\lambda) \end{bmatrix} \begin{Bmatrix} x_1 \\ x_2 \end{Bmatrix} = \begin{Bmatrix} 0 \\ 0 \end{Bmatrix}$$

For a non-zero solution,

$$\det \begin{bmatrix} (1-\lambda) & 4 \\ 2 & (1-\lambda) \end{bmatrix} = 0$$

or

$$\lambda^2 - 2\lambda - 8 = 0 \quad \text{factoring} \quad (\lambda + 4)(\lambda - 2) = 0$$

The eigenvalues (EV) for the above equation are $\lambda_1 = 2, \lambda_2 = -4$

To determine the eigenvectors [X] for each λ, we substitute the λ value back into the original linear system, as shown below:

For $\lambda_1 = 2$

$$\begin{aligned} x_1 + 4x_2 &= 2 x_1 \\ 2 x_1 + x_2 &= 2 x_2 \end{aligned} \quad \text{or} \quad \begin{aligned} x_1 + 2 x_2 &= 0 \\ 2 x_1 - x_2 &= 0 \end{aligned}$$

Merging two equations, we get,

$$3x_1 - x_2 = 0 \quad \text{or} \quad \frac{x_1}{x_2} = \frac{1}{3}$$

This is a representation of eigenvector. We cannot tell the magnitude of $[X]_1$, but we can know the amplitude ratios among x_1 and x_2. Other representation of the eigenvector is shown below,

$$\begin{bmatrix} x_1 \\ x_2 \end{bmatrix}_1 = k \begin{Bmatrix} 1 \\ 3 \end{Bmatrix}$$

Normally we call this representation the normalization of the eigenvector to $x_1 = 1$.

Similarly, for $\lambda_2 = -4$

$$x_1 + 2 x_2 = -4 x_1$$
$$2 x_1 + x_2 = -4 x_2$$

or

$$-3 x_1 + 2 x_2 = 0$$
$$2 x_1 + 5 x_2 = 0$$

Two non-independent equations are combined as

$$-x_1 + 7 x_2 = 0 \quad \text{or} \quad \frac{x_1}{x_2} = 7$$

This is a representation of eigenvector. Set $x_1 = 1$ and

$$\begin{bmatrix} x_1 \\ x_2 \end{bmatrix}_2 = k \begin{Bmatrix} 1 \\ \dfrac{1}{7} \end{Bmatrix}$$

Many engineering problems can be solved through the use of eigenvalues and eigenvectors. Typical problems include those in the areas of vibrations and dynamics of physical systems, stability of systems, and resonance of acoustical and electrical systems. Applications of eigenvalues and eigenvectors in these areas are beyond the scope of the book. You can refer to other textbooks if you are interested in eigenvalue applications.

16.5   Questions

Q1.   Solve the following equation using the Direct Inverse, Cramer method, and Gaussian Elimination method:

$$2x_1 + 2x_2 - 3x_3 = -4$$
$$-2x_1 - 2x_2 + 5x_3 = 1$$
$$x_1 - 4x_2 + 6x_3 = 0$$

Q2.   Solve Problem Q1 using Choleski method.

Q3.   Given the below 3 x 3 system of linear equations:

$$3x_1 + 9x_2 - 6x_3 = 15$$
$$-2x_1 - 2x_2 + 7x_3 = 1$$
$$2x_1 - 4x_2 + 6x_3 = 6$$

Find the solution using Jacobi's and Gauss-Seidel iteration methods. Stop iterations when all the current and previous iteration values are within 0.01

Q4.   What is an Eigenvalue? Find an example of Eigenvalue problems on Internet.

Chapter 17
Getting to Know MATLAB

As discussed in the previous chapters, numerical methods are techniques used to solve science and engineering problems. Many software packages have been developed to use computers to implement these numerical methods. MATLAB, Maple, and Mathematica, to name a few, are commercially available for engineers and scientists. MATLAB stands for Matrix Laboratory. It is an interactive software system for numerical computations and graphics. It has powerful capabilities for solving systems of linear equations, computing eigenvalues and eigenvectors, factoring matrices, and so forth. In addition, it has a variety of graphical capabilities and a built-in programming language to extend its functions for matrix computations.

Maple is a general-purpose computer algebra system designed to solve problems and produce high-quality technical graphics. It is easy to learn, but powerful enough to execute complex numerical methods in seconds. Maple incorporates a high-level programming language and built-in functions to make users define their own procedures for statistical and mathematical computing.

Mathematica, similar to Maple, is a powerful computer software package. It helps engineers solve complex algebraic problems by formulating algorithms through symbolic expressions.

These three software packages are all useful in solving engineering problems. However this book is not intended to cover all these three software packages. Instead it concentrates only on MATLAB and its use in implementing numerical methods often used in engineering. Through the implementation, you can not only understand the principles of numerical methods, but also use them as an efficient vehicle for learning computer programming. This chapter will introduce MATLAB and its basic features and functions. Chapter 18 will describe the implementation of numerical methods discussed in the previous chapters.

17.1   What is MATLAB?

MATLAB is a computer system that integrates powerful tools for computation, visualization, and programming in an easy-to-use environment where problems and solutions are expressed in numerical methods and mathematical notation.

Typical uses of MATLAB include:

> Math and computation
> Algorithm development
> Numerical modeling and analysis
> Data analysis, exploration, and visualization

Scientific and engineering graphics
Application development, including graphical user interface building

MATLAB was originally written to provide for matrix operations. It has evolved to be the standard instructional tool for introductory and advanced courses in mathematics, engineering, and science in universities and computing industry.

17.2   Starting MATLAB

To start MATLAB from Windows XP (Assume MATLAB 7.0.1 has been already installed on Windows XP):

- Click *Start*
- Select *Programs* and then *MATLAB 7.0.1* or
- Click on the *MATLAB 7.0.1* icon on the Windows Desktop if the icon is available

Finishing the above steps, you will see the MATLAB working environment (see Figure 17-1). The key functions provided in this environment include:

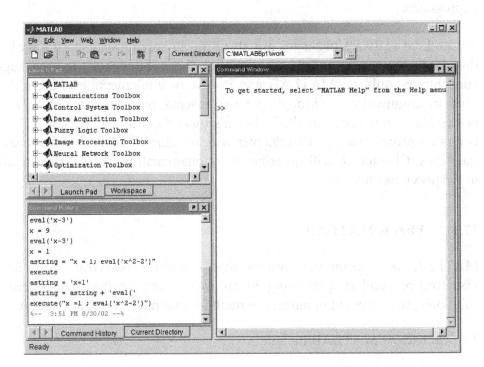

Figure 17-1   MATLAB Working Environment

- Command Window
- Command History
- Launch Pad
- Help Browser
- Current Directory Browser
- Workspace Browser
- Array Editor
- Editor/Debugger

The Command Window is the place in which you can enter and run MATLAB commands. To perform a simple MATLAB operation, just type a command within the Command window and press the *Enter* key. For example, if you want to calculate the value of the quadratic expression "x^2 –2x +1" with x = 2, you will have the following commands within the Command window:

```
>>    x = 2
x   =

      2
>>    y = x^2 -2*x +1

y   =

      1
```

The first command assigns 2 to a MATLAB variable called x. The naming convention of MATLAB variables is similar to that of VB.Net. Typically, a MATLAB variable name begins with a letter, followed by letters, numbers or underscores. MATLAB recognizes only the first 31 characters of a variable name.

The second command involves a MATLAB expression "x^2 - 2*x +1". When the *Enter* key is pressed, MATLAB will get a value from variable x and use it in the execution of the expression and assigns the result to another MATLAB variable called y.

As you can see, the execution logic of a command in MATLAB is similar to that in VB.NET. You can use MATLAB help to learn the topics of the Command History window, the Launch Pad, the Help Browser, the Current Directory Browser, the Workspace Browser, the Array Editor, and the Editor/Debugger.

MATLAB has a comprehensive set of online help tools that can be activated when you type `help` in the Command window. When you type `Help CommandName` within the Command window, you should know the name of the MATLAB command before you want to get the detailed description of its use. More discussion of MATLAB commands will be provided in later sections of this chapter.

To clear all the previous commands in the Command window, type *clc* and then press the *Enter* key. To clear all the variables in MATLAB, type *Clear* in the Command window.

To close MATLAB, you type *Exit* or *Quit* in the Command window and press the *Enter* key.

17.3   Vectors in MATLAB

MATLAB allows users to enter and manipulate vectors. To create the vector a, type:

```
» a = [1        2        3        4        5        8        7]
a =
      1      2    3     4    5    8    7
```

You need to separate the above elements by spaces. If you want to create a column vector b, separate the elements by semicolons:

```
» b = [1;    2;    3;    4;    5;    6]
b =
      1
      2
      3
      4
      5
      6
```

You can also define a vector by specifying the first entry, an increment, and the last entry. MATLAB can automatically figure out the elements and their values for the vector. For example, to create a vector whose elements are 0, 2, 4, 6, 8 and 10, you can type in the following line:

```
>> A = [0:2:10]

A =

    0    2    4    6    8    10
```

The variable A is created to store the vector for later use. It is noted that within MATLAB, variables are case sensitive. Variables A and a are not the same.

The command length returns the number of components or elements in a vector. For example,

```
» length(A)
```

```
        ans =

            6
```

Note that if you do not assign the result of an execution to a variable, MATLAB will automatically assign the result to the default variable called *ans*.

You can specify a vector with only one element in it. We call this element a scalar element. For example, if you want to type a scalar, just enter:

```
    » x = 2006

    x =

        2006
```

A typical use of a scalar element is to calculate a value of a function *f(x)*. Assume we want to calculate the value of the below quadratic function

$$f(x) = x^2 - 2, \qquad x = 5$$

We will have the following commands in MATLAB,

```
    >> x = 5
    x =
        5

    >>  y = eval('x^2-3*x+2')
    y =

        12
```

Note that *eval()* is the MATLAB function that calculates the value of a symbolic expression. The independent variables inside the expression are assigned with values. The *eval()* function has only one argument of a string type. Also note that the "*" is needed in the expression to represent the multiplication.

To list variables in the current working session of MATLAB, you can use the following command,

```
>> whos
        Name        Size        Elements        Bytes

          A        3 by 3             9            72
          B        3 by 3             9            72
        ans        1 by 3             3            24

Grand total is 21 elements using 168 bytes
```

The command displays the names of all defined variables and their types.

17.4   Matrix Operations with MATLAB

Matrices in MATLAB are considered as vectors, except each row of elements is separated by a semicolon (;) or a return. For example, to define a matrix, you can enter each row of elements as a vector (**note that the spaces are required!**):

```
>> A = [1    2    3; 3    4    5; 6    7    8]

A =

    1    2    3
    3    4    5
    6    7    8
```

You can also enter columns of matrix elements as a set of column vectors separated by spaces. For example,

```
>> B = [[1 2 3 4]'      [2 4 7 6]'      [3 5 8 7]']

B =

    1    2    3
    2    4    5
    3    7    8
    4    6    7
```

You can also use MATLAB functions to create matrices that have a specific nature. For example, you can use the below functions to create special matrices:

```
zeros(m,n)        It creates an m x n matrix of zeros
ones(m,n)         It creates an m x n matrix of ones
eye(n)            It creates the n x n identity matrix
```

Type the following command within the Command window, you will see:

```
>>      eye(4)

ans =

    1    0    0    0
    0    1    0    0
    0    0    1    0
    0    0    0    1
```

Once matrices are created in MATLAB, you can perform many matrix manipulations and operations.

a)   Transpose of a matrix

You can find the transpose of a matrix using the apostrophe key. For example,

```
>> B =        [1 2 3 ; 3 4 5]
B=

        1       2       3
        3       4       5

>> C = B'
C =

        1       3
        2       4
        3       5
```

b)   Multiplication of matrices

We can use MATLAB to calculate dot and cross products of two matrices. Before we calculate the dot product, we need to make sure the dimensions of two matrices are the same.

The syntax of dot operations is as follows:

A .* B   It multiplies each element of matrix A by the corresponding element of B

A ./ B   It divides each element of matrix A by the corresponding element of B

A .^ B   It raises each element of matrix A to the power of the corresponding element of B

For example,

```
>> A = [4 5;        6 7]
A =
        4       5
        6       7
```

```
>> B = [2 3; 4 5]

B =
        2     3
        4     5


>>  C = A .* B


C =
        8    15
       24    35
```

As to a cross product of two matrices, we need to check the order of the two matrices. The number of columns in the first matrix must be the same as the number of rows in the second matrix. Assume you have entered the following matrices:

```
>>  A = [1 2 ; 3 4]

A =    1     2
       3     4

>> B = [ 3  4; 4   6]
B =    3     4
       4     6
```

As matrix A has two columns and B has two rows, we can determine the cross product of A and B as follows:

```
>>     C = A * B

C =
       11    16
       25    36
```

c)   Inverse of a matrix

The inverse of a matrix can be implemented in MATLAB. For example,

```
>>              A = [2 3 0; 0 1 2 ; 1 0 1]

A =

        2     3     0
        0     1     2
        1     0     1
```

The inverse of the A is as follow:

```
>>              inv(A)

ans =

        0.125       -0.375       0.75
        0.250        0.250      -0.50
       -0.125        0.375       0.25
```

d)   Addition and Subtraction of matrices

Two matrices can be added or subtracted one from another when they have the same order. For example,

```
>> A = [1 2 3; 4 5 6; 7 8 9]

A =
        1       2       3
        4       5       6
        7       8       9


>> B = [1 1 1; 2 2 2; -1 -1 -1]

B =

        1       1       1
        2       2       2
       -1      -1      -1


>> C = A+B

C   =
        2       3       4
        6       7       8
        6       7       8

>> D = A - B

D =

        0       1       2
        2       3       4
        8       9      10
```

17.5   Solving Systems of Linear Equations with MATLAB

A system of linear equations as described in Chapter 16 is formulated as follows:

$$AX = B$$

Where A is a square matrix whose determinant is not 0

The solution of the above equation using the direct inverse method is

$$X = A^{-1}B$$

MATLAB implements this operation with the backslash operator. Suppose we have a system of linear equations listed below:

$$
\begin{aligned}
2\ x_1 - 1\ x_2 + 3\ x_3 &= -1 \\
3\ x_1 + 1\ x_2 - 2\ x_3 &= 1 \\
2\ x_1 + 2\ x_2 + 2\ x_3 &= 5
\end{aligned}
$$

Note that you can write this system as Ax = B in MatLab as follows:

```
>>    A = [ 2 -1 3;     3 1 -2;     2 2 2]
A =

    2      -1       3
    3       1      -2
    2       2       2


>>    B = [ -1     1      5]'
B =

          -1
           1
           5

>> x = A\B

x =

       -0.0882
        2.1471
        0.4412
```

More discussion on how to use MATLAB to implement numerical methods is provided in Chapter 18.

17.6   MATLAB Programming

In the previous sections we have discussed individual commands that are related to matrix operations. We will group commands together and use them for specific tasks. MATLAB has a language similar to VB.Net. We introduce MATLAB conditions and loop statements here because other statements are pretty easy to understand.

a)   IF-THEN-ELSE Statement

The IF-THEN-ELSE statement in MATLAB is similar to that in VB.Net. Its syntax is as follows:

```
if expression
      MATLAB Commands or statements
else
      MATLAB Commands or statements
end
```

For example:

```
>> x = rand(1);
>> if x < 0.50
      y = 0;
   else
      y = 10-2*(x-0.50);
   end;
>> x
x =
      0.9501
>> y
y =
      9.0997
```

Note that a semicolon appears at the end of the first two MATLAB commands. The semicolon indicates that MATLAB does not display the execution results of the first two commands. Because the third and fourth commands do not have semicolon at the end of the statement, you can see the result of the MATLAB commands, in this case, just show the value of the variable x and y.

b)   For Statement

For statement in MATLAB is similar to that of VB.Net. Its syntax is as follows:

```
for variable = expression
    statements or commands
end
```

For statement repeats looping statements or commands in a specific number of times. For example,

```
>> A = [1 2 3; 0 2 1; 2 1 3]

A =

    1    2    3
    0    2    1
    2    1    3


>> for i = [2 3]
        For j = [1 2 3]

            A(i, j) = A(i, j) - A (i-1, j)
        end
    end


A =

    1    2    3
   -1    0   -2
    2    1    3


A =

    1    2    3
   -1    0   -2
    3    1    5
```

c)   While Statement

While statement in MATLAB is similar to that of VB.Net. Its syntax is as follows:

```
while expression
        statements or commands
end
```

While statement repeats looping statements in an indefinite number of times. The looping statements are executed until the *expression* turns to be false. For example,

```
>> sum = 0;
   I = 1;
   while I <= 10
     sum = sum + I;
     I = I + 1;
   end
   I
   Sum
```

The above while-statement compares the value in variable I and see if it is less than and equal to 10. If the comparison turns to be true, then the two loop statements are executed and the value of I is increased by 1. The above procedure repeats until the comparison turns to be false.

17.7   M-Files

A MATLAB program is stored in an M-file with .m suffix. An M-file is a text file in which a series of MATLAB statements or commands are stored.

In the Command Window, type the following command:

```
>> cd c:\temp
```

The `cd` command changes MATLAB's current working directory to be `C:\temp` folder, so any M-files you create will save into `C:\temp`.

With the current working directory to be `c:\temp`, type the following command:

```
>>      !notepad MyFirstMFile.m &
```

This command invokes a Windows application called *Notepad*. The letter "!" in the command indicates *Notepad* is a Windows application. The letter "&" indicates *NotePad* application will be executed in background mode. After the command is entered, A *Notepad* window appears. It provides a text editor in which you can type the following MATLAB statements:

```
x = rand(1);
if x < 0.5
        y = 0;
else
        y = 10-2*(x-0.50);
end;
x
y
```

In the Notepad,

Select *File->Save*

It will save the above statements in the *MyFirstMFile.m* file. The file is located at `C:\Temp` folder.

Exit

Exit out of *Notepad* and come back to the MATLAB environment.

In MATLAB Command Window, type the following command:

>> MyFirstMFile

Compare the results with those produced previously from the MATLAB commands.

17.8   MATLAB Functions

MATLAB includes many built-in functions that can be used in programming. Each function is a block of code that works on a specific task. MATLAB contains mathematical functions such as sin(), cos (), log(), exp(), sqrt(), as well as others. Commonly used constants such as pi, and i or j for the square root of -1, are also incorporated into MATLAB.

For example,

```
cos(pi/4)
ans =

    0.7071
```

A list of MATLAB functions for matrices and their manipulations is provided below:

a)   Elementary Matrices

```
zeros         - Zeros array.
ones          - Ones array.
eye           - Identity matrix.
repmat        - Replicate and tile array.
rand          - Uniformly distributed random numbers.
randn         - Normally distributed random numbers.
linspace      - Linearly spaced vector.
logspace      - Logarithmically spaced vector.
freqspace     - Frequency spacing for frequency response.
```

```
    meshgrid    - X and Y arrays for 3-D plots.
```

b)   Basic Array Information

```
    size        - Size of matrix.
    length      - Length of vector.
    ndims       - Number of dimensions.
    numel       - Number of elements.
    disp        - Display matrix or text.
    isempty     - True for empty matrix.
    isequal     - True if arrays are identical.
    isnumeric   - True for numeric arrays.
    islogical   - True for logical array.
    logical     - Convert numeric values to logical.
```

c)   Matrix Manipulation
```
    reshape     - Change size.
    diag        - Diagonal matrices and diagonals of matrix.
    blkdiag     - Block diagonal concatenation.
    tril        - Extract lower triangular part.
    triu        - Extract upper triangular part.
    fliplr      - Flip matrix in left/right direction.
    flipud      - Flip matrix in up/down direction.
    flipdim     - Flip matrix along specified dimension.
    rot90       - Rotate matrix 90 degrees.
    find        - Find indices of nonzero elements.
    end         - Last index.
    sub2ind     - Linear index from multiple subscripts.
    ind2sub     - Multiple subscripts from linear index.
```

d)   Special Variables and Constants
```
    ans         - Most recent answer.
    eps         - Floating point relative accuracy.
    realmax     - Largest positive floating point number.
    realmin     - Smallest positive floating point number.
    pi          - 3.1415926535897....
    i, j        - Imaginary unit.
    inf         - Infinity.
    NaN         - Not-a-Number.
    isnan       - True for Not-a-Number.
    isinf       - True for infinite elements.
    isfinite    - True for finite elements.
    why         - Succinct answer.
```

e)   Specialized Matrices
```
    compan      - Companion matrix.
    gallery     - Higham test matrices.
    hadamard    - Hadamard matrix.
    hankel      - Hankel matrix.
    hilb        - Hilbert matrix.
    invhilb     - Inverse Hilbert matrix.
    magic       - Magic square.
    pascal      - Pascal matrix.
    rosser      - Classic symmetric eigenvalue test problem.
    toeplitz    - Toeplitz matrix.
    vander      - Vandermonde matrix.
    wilkinson   - Wilkinson's eigenvalue test matrix.
```

A list of functions for numerical linear algebra is provided below:

a) Matrix Analysis
```
     norm          - Matrix or vector norm.
     normest       - Estimate the matrix 2-norm.
     rank          - Matrix rank.
     det           - Determinant.
     trace         - Sum of diagonal elements.
     null          - Null space.
     orth          - Orthogonalization.
     rref          - Reduced row echelon form.
     subspace      - Angle between two subspaces.
```

b) Linear Equations
```
     \ and /       - Linear equation solution; use "help slash".
     inv           - Matrix inverse.
     rcond         - LAPACK reciprocal condition estimator
     cond          - Condition number with respect to inversion.
     condest       - 1-norm condition number estimate.
     normest1      - 1-norm estimate.
     chol          - Cholesky factorization.
     cholinc       - Incomplete Cholesky factorization.
     lu            - LU factorization.
     luinc         - Incomplete LU factorization.
     qr            - Orthogonal-triangular decomposition.
     lsqnonneg     - Linear least squares with nonnegativity constraints.
     pinv          - Pseudoinverse.
     lscov         - Least squares with known covariance.
```

c) Eigenvalues and Singular Values
```
     eig           - Eigenvalues and eigenvectors.
     svd           - Singular value decomposition.
     gsvd          - Generalized singular value decomposition.
     eigs          - A few eigenvalues.
     svds          - A few singular values.
     poly          - Characteristic polynomial.
     polyeig       - Polynomial eigenvalue problem.
     condeig       - Condition number with respect to eigenvalues.
     hess          - Hessenberg form.
     qz            - QZ factorization for generalized eigenvalues.
     schur         - Schur decomposition.
```

d) Matrix Functions
```
     expm          - Matrix exponential.
     logm          - Matrix logarithm.
     sqrtm         - Matrix square root.
     funm          - Evaluate general matrix function.
```

e) Factorization Utilities
```
     qrdelete      - Delete column from QR factorization.
     qrinsert      - Insert column in QR factorization.
```

```
rsf2csf    - Real block diagonal form to complex diagonal form.
cdf2rdf    - Complex diagonal form to real block diagonal form.
balance    - Diagonal scaling to improve eigenvalue accuracy.
planerot   - Givens plane rotation.
cholupdate - rank 1 update to Cholesky factorization.
qrupdate   - rank 1 update to QR factorization.
```

MATLAB also allows users to develop their own functions. User-defined functions are stored in M-Files. Suppose we want to calculate the sum of the following expression

$$F(n) = 1^2 + 2^2 + 3^2 + 4^2 + \ldots + n^2$$

We can create a function listed below:

```
function y = SquareSum(n)
    sum = 0;
    for  i = 1:n
        sum = sum + i ^2;
    end
    y = sum;
end
```

We save this function in an M-File called `SquareSum.m`. The procedures to save the M-file are as follows:

1)   Type the below statement in the MATLAB's Command Window

```
>> !notepad SquareSum.m &
```

2)   Copy the above function in the Notepad editor
3)   Save and Exit the Notepad Editor
4)   Type the following statement in MATLAB Command Window

```
>> SquareSum(5)
```

```
55
```

17.9   Plotting

You can plot a function graphically in MATLAB. Suppose you want to plot a `cos(x)` function. You can have the following MATLAB commands (see Figure 17-2).

```
x=0:0.25:10;
y = cos(x);
plot(x,y)
```

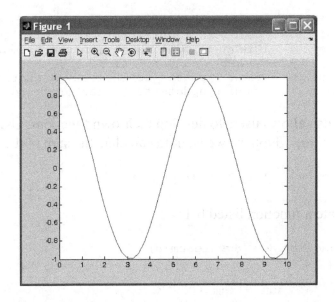

Figure 17-2 Curve for cos(x)

Note that the plot (x,y) command plots the elements of vector x on the horizontal axis of the figure and the elements of the vector y on the vertical axis of the figure. More information about the plot command can be found in the MATLAB online help.

MATLAB function fplot() is very important in the implementation of numerical methods. Its syntax is `fplot(func(x),lims)`. It plots the function `func(x)` between the x-axis limits specified by `lims = [xmin xmax]`. The function `func(x)` returns a row vector for each element of vector x. For example, if we want to plot function $f(x) = x^2 - 2$ with the x in the range of [-10, 10] (see Figure 17-3), you can do:

```
>> fplot('x^2-3', [-10,10])
```

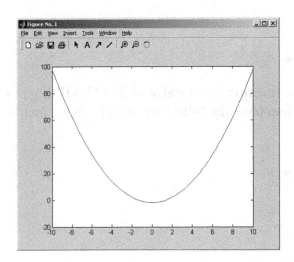

Figure 17-3 Result of the Plot `fplot('x^2-3', [-10,10])`

Another MATLAB function called `ezmesh(func(x,y))` is often used for 3-D surface plotting. It creates a graph of `func(x,y)` using the ezmesh function. The argument func(x, y) is plotted over the default domain: $-2\pi < x < 2\pi, -2\pi < y < 2\pi$.

For example, if we want to plot a function `f(x,y) = x^2 - y^2` with x and y values in the range of [-10, +10] and [-20, 20], respectively, we can do:

```
ezmesh('x^2-y^2', [-10,10], [-20, 20])
```

Figure 17-4 shows the graph of the function `f(x,y) = x^2- y^2`.

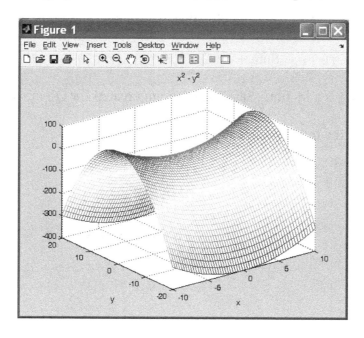

Figure 17-4   3-D Plot of f(x,y) = x^2-y^2

17.10 Questions

Q1.   Besides MATLAB, list two more software packages that are widely used for implementing numerical methods.

Q2.   When you work in the MATLAB environment, you see a lot of commands displayed within the Command window. Which command do you need to use to clear all these commands?

Q3.   Assume you enter the following vector within the Command window:

```
>> A = [1    2    3    4    55    6]
```

```
>> length(A)
```

What is the result of the length () function?

Q4.   Given $A = \begin{bmatrix} 1 & 2 & 4 \\ 7 & 4 & 3 \\ 0 & 2 & 5 \end{bmatrix}$ $B = \begin{bmatrix} 1 & 2 & 0 \\ 5 & 3 & 3 \\ 0 & 2 & 3 \end{bmatrix}$

Use MATLAB to get the dot and cross products of A and B

Q5.   Write a MATLAB function that can do the following

$$Sum = 1 + 2 + 3 + \quad \ldots + n$$

Q6.   What is a M-file? Save the program created for Q5 into a M-file called Q5.m

Q7.   Plot the following two functions on a graph:

$$f(x) = 2x$$
$$f(x) = x^2 - 2x + 1$$

x is within [−5, 5]

Chapter 18
Numerical Methods Using MATLAB and EXCEL

We have discussed numerical methods, matrices and systems of linear equations in the previous chapters. In this chapter we will use EXCEL and MATLAB to implement various numerical methods for finding roots of equations, performing various operations of matrices, and solving systems of linear equations.

18.1   Finding Roots of Equations Using MATLAB

As described in the previous chapters, there are three commonly used numerical methods for finding roots of equations: Bisection, False-Position, and Newton-Raphson methods. When we use these methods manually, the searching process to get a satisfactory approximation of a root is tedious and time-consuming. Practically we use MATLAB or other software packages for the search. In this section we will discuss how to use MATLAB to find roots of equations.

18.1.1   Bisection Method with MATLAB

Assume you are in the MATLAB environment (MATLAB 7.0.1 or higher version). The steps used to create the MATLAB bisection function are as follows:

Step 1:   Change the working directory or folder in MATLAB to your preferred one. If you want to change the working folder to be `c:\temp`, you need to enter the below command within the *Commands* window:

```
>> cd c:\temp
```

Step 2:   Open Notepad to create an MATLAB M-file in which the bisection function is stored. The name of the M-file is called `bisection.m`.

Step 3:   Inside the Notepad, type the following MATLAB statements

```
function    root = bisection(Func, x1, x2, SmallVal)

% bisection is the MATLAB-based function that can
% be executed only in MATLAB.
% Func is the string that contains a function f(x),
% where x is the independent variable.
% x1 and x2 specifies an interval [x1, x2] in which
% a root exists.
% SmallVal is the small value used to terminate the
% the search process.
```

```
x = x1;
fx1 = eval(Func);
x = x2;
fx2 = eval (Func);

% Check if a root exists in [x1, x2]
% If not, exit the function.

if  fx1 * fx2 > 0
        disp (' A root not in [x1, x2] …');
        return;
end

% If a root exists in [x1,x2],
% Search for the root.

while abs (x1 - x2) > SmallVal
        xmid = x1 + (x2 - x1)/2;
        x = xmid;
        fxmid = eval(Func);

        if fx1 * fxmid <= 0
                % A root in [x1, xmid]
                x2 = xmid;
                fx2 = fxmid;
        else
                % a root in [xmid, x2]
                x1 = xmid;
                fx1 = fxmid;
        end
end
root = xmid;
```

Step 4:   Save the `bisection.m` file and back to MATLAB

Step 5:   Assume the function $f(x) = x^2 - 2$, $[x1, x2] = [1, 2]$, and the small value is 0.01. We will have

```
>>   bisection ('x^2-2', 1, 2, 0.01)
```

You will get the result as follows:

```
>> ans = 1.4141
```

18.1.2 False Position Method with MATLAB

The steps used to create the MATLAB false-position function are as follows:

Step 1:   Change your working directory or folder in MATLAB. If you want to change the working folder to be `C:\temp`, you need to enter the below command within the *Commands* window:

```
>> cd c:\temp
```

Step 2:   Open Notepad to create an MATLAB M-file in which the false_position function is stored. The name of the M-file is called `false_position.m`.

Step 3:   Inside the Notepad, type the following MATLAB statements

```
function root = false_position(Func, x1, x2, SmallVal, looplimits)

    % false_position is the MATLAB function that can
    % be executed only in MATLAB.
    % Func is the string that contains a function f(x),
    % where x is the independent variable.
    % x1 and x2 specifies an interval [x1, x2] in which
    % a root should be searched if it exists in
    % the interval.
    % SmallVal is the small value used to terminate the
    % the search process.
    % looplimits is the limit of the loops. If the repetition
    % is greater than the limit, the search stops.

    x = x1;
    fx1 = eval (Func);
    x = x2;
    fx2 = eval (Func);

    % Check if a root exists in [x1, x2]
    % If not, exit the function.

    if  fx1 * fx2 > 0
        disp ('A root not in [x1, x2] …');
        return;
    end

    % If a root exists in [x1, x2],
    % Search for the root.

    Loops = 0;
    while abs (x1 - x2) > SmallVal
        loops = loops +
        if loops > looplimits
            break;
        end
        xfp = (x1*fx2 - x2* fx1)/(fx2 -fx1);
        x = xfp;
        fxfp = eval(Func);

        if fx1 * fxfp <= 0
            % A root in [x1, xfp]
            x2 = xfp;
            fx2 = fxfp;
        else
            % a root in [xfp, x2]
            x1 = xfp;
```

```
                fx1 = fxfp;
         end
   end
root = (x1+x2)/2;
```

Step 4:   Save the `false_position.m` file and back to MATLAB

Step 5:   Assume the function f(x) = x^2 –3, [x1, x2] = [1, 2], the small value is 0.01, and the looping limit is 10000. We will have

```
>>    false_position ('x^2 - 3', 1, 2, 0.001, 10000)
```

You will get the result as follows:

```
>> ans = 1.7321
```

As you know the MATLAB false-position function is the implementation of the original false-position method. The below function called `false_position_advanced` implements the search process described in Section 14.3.4.

```
function    root = false_position_advanced(Func, x1, x2, SmallVal)

   % false_position is the MATLAB function that can
   % be executed only in MATLAB.
   % Func is the string that contains a function f(x),
   % where x is the independent variable.
   % x1 and x2 specifies an interval [x1, x2] in which
   % a root should be searched if it exists in
   % the interval.
   % SmallVal is the small value used to terminate the
   % the search process.

            x = x1;
            fx1 = eval (Func);
            x = x2;
            fx2 = eval (Func);

            % Check if a root exists in [x1, x2]
            % If not, exit the function.

            if  fx1 * fx2 > 0
                  disp (' A root not in [x1, x2] …');
                  return;
            end

            % If a root exists in [x1, x2],
            % Search for the root.

            while abs (x1 - x2) > SmallVal
```

```
xfp = (x1*fx2 - x2* fx1)/(fx2 -fx1);
x = xfp;
fxfp = eval(Func);

if fx1 * fxfp <= 0
        % A root in [x1, xfp]
        x2 = xfp;
        fx2 = fxfp;
% This is statement that shows the
% improvement of the search

        fx1 = fx1/2;
else
        % a root in [xfp, x2]
        x1 = xfp;
        fx1 = fxfp;
% This is statement that shows the
% improvement of the search
        fx2 = fx2/2;
end
        end
root = (x1+x2)/2;
```

Save the `false_position_advanced.m` file and run the function f(x) = xe^x-1 with [x1, x2] = [0, 1], and the small value is 0.035. We will have

```
>>      false_position ('x*exp(x) - 1', 0, 1, 0.035)
```

You will get the result as follows:

```
>> ans = 0.5581
```

18.1.3 Newton-Raphson Method with MATLAB

The steps used to create the MATLAB Newton-Raphson function are as follows:

Step 1:   Change your working directory or folder in MATLAB. If you want to change the working folder to be `c:\temp`, you need to enter the below command within the *Commands* window:

```
>> cd c:\temp
```

Step 2:   Open Notepad to create an MATLAB M-file in which the `Newton-Raphson` function is stored. The name of the M-file is called `Newton_Raphson.m`.

Step 3:   Inside the Notepad, type the following MATLAB statements

```
function root = newton_raphson(Func, x0, SmallValue)

    % Newton_Raphson is the MATLAB function that can
    % be executed only in MATLAB.
    % Func is the string that contains a function f(x),
    % where x is the independent variable.
    % x0 specifies a seed value from which the search starts
    % SmallVal is the small value used to terminate the
    % the search process.

    x = x0;
    fx = eval(Func);

    % Diff() is the MATLAB function to get a derivative
    % function of a function.

    derivFunc = diff(Func);
    derivfx = eval(derivFunc);
    x_previous = x0;
    x_current =  x_previous - fx/derivfx;

    while abs ((x_current-x_previous)/x_current) > SmallValue

        x = x_current;
        fx = eval(Func);
        derivfx = eval(derivFunc);
        x_previous = x_current;
        x_current  = x_previous - fx/derivfx;
    end
    root = x_current;
```

Step 4:   Save the `newton_raphson.m` file and back to MATLAB

Step 5:   Assume the function $f(x) = x^4 - 4x^3 - 7x^2 + 34x - 24 = 0$, x_0 = -5, and the small value is 0.02, we will have

>>   `newton_raphson ('x^4-4*x^3-7*x^2+34*x-24', -5, 0.02)`

You will get the result as follows:

>> `ans = -3.0009`

18.2   Matrix Operations Using EXCEL

Microsoft's EXCEL provides an environment for matrix computations. Before we introduce the standard procedures for matrix computations, we need to have a good understanding of the important term, named ranges, used in EXCEL. Below is the brief discussion of the term.

18.2.1 Named Ranges

Many EXCEL formulas require the specification of one or more *ranges* of cells as arguments. The easiest way to indicate such a range is to *select* it by highlighting a group of continuous cells through a mouse and name the group a range.

Suppose we would like to name the range A1:C4 (see Figure 18-1) to be *Array1*, the following are the steps:

Step 1:   *Insert -> Name-> Define*

Step 2:   Type *Array1* in the textbox below the *Names in Workbook* field (see Figure 18-2) and click on the arrow shown in the *Refers to:* field.

Step 3:   Specify the range and Click OK (see Figure 18-3)

18.2.2 Matrix Formula

In order to perform matrix operations in EXCEL, we should have a clear understanding of the concept of *Matrix (Array) formula*. A matrix formula is an expression that consists of named ranges and matrix operators. Execution of a matrix formula returns a result that can be a matrix, a vector, or a scalar, depending on the computations involved. Whatever the result may be, an area with a correct size on the spreadsheet must be specified before the formula is typed in and executed.

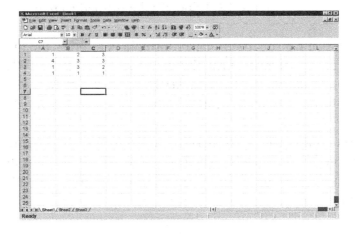

Figure 18-1   An EXCEL Range

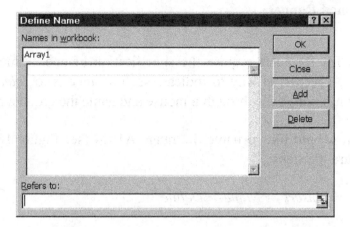

Figure 18-2   Named Range Window

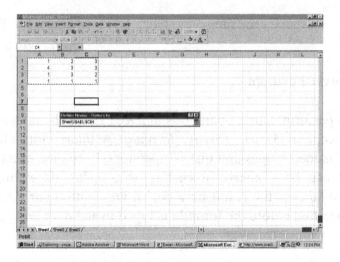

Figure 18-3 Specify the Named Range

The way to execute a specified matrix formula is to press the three keys CTRL, SHIFT and ENTER at the same time (or first press and hold the CTRL key, second press the SHIFT key and hold the CTRL and SHIFT keys together, and third press the ENTER key). This indicates that matrix (array) operations are performed.

When matrix computations are performed using specified matrix formulas, the results will be updated immediately whenever any of the values in the matrix formulas changes. This feature allows you to evaluate the effects of changes in assumptions, initial conditions, etc.

Using specified formulas, we can add two matrices together, subtract one matrix from another, multiply two matrices, get the inverse of a matrix, and transpose a matrix.

18.2.3 Matrix Addition

Assume that *Students1* and *Students2* are two named ranges of the same size. Do the following to add these two matrices:

Step 1: Select an empty range with the same size as *Students1* on the worksheet,

Step 2: Type in the formula:

= Students1 + Students2

Step 3: Press CTRL+SHIFT+ENTER.

Note that any two matrices of the same size can be added in this manner, with the result placed in the specified range of the same size.

18.2.4 Matrix Subtraction

A matrix can be subtracted from another one if their size is same. For example we will have the following steps to subtract *Students2* from *Students1*:

Step1: Specify an empty range with the same size as *Students1*

Step 2: Create the following matrix formula

= Students1 – Students2

Step3: Press CTRL+SHIFT+ENTER.

18.2.5 Matrices with Scalars

To multiply a constant to every element of a matrix with the named range called *students*, simply do the following steps:

Step 1: Specify an empty range with the same size as *students*

Step 2: Create the following matrix formula

= students * 100

Step3: Press CTRL+SHIFT+ENTER.

18.2.6 Matrix Multiplication

To multiply two matrices, use the MMULT function. Thus, if *array1* and array2 are compatible for multiplication, you could compute the cross product matrix using the following steps:

Step 1: Specify an empty range with a correct size. For example, if you have an m by k matrix *array1* and a k by n matrix *array2*, the size of the result matrix is m by n.

Step 2: Create the following matrix formula

= MMULT(array1, array2)

Step3: Press CTRL+SHIFT+ENTER.

18.2.7 Matrix Transpose

We can use the TRANSPOSE function in EXCEL to get a transpose of a matrix. Assume *array1* is a matrix $[A]_{mn}$, we can do the following steps to get the transpose of matrix [A]:

Step 1: Specify an n by m empty range

Step 2: Create the following matrix formula

= TRANSPOSE(array1)

Step2: Press CTRL+SHIFT+ENTER.

18.2.8 Matrix Inversion

To produce the inverse of a matrix, we can use the MINVERSE function provided in EXCEL. Given a named range *array1* to represent a matrix $[A]_{nn}$, we can do the following:

Step 1: Specify an n by n empty range

Step 2: Create the following matrix formula

= MINVERSE(array1)

Step2: Press CTRL+SHIFT+ENTER.

18.3   Solving Linear Equations Using EXCEL

In EXCEL you may combine matrix operations in formulas to solve a system of linear equations. A system of linear equations as described in the previous chapters can be written in a matrix form

$$AX=B$$

Using the Direct Inverse method, the solutions of the equations can be obtained from the following formula:

$$X=A^{-1}B.$$

To find the inverted matrix you can use the EXCEL matrix inversion operation.

For Example,

$$\begin{bmatrix} 3 & -3 & 5 \\ 1 & 2 & -6 \\ 2 & -1 & 3 \end{bmatrix} \begin{Bmatrix} x_1 \\ x_2 \\ x_3 \end{Bmatrix} = \begin{Bmatrix} 4 \\ 3 \\ 1 \end{Bmatrix}$$

Step 1:   Enter the elements of the matrix **A** into cells A1 through C3
               Enter the elements of the matrix **X** into cells E1 to E3
               Enter the elements of the Matrix **B** into cells F1 to F3 (see Figure 18-4)

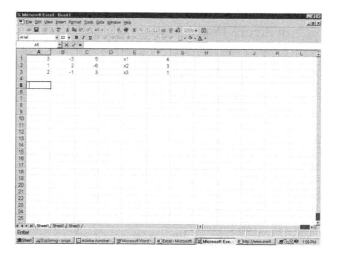

Figure 18-4 Enter the Equation into EXCEL

Step 2:   Highlight cells E1 through G3
               Type   = MINVERSE(A1:C3).

Press CTRL+SHIFT+ENTER. EXCEL will show the elements of the inverted matrix. The result of the inverse of A is as shown in Figure 18-5:

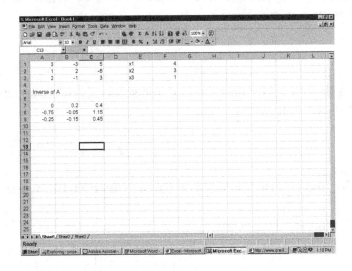

Figure 18-5 Result of Inverse of A

Step 3:   The cross product matrix can be calculated by using the EXCEL MMULT function.

Highlight cells A7 through C9
Type = MMULT(A7:C9,F1:F3).

Press CTRL+SHIFT+ENTER to enter the formula. The result is shown in Figure 18-6.

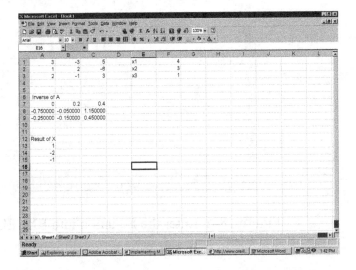

Figure 18-6   Results for a System of Linear Equations

18.4   Questions

Q1.   Use EXCEL to solve the following equation using the Direct Inverse, Cramer method, and Gaussian Elimination method:

$$2x_1 + 2x_2 - 3x_3 = -4$$
$$-2x_1 - 2x_2 + 5x_3 = 1$$
$$x_1 - 4x_2 + 6x_3 = 0$$

Q2.   Use EXCEL to solve Problem Q1 using Choleski method.

Q3.   Given the below 3 x 3 system of linear equations:

$$3x_1 + 9x_2 - 6x_3 = 15$$
$$-2x_1 - 2x_2 + 7x_3 = 1$$
$$2x_1 - 4x_2 + 6x_3 = 6$$

Use EXCEL to find the solution based on Jacobi's and Gauss-Seidel iteration methods. Stop iterations when all the current and previous iteration values are within 0.01.

Q4.   Use MATLAB `bisection` function described in this book to determine a root for the following function:

$$F(x) = x^2 - 5 = 0$$

Q5.   Use MATLAB `false_position` function described in this book to determine the function:

$$F(x) = x^3 - 3 = 0$$

Q6.   Use MATLAB `false_position_advanced` function described in this book to determine a root for the following function:

$$F(x) = x^2 - 3 = 0$$

Chapter 19
Curve Fitting and Numerical Integration

In this chapter we will introduce numerical methods for curve fitting and integral estimation. One of the commonly used methods for curve fitting is least square method. We will describe the fundamental principles of this method before we use it to solve problems in EXCEL and MATLAB.

An integral is the area under a continuous and monotonic function $y = f(x)$ between an interval [a, b]. In other words,

$$I = \int_a^b f(x)dx$$

A primary technique to estimate the area is the trapezoidal method. We will discuss the procedures of using this method to estimate integrals in MATLAB and EXCEL.

19.1   Curve Fitting

Engineers often collect paired data in order to observe and understand the characteristics of features and the operational behavior of engineering systems. These paired data are formulated as

$$
\begin{array}{cc}
x_1 & f(x_1) \\
x_2 & f(x_2) \\
x_3 & f(x_3) \\
\vdots & \vdots \\
x_n & f(x_n)
\end{array}
$$

Engineers need to capture the deterministic or statistical relationships shown in the paired data through a fitted curve.

19.1.1 Least Square Method

The least square method is a technique of "fitting" a curve to a set of paired data points based on a criterion of "best fit". A commonly used criterion of *best fit* is the **least squares** of the deviations of a curve from the data points (see Figure 19-1).

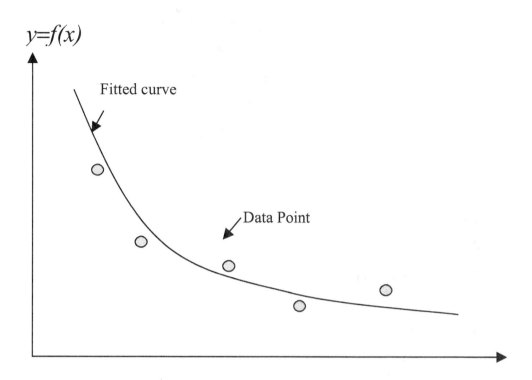

Figure 19-1 Concept of Least Squares in Curve Fitting

Which curve do we use to fit the data points? Normally we do not know. We try to fit a family of functions to the data points. Typical curves are

$$\text{Straight line:} \quad y = f(x) = p_1 + p_2 x$$
$$\text{Parabola:} \quad\quad y = f(x) = p_1 + p_2 x^2$$

The *coefficients* (p_1 and p_2) can be determined through the curve fitting process.

In general, we can fit any linear set of functions (of any type)

$$y = f(x, p_1, p_2, \ldots\ldots, p_m) = p_1 f_1(x) + p_2 f_2(x) + \ldots\ldots + p_m f_m(x)$$

We need to determine coefficients p_1, p_2, $\ldots$ p_m based on the least square criterion. The criterion minimizes the sum of the squares of the differences between the curve values and the data point values.

For example, given the four data points as shown in Figure 19-2, we try to use $y = f(x) = p_1 + p_2 x^2$ to fit them. The errors or residuals between the y_i data values and the y function values at a given x_i are as follows:

$$c_1 = p_1 + p_2 x_1^2 - y_1$$
$$c_2 = p_1 + p_2 x_2^2 - y_2$$
$$c_3 = p_1 + p_2 x_3^2 - y_3$$
$$c_4 = p_1 + p_2 x_4^2 - y_4$$
$$c_5 = p_1 + p_2 x_5^2 - y_5$$

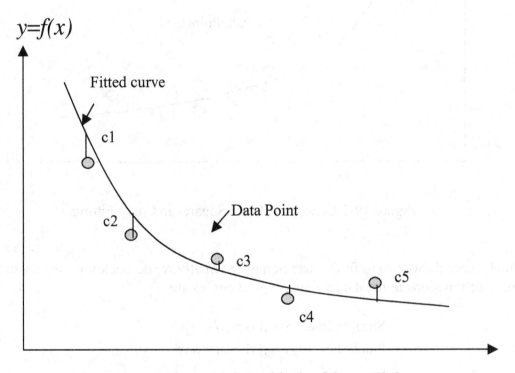

Figure 19-2 Residuals of Curve Fitting

Our goal is to determine p_1 and p_2 to minimize the sum of the square of the residuals, i.e.

$$\sum_{i=1}^{n} (c_i)^2 = minimum$$

To minimize the sum of residuals, we need to set up n differentiation equations for each $p_i(1, 2, 3, \ldots, m)$, as shown below,

$$\frac{\partial}{\partial p_k} \sum_{i=1}^{n} (c_i)^2 = 0 \quad \text{or} \quad \sum_{i=1}^{n} (c_i \frac{\partial c_i}{\partial p_k}) = 0 \quad \text{for} \quad k = 1, \ 2, \cdots, m$$

With the five data points to be fitted, $m = 2$ and $n = 5$. We obtain the two equations

$$c_1 \frac{\partial c_1}{\partial p_1} + c_2 \frac{\partial c_2}{\partial p_1} + c_3 \frac{\partial c_3}{\partial p_1} + c_4 \frac{\partial c_4}{\partial p_1} + c_5 \frac{\partial c_5}{\partial p_1} = 0 \qquad k = 1$$

$$c_1 \frac{\partial c_1}{\partial p_2} + c_2 \frac{\partial c_2}{\partial p_2} + c_3 \frac{\partial c_3}{\partial p_2} + c_4 \frac{\partial c_4}{\partial p_2} + c_5 \frac{\partial c_5}{\partial p_5} = 0 \qquad k = 2$$

Note that

$$\frac{\partial c_i}{\partial p_1} = 1 \quad \text{and} \quad \frac{\partial c_i}{\partial p_2} = x_i^2 \quad \text{for} \quad i = 1, 2, 3, 4, 5$$

The two equations have the form

$$5 p_1 \quad + p_2 \sum_{i=1}^{5} x_i^2 - \sum_{i=1}^{5} y_i = 0$$

$$p_1 \sum_{i=1}^{5} x_i^2 + p_2 \sum_{i=1}^{5} x_i^4 - \sum_{i=1}^{5} y_i x_i^2 = 0$$

or

$$\begin{bmatrix} 5 & \sum_{i=1}^{5} x_i^2 \\ \sum_{i=1}^{5} x_i^2 & \sum_{i=1}^{5} x_i^4 \end{bmatrix} \begin{Bmatrix} p_1 \\ p_2 \end{Bmatrix} = \begin{Bmatrix} \sum_{i=1}^{5} y_i \\ \sum_{i=1}^{5} y_i x_i^2 \end{Bmatrix}$$

Assume the paired data points are $(1.0, 4.3)$, $(2.0, 7.5)$, $(3.0, 20.0)$, $(4.0, 30.0)$ and $(5.0, 23.0)$. Also assume the curve used to fit the data points are

$$y = p_1 + p_2 x^2$$

We will have

$$\sum_{i=1}^{5} x_i^2 = 1.0^2 + 2.0^2 + 3.0^2 + 4.0^2 + 5.0^2 = 55.0$$

$$\sum_{i=1}^{5} x_i^4 = 1.0^4 + 2.0^4 + 3.0^4 + 4.0^4 + 5.0^4 = 979$$

$$\sum_{i=1}^{5} y_i = 4.3 + 7.5 + 20.0 + 30.0 + 23.0 = 84.8$$

$$\sum_{i=1}^{5} y_i x_i^2 = (4.3)1.0^2 + (7.5)2.0^2 + (20.0)3.0^2 + (30.0)4.0^2 + (23.0)5.0^2 = 1269.3$$

Thus $5p_1 + 55.0p_2 = 84.8$

$55.0p_1 + 979p_2 = 1269.3$

Solving the equations, we have

$$p_1 = 7.0629$$
$$p_2 = 0.8997$$

The fitted curve follows: $y = 7.0629 + 0.8997x^2$

The least square method has a statistical basis. When measured values (y_i) follow a normal distribution at each x_i, the resulting curve obtained from the minimization is proven to be the most probable curve. In fact, when statistical error (deviation) follows any distribution with fixed variance, the least squares produces the most probable solution.

There are three terms or indicators that show how well a curve fits data points: Sum of the Square of Errors or Residuals (SSE or SSR), Sum of the Squares of the derivations about the mean (SST), and R-Squared value.

$$SSE \ \ or \ \ SSR = \sum_{i=1}^{n} (c_i)^2$$

$$SST = \sum_{i=1}^{n} (y_i - \overline{y})^2$$

$$R^2 = 1 - \frac{SSE}{SST}$$

The R-Squared value is in the range of [0, 1]. Typically the higher the R-squared value, the better the curve fits the data points. An R-squared value close to 1 means a good fit.

19.1.2   Curve Fitting in EXCEL

EXCEL provides a set of curve fitting functions that allow us to use the least square method. Consider the following data collected through a test (See Table 19-1). We would like to fit these data by a linear function $\hat{y} = ax + b$.

The procedures to find this linear function in EXCEL are as follows:

1)   Open EXCEL and enter the data into two columns (see Example 19-1 in CD).
2)   Plot the data as a line graph (i.e., an XY chart) (see Figure 19-3)

Table 19-1 Data Used for Curve Fitting

y	x
8.35	0.13
16.9	0.54
26.8	0.77
34.5	1.11
38.5	1.14
40.8	1.44
51.3	1.52
50.5	1.65
61.3	1.88
65.5	2.19
72.4	2.25
76.5	2.55
83.4	2.66
88.3	3.09

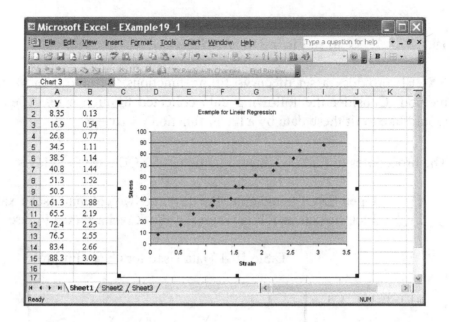

Figure 19-3 Line Graph for the Example Data Set

3)   Right click on one of the plotted data points (see Figure 19-3).
4)   Choose *Trendline* from the context menu
5)   Specify the *linear* type of curve
6)   Press the *OK* button. EXCEL carries out the curve fitting and draws a line through the plotted data points.
7)   Right click on the trend line, select *Options* tab, and check on *Display Equation on Chart* and *Display R-Squared Value on Chart* (See Figure 19-4)

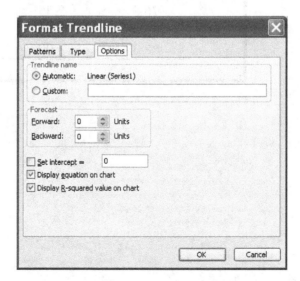

Figure 19-4 Format Trendline Window

We see that the equation of the trend line is

$$Y = 28.714 + 4.0662$$

$$R^2 = 0.987$$

Note that the R-squared value is close to 1. It means the trend line is a good fit.

19.1.3   Curve Fitting with MATLAB

MATLAB has built-in functions and toolboxes that can help us find probable curves for paired data points. One of the commonly used built-in functions is polyfit (x, y, n). This function fits a series of paired data by a polynomial function with the following form:

$$y = a_0 x^n + a_1 x^{n-1} + a_2 x^{n-2} + \cdots + a_{n-1} x + a_n$$

It has three parameters: a vector of x values, a vector of y values, and an integer value n that indicates the order of a polynomial function used to fit the paired data. For example,

```
>> polyfit (x, y, 1)
>> polyfit (x, y, 2)
```

The above two functions use $y = a_1 x + a_0$ and $y = a_2 x^2 + a_1 x + a_0$ to fit paired data points, respectively.

The polyval (y, x) function is another commonly used function. It returns the value of a polynomial of degree n evaluated at x. It has two arguments. The first is a coefficient vector created by the polyfit (x, y, n) function. The second is a vector of x values from which y values will be calculated based on the fitted curve.

For example, we can use the polyfit () and polyval() functions to fit a linear curve for the data points shown in Table 19-1. The MATLAB commands are as follows:

```
>> xdata =[0.13, 0.54, 0.77, 1.11, 1.14, 1.44, 1.52, 1.65, 1.88, 2.19,
2.25, 2.55, 2.66, 3.09];

>> ydata=[8.35, 16.9, 26.8, 34.5, 38.5, 40.8, 51.3, 50.5, 61.3, 65.5,
72.4, 76.5, 83.4, 88.3];

>> coef = polyfit(xdata,ydata,1)
```

```
coef =

   28.7140     4.0662

>> y_fit_value = polyval(coef, xdata)

y_fit_value =

  Columns 1 through 8

   7.7990    19.5717    26.1759    35.9386    36.8001    45.4142    47.7114    51.4442

  Columns 9 through 14

   58.0484    66.9497    68.6726    77.2867    80.4453    92.7923
```

```
>> plot (xdata, ydata, '*', xdata, y_fit_value)
```

You will see a MATLAB Window that plots the fitted curve and the actual paired data points (see Figure 19-5).

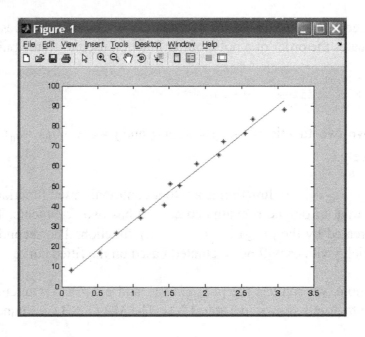

Figure 19-5 A Plot for a Fitted Curve

This MATLAB window contains a set of interactive tools that help you annotate your fitted curves. To activate these interactive tools, you need to select *Tools -> Basic Fitting* from the window (see Figure 19-6).

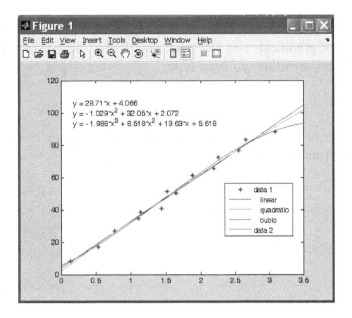

Figure 19-6 Interactive Tools for Basic Fitting

Within the Basic Fitting window,

1)   Check on linear, quadratic, and cubic
2)   Check on Show equations with 4 Significant digits
3)   Check on Plot Residuals

You can see the three fitted curves (linear, quadratic, and cubic curves) with their equations in Figure 19-7. Also you can see the residuals of the three fitted curves against the actual data points.

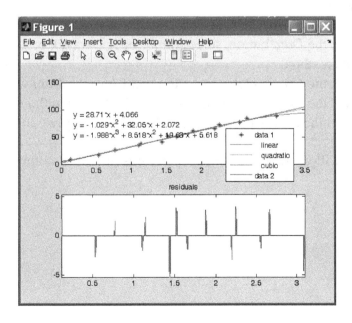

Figure 19-7   Basic Fitting Results

In addition to the built-in functions, MATLAB also provides a curve fitting toolbox. The toolbox has a graphical user interface (GUI) that helps you visualize fitted curves. To activate the curve-fitting, you just type:

```
>> cftool
```

The curve-fitting tool window should appear (see Figure 19-8). If it is not, it means that you need to install this toolbox.

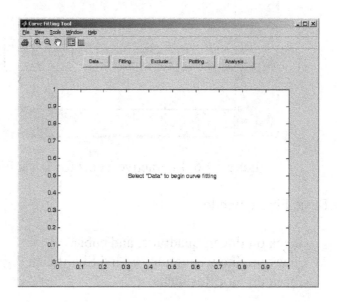

Figure 19-8   Curve-Fitting Toolbox Window

Assume you have the previous *xdata* and *ydata* vectors within the MATLAB. You can do the following:

1) Click the *Data* button, select *xdata* for X Data textbox, and select *ydata* for Y Data textbox.
2) Click the *Create Data Set* button and *Close* the *Data* window.
3) Click the *Fitting* button and the *New Fit* button in the *Fitting* window.
4) Select the Linear Polynomial and Click the Apply button.

MATLAB will conduct the fitting operations and display the results as shown in Figure 19-9.

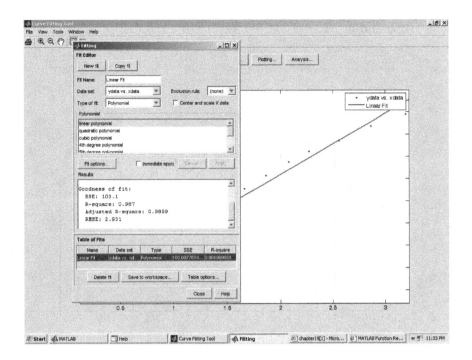

Figure 19-9 Results Using Curve-Fitting Toolbox.

19.2   Numerical Integration

Numerical integration is a method that approximates an integral of a continuous function $f(x)$. When we cannot use the fundamental theorem of calculus to formulate an exact anti-derivative function, numerical integration provides an alternative way of computing the integral of $f(x)$ for a given interval of x.

There are a number of methods used for numerical approximation to an integral. The most efficient approximation is the trapezoidal approximation. The trapezoidal method assumes the area under $f(x)$ over an interval [a, b] is the sum of smaller trapezoidal areas. Figure 19-10 shows the process of the trapezoidal approximation. Each trapezoidal area over a small interval $[x_i, x_{i+1}]$ is the average values of $f(x_i)$ and $f(x_{i+1})$ times the distance between x_i and x_{i+1} (or Δx).

The areas of the individual trapezoids (from left to right) are as follows.

Trapezoid 1 $0.5 * (f(x_0) + f(x_1)) * \Delta x$

Trapezoid 2 $0.5 * (f(x_1) + f(x_2)) * \Delta x$

. . .   . . .

Trapezoid i $0.5 * (f(x_{i-1}) + f(x_i)) * \Delta x$

Trapezoid n $0.5 * (f(x_{n-1}) + f(x_n)) * \Delta x$

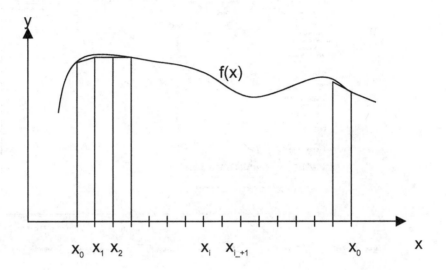

Figure 19-10 Trapezoidal Approximation to an Integral

Adding these together, gives the trapezoid sum:

$$I = \int_a^b f(x)dx = \text{Trapezoid Sum} = \sum_{i=1}^{n} 0.5 * (f(x_{i-1}) + f(x_i)) * \Delta x$$

Obviously, the smaller the interval between x_i and x_{i+1}, the more accurate the approximation is.

19.2.1   Numerical Integration with EXCEL

We implement the trapezoidal method in EXCEL to compute the integral of $f(x)$. Assume we have the following integral:

$$I = \int_0^2 (x^2 - 2)dx$$

We can have the following steps to estimate the integral:

Step 1:   Assume the interval used for the trapezoidal approximation is 0.1, we will
             get the x values in the first colume (see Figure 19-11)

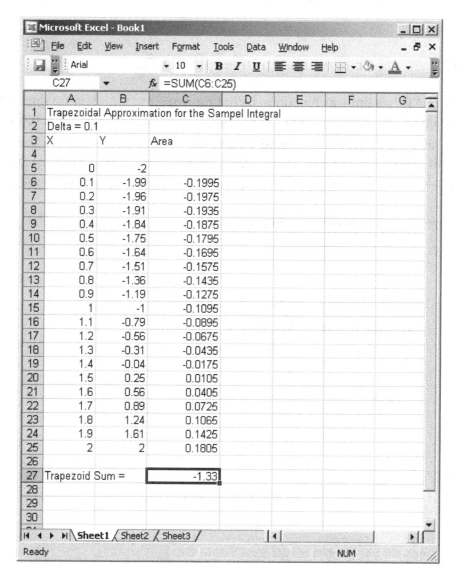

Figure 19-11 Trapezoidal Approximation of an Integral Using Excel

Step 2:   Calculate y values using cell formulas. For example, the value of -1.99 shown
             in cell B6 is calculated based on the formula = A6 * A6 – 2.

Step 3:   Calculate the area for each interval using the trapezoidal method. For
             example, the value of -0.1995 in cell C6 is calculated based on the formula =
             0.1 * (A5 + A6)/2.

Step 4:   Sum the trapezoidal areas. The approximation of the integral is calculated as
            1.33.

19.2.2   Numerical Integration with MATLAB

MATLAB has built-in functions including *trapz ( )* and *quad ( )* that help us to find the
area under the curve of $f(x)$. The *trapz (x, y)* function computes the integral of y with
respect to x using the trapezoidal method.   The x and y vectors must be of the same
length. The *quad (f(x), a, b)* function has three arguments: $f(x)$, a, and b. The values *a*
and *b* form an interval [a, b] where the area under the curve is to be computed.

For example, to compute the integral

$$I = \int_0^2 (x^2 - 2)dx$$

We can have the following MATLAB commands:

```
>> x = 0:0.1:2

x =

  Columns 1 through 10

    0       0.1000      0.2000     0.3000      0.4000      0.5000      0.6000
  0.7000    0.8000      0.9000

  Columns 11 through 20

  1.0000    1.1000      1.2000     1.3000      1.4000     1.5000      1.6000
  1.7000    1.8000      1.9000

  Column 21

  2.0000

>> y = x.^2 -2

y =

  Columns 1 through 10

   -2.0000    -1.9900     -1.9600     -1.9100     -1.8400     -1.7500     -1.6400
   -1.5100    -1.3600     -1.1900
```

```
  Columns 11 through 20

   -1.0000    -0.7900    -0.5600    -0.3100    -0.0400    0.2500    0.5600
    0.8900     1.2400     1.6100

  Column 21

    2.0000

>> z = trapz(x, y)

z =

   -1.3300

>> z = quad('x.^2 - 2', 0, 2)

z =

   -1.3333
```

As you can see all the three numerical methods get an approximate value close to the actual value of -4/3.

19.3   Questions

Q1.   Use the trapezoidal method to estimate the following integral in EXCEL:

$$I = \int_{0}^{2} (x^2 - 5)dx$$

Q2.   Use the trapezoidal method to estimate the following integral in MATLAB:

$$I = \int_{0}^{2} (x^2 - 5)dx$$

(Hint: Use the *trapz ()* and *quad ( )* functions.)

Q3. Given the following paired data points, Use EXCEL and MATLAB to create a
linear line to fit them:

y	x
8.35	0.13
16.9	0.54
26.8	0.77
34.5	1.11
38.5	1.14
40.8	1.44
51.3	1.52
50.5	1.65
61.3	1.88
65.5	2.19
72.4	2.25
76.5	2.55
83.4	2.66
88.3	3.09